Router
Projects and Techniques

Router
Projects and Techniques

The Best Of Fine WoodWorking

The Taunton Press

Cover photo by Susan Kahn

Taunton
BOOKS & VIDEOS

for fellow enthusiasts

10 9 8 7 6 5 4
Printed in the United States of America

A FINE WOODWORKING Book

FINE WOODWORKING® is a trademark of The Taunton Press, Inc.,
registered in the U.S. Patent and Trademark Office.

The Taunton Press, Inc.
63 South Main Street
Box 5506
Newtown, Connecticut 06470-5506
e-mail: tp@taunton.com

Distributed by Publishers Group West

Library of Congress Cataloging-in-Publication Data

Router projects and techniques.
    p. cm. — (The Best of fine Woodworking)
    "A Fine woodworking book" — T.p. verso.
    Includes index.
    ISBN 1-56158-002-3
    1. Routers (Tools).   2. Woodwork   I. Series.
TT203.5.R68   1991
684'.083–dc20
                                    92-830
                                    CIP

Contents

Introduction

When routers first became popular in home shops, they were used primarily as portable mini-shapers to mold the edges of tabletops, drawer fronts and cabinet doors. Eventually, weekend woodworkers discovered this humble tool could extend their skills to include dovetails (previously the sacred territory of old-world craftsmen). This realization opened the floodgates, and shopmade jigs were developed to help routers do tasks of every conceivable kind.

Routers really didn't begin living up to their full potential until woodworkers took to mounting them under tabletops, which transformed them into full-fledged mini-shapers. But unlike a shaper, a table-mounted router can cut dadoes that stop on a dime in the middle of wide panels (better than the gradually arching end of tablesawn dadoes), and they can also cut deep mortises nearly as efficiently as an expensive mortising machine. Of course, it wasn't long before someone mounted a router horizontally above a movable table so that it could truly fulfill the functions of a mortising machine. The latest advancement in router technology is the plunge router. Its redesigned base makes it possible to plunge the bit directly into the work at a precise spot, to a precise depth and perfectly perpendicular to the surface.

The 32 articles in this book, reprinted from past issues of *Fine Woodworking* magazine, will help you get the most out of your router, and may even inspire you to come up with a few ingenious ways of your own to put this woodshop jack-of-all-trades to work.

—Jim Boesel, executive editor

The "Best of *Fine Woodworking*" series spans issues 48 through 90 of *Fine Woodworking* magazine, originally published between mid-1984 and the end of 1990. There is no duplication between these books and the popular *"Fine Woodworking on..."* series. A footnote with each article gives the date of first publication; product availability, suppliers' addresses and prices may have changed since then.

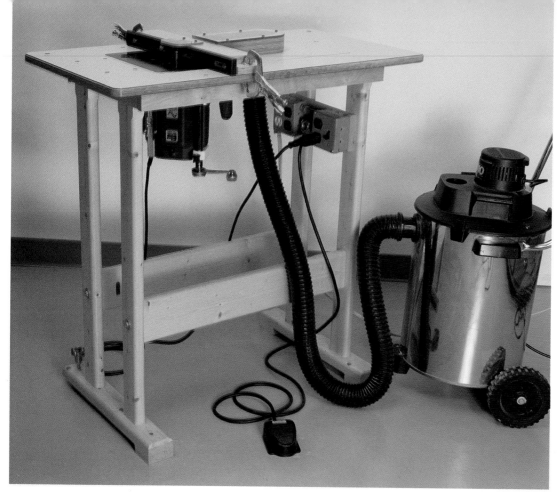

This shop-built router table is sturdy yet lightweight and knocks down for portability. It also has a quick-clamping fence with an adjustable bit opening, a dual-router setup and a built-in dust-collection system.

Building a Router Table

A *drop-in baseplate for easy access*

by Ed Walker

There is no quicker or cheaper way to increase your shop's versatility than by table-mounting your router. A table-mounted router is an excellent substitute for a light-duty shaper. With an almost endless variety of reasonably priced bits to choose from, a router table lets you shape, mold, bevel, groove, dado, mortise or trim just about any wood part you can balance on a tabletop.

A router table can be as simple as a piece of plywood sitting on sawhorses, or it can include an elaborate base cabinet full of drawers. Many woodworkers have installed a router in their workbench or tablesaw extension. Others have made router tabletops that can be clamped in a vise and supported on hinged legs and then stored out of the way when not in use. Some of these options are discussed in the sidebar on pp. 12-13. The popularity of shop-built router tables has led to the recent proliferation of commercially available models offered by both small and large manufacturers. When I was in the market for a router table, I examined most of the commericial tables. I concluded that because of their simplicity and because most of them incorporated different ideas developed

by ingenious woodworkers in the first place, I could build a router table that would suit me better than any I could buy.

I thought my first router table was the ultimate design. It included a large, heavy base cabinet with lots of storage, and it had built-in retractable casters so I could move the table around the shop. However, my second router table, shown in the photo above and in figure 1 on the facing page, has become my favorite. The base of this router table is designed to be easily disassembled so I can transport it to job sites or to demonstrations that I conduct. My portable router table incorporates one of the most significant advancements in table-mounting routers: The concept of mounting the router to an oversized baseplate that can be inserted flush into a rabbeted hole in the tabletop. There's no need to screw the plate to the table because the weight of the router holds it down. This method of mounting allows fast removal of the router from the table for changing bits or for using the router by hand. I decided to make two cutouts in my tabletop so I could insert two routers with different bits. Occasionally, this is a handy feature, but since I

(continued on p. 10)

From *Fine Woodworking* magazine (September 1991) 90:56-61

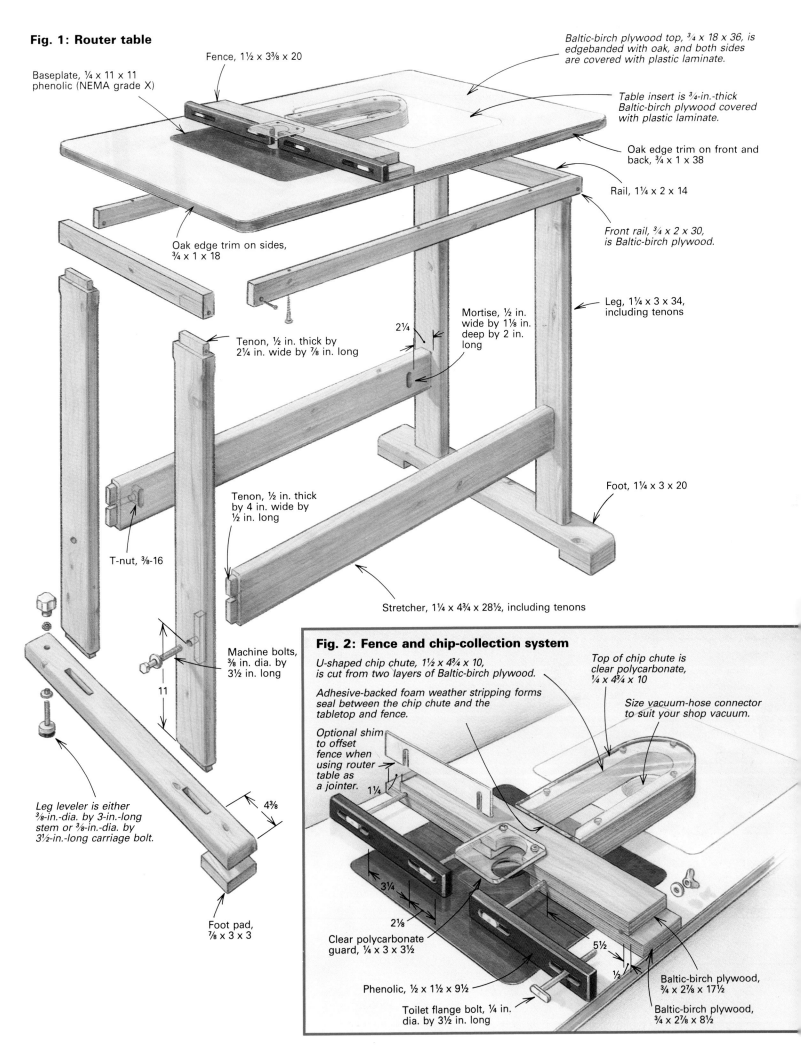

Fig. 1: Router table

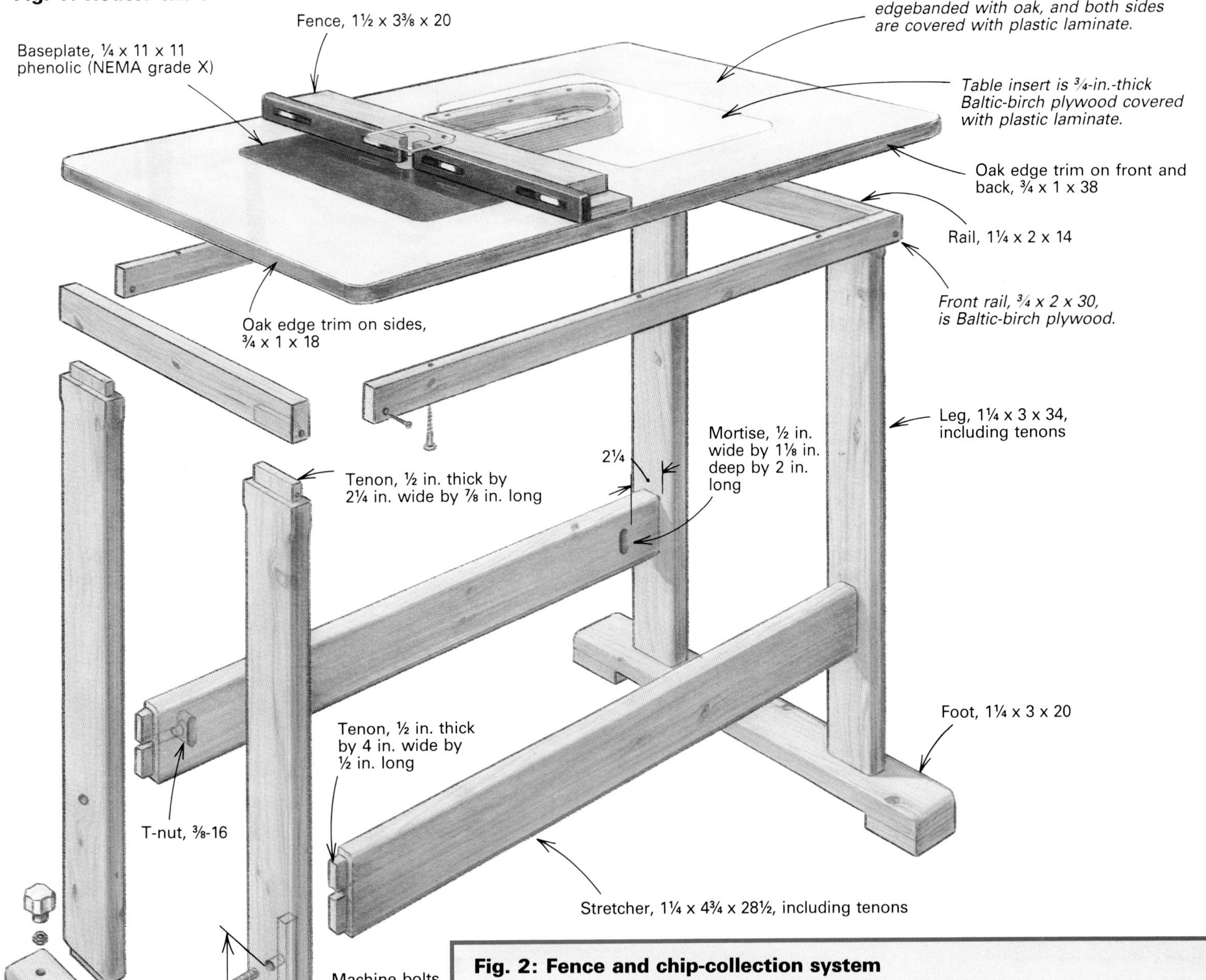
Fence, 1½ x 3⅜ x 20
Baseplate, ¼ x 11 x 11 phenolic (NEMA grade X)
Baltic-birch plywood top, ¾ x 18 x 36, is edgebanded with oak, and both sides are covered with plastic laminate.
Table insert is ¾-in.-thick Baltic-birch plywood covered with plastic laminate.
Oak edge trim on front and back, ¾ x 1 x 38
Rail, 1¼ x 2 x 14
Front rail, ¾ x 2 x 30, is Baltic-birch plywood.
Oak edge trim on sides, ¾ x 1 x 18
Leg, 1¼ x 3 x 34, including tenons
Mortise, ½ in. wide by 1⅛ in. deep by 2 in. long
2¼
Tenon, ½ in. thick by 2¼ in. wide by ⅞ in. long
Tenon, ½ in. thick by 4 in. wide by ½ in. long
Foot, 1¼ x 3 x 20
T-nut, ⅜-16
Stretcher, 1¼ x 4¾ x 28½, including tenons
Machine bolts, ⅜ in. dia. by 3½ in. long
11
4⅜
Leg leveler is either ⅜-in.-dia. by 3-in.-long stem or ⅜-in.-dia. by 3½-in.-long carriage bolt.
Foot pad, ⅞ x 3 x 3

Fig. 2: Fence and chip-collection system

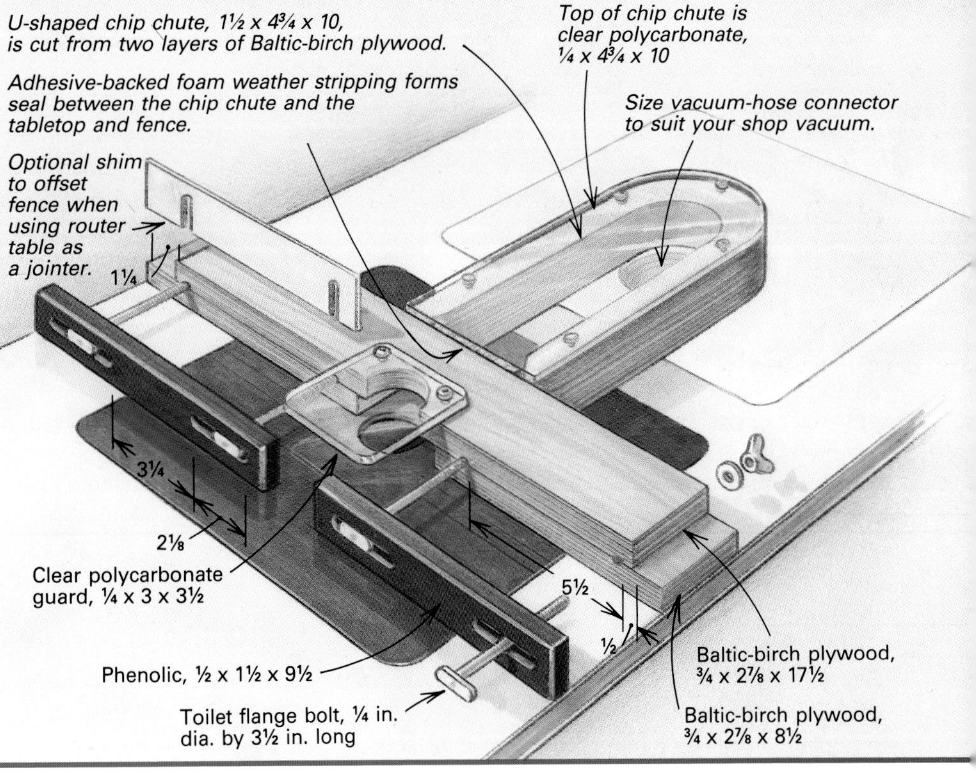
U-shaped chip chute, 1½ x 4¾ x 10, is cut from two layers of Baltic-birch plywood.
Top of chip chute is clear polycarbonate, ¼ x 4¾ x 10
Adhesive-backed foam weather stripping forms seal between the chip chute and the tabletop and fence.
Size vacuum-hose connector to suit your shop vacuum.
Optional shim to offset fence when using router table as a jointer.
1¼
3¼
2⅛
Clear polycarbonate guard, ¼ x 3 x 3½
5½
½
Phenolic, ½ x 1½ x 9½
Baltic-birch plywood, ¾ x 2⅞ x 17½
Toilet flange bolt, ¼ in. dia. by 3½ in. long
Baltic-birch plywood, ¾ x 2⅞ x 8½

Photos except where noted: Charley Robinson; drawings: Bob La Pointe

usually only have one router mounted in the table, I made a special table insert for the other cutout that allows me to hook up a shop vacuum for chip removal (see the photo on p. 8).

You may choose to build a more elaborate router table than the one I'm describing in this article, or you may go for the piece of plywood on sawhorses. But no matter what type of table you decide to build, I think you'll find the tips and guidelines I present on the main components of my router table helpful.

The router-table base

The primary function of the base is to place the work surface at a comfortable height. The tabletop should be at least as high as the distance from the floor to your wrist, but lower than the distance from the floor to your elbow; 34 in. to 38 in. is about right for most people. The type of work you do will help determine the best height. Generally, small, detailed work will be most comfortable at elbow height.

As I mentioned earlier, I needed a portable but steady router table to take to demonstrations. To reduce both costs and weight, I built the base from construction-grade spruce 2x4s and 2x6s. The legs are mortised, tenoned and glued to the top rails and feet, but the stretchers are attached to the legs with ⅜-in. machine bolts that thread into T-nuts captured in mortises in the stretchers, as shown in figure 1 on the previous page. The front and back rails are screwed into the ends of the side rails and to the underside of the top. After mortising and tenoning the legs and stretchers, I routed blind mortises in the stretchers for the T-nuts. Then I drilled ⁷⁄₁₆-in.-dia. holes through the legs and through the ends of the stretchers to meet the mortises. I dry-assembled the base to make sure everything fit properly. Then I rounded over all the edges except the top rail and the top inch of the legs, and sanded the individual components. I glued up the two leg assemblies (each consisting of two legs, a side rail and a foot), making sure they were flat and square. To complete the leg assemblies, I glued three pads onto the feet and installed a leg leveler in place of the fourth foot pad. One leveler is all that's needed to stabilize the base on uneven floors. If you cannot find a suitable leg leveler at your local hardware store, you can substitute a carriage bolt screwed through a T-nut on the bottom of the foot with a threaded knob locked in place on the threaded end of the carriage bolt.

After bolting the leg assemblies to the stretchers, I fastened the front and back rails to the ends of the side rails with #10 by 2½-in.-long washer-head screws countersunk ⅜ in. deep. These screws reach into the leg tenons, providing much better holding power than the endgrain of the side rails alone. The top is later secured by screwing through the front and back rails into the underside of the top.

The router-table top

A router-table top needs to be strong, stable and smooth. I made my top from ¾-in.-thick Baltic-birch plywood. I glued on oak edgebanding and then covered both sides of the top with plastic laminate, as shown in figure 1 on the previous page. The front and back rails attached to the underside of the top help keep it flat. Medium-density fiberboard (MDF), at least 1 in. thick, also makes an excellent top. Particleboard could be used, but I don't recommend anything less than 1¼ in. thick because I've heard of router baseplates tearing through the ½-in. thickness left after rabbeting ¾-in.-thick particleboard. No matter what material you use, both sides of the top should be covered with high-pressure plastic laminate, and all edges should be laminated, banded with hardwood strips or otherwise sealed for stability. A light-colored, matte laminate allows temporary layout lines to be marked on the top and

then cleaned off easily. An occasional coat of paste wax will prolong the top's life and make sliding material over the top easier.

A top that is 16 in. to 24 in. wide by 30 in. to 48 in. long will suit most needs, although you may want to modify these dimensions to suit your situation. Keep in mind, however, that with router tables, bigger isn't necessarily better. If the work is too large for the table, the router can be removed from the table and hand-guided over the stationary work. Mounting the router on one end of the top instead of in the middle provides space for work in progress or for mounting a second router, which greatly facilitates multiple-setup operations. In addition, the top should overhang the base by at least 2 in. to provide space for clamping the fence and other fixtures.

Router baseplates

An integral part of the router-table top is the drop-in baseplate to which the router is mounted. A variety of baseplate materials can be used. Clear acrylic is often used for baseplates to increase visibility, which is beneficial if the router is operated freehand. However, concentration of stresses around mounting screws in acrylic can cause chipping and even breakage, allowing the router to fall out of the table. If acrylic is the only material available, it should be at least ⅜ in. thick, and the baseplate should be as small as possible. The baseplate must be checked regularly and discarded if cracks radiate from the screw holes. Polycarbonate, another clear plastic, is safe to use, but it will sag over time. In addition, heat from the router can cause the polycarbonate to expand enough to jam in the recess. I think ¼-in.-thick phenolic resin board is the best choice for a router baseplate. The phenolic securely holds the router without danger of breaking or flexing, which can affect the accuracy of setups. And phenolic's strength allows the use of a thinner and larger baseplate, which makes inserting and removing the router easier and maximizes the cutting depth of router bits. Phenolic comes in a bewildering assortment of grades for various purposes, but paper-base phenolic resin board (NEMA Grade X) makes an excellent baseplate; it is available in natural (brown) or black from most plastic-supply stores.

I made an 11-in.-sq. baseplate to accommodate even the largest router without requiring a lot of twisting and turning to get the router through the table opening. A square baseplate can also be rotated 90° to reposition the router controls in relation to the table—a handy feature at times.

Routing the baseplate recess

The baseplate should fit snugly into its recess in the top so that the baseplate is flush or about ¹⁄₆₄ in. proud of the top. If the baseplate is low, stock will catch on the edge of the recess and depth of cut will change as the work passes from the baseplate to the table surface. A ⅜-in.-wide rabbet around the perimeter of the recess will adequately support any of the various baseplate materials. I've developed a method for routing the recess that takes into account the fact that most router bases are not concentric with the router bit. I made separate templates of ¼-in.-thick hardboard for each side of the router and used them in conjunction with the phenolic baseplate to set up router guides on the tabletop. This procedure has yielded extremely accurate baseplate rabbets with non-concentric circular bases or any other shape router base. I recommend practicing routing with the templates on some scrap before cutting into a nice, new router-table top.

To make the templates, I first cut four pieces of hardboard slightly shorter than the sides of the phenolic baseplate and slightly wider than the distance from the edge of the router base to the cutting edge of a 1-in.-dia. straight bit chucked in the router. Next, I marked one of the template blanks "left" and butted it against a

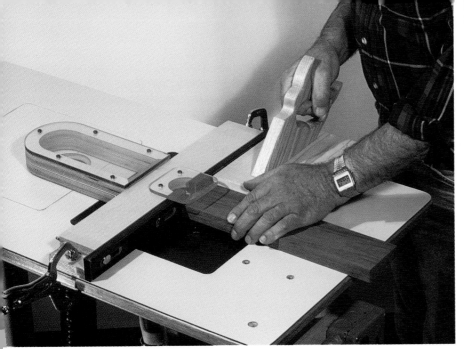

The router jig above is used to trim templates that are the same width as the distance between the router's edge and the cutting edge of the bit.

This chip-collection system is a chute that connects an opening on the back of the fence with a vacuum port in the tabletop or in a second insert plate (left).

straightedge tacked to a piece of scrap plywood, as shown in the photo above at right. A piece of double-sided tape secured the template to the plywood. With the left edge of the router base held firmly against the same straightedge, I routed off the edge of the template, making it exactly the same width as the distance from the router base's edge to the straight bit's edge. I repeated this operation to make templates for the front, right and back sides.

Next, I positioned the baseplate on the router table where I wanted the cutout and placed the templates on their respective sides of the baseplate. This way, I could clamp straightedge guides firmly against the templates and then remove the templates and the baseplate. With the router oriented correctly in relation to the templates that I used to set up the guides, I am ensured of a perfectly sized recess. After setting the router depth of cut about 1/64 in. shy of the baseplate's thickness, I routed a recess with the 1-in.-dia. bit used to make the templates. This recess is the rabbet that will support the baseplate. I cleared out chips that built up along the guides and made passes until the bit no longer cut. Then I checked to be sure no chips were holding the router away from the guides.

To remove the waste in the center of the cutout, I switched to a 1/4-in.-dia. straight bit, and, without moving the straightedge guides, I routed all the way through the top. Because of the difference between the 1-in.-dia. bit that cuts the recess and the 1/4-in.-dia. bit that cuts through the top, I was left with a 3/8-in.-wide rabbet. Before removing the straightedge guides, I eased the sharp edges of the recess with a file, rounded the corners of the baseplate to match the recess and test-fit the plate. If necessary, additional passes can be made with the 1-in.-dia. bit until the baseplate is just barely higher than the top. If the recess is too small, the baseplate can be filed until it fits, or the appropriate guide can be lightly tapped and then the recess can be trimmed with one more router pass. Conversely, if the recess is too deep or too large, the rabbet can be shimmed. I make shims by sanding the back sides of thin strips of plastic laminate until they are the proper thickness, and then I glue them into the recess. A snug fit is essential. When the baseplate was properly fitted to the table, I drilled two 1-in.-dia. finger holes in opposite corners of the baseplate and removed the sharp edges with a 1/8-in.-radius roundover bit. This makes the baseplate easy to grasp when placing it in or lifting it out of the table.

Fitting the router to the baseplate

I positioned my Elu router diagonally on the baseplate; this diagonal orientation makes it easier to get the router in and out of the table and moves the height-adjustment mechanism toward the front of the table. To mount the router, I first located the center of the baseplate. Then, using the router's subbase as a pattern, I marked, drilled and countersunk the mounting-screw holes. If your router does not have a removable subbase, or if you wish to locate the router precisely in the center of the baseplate, you can easily make a subbase from a piece of clear plastic large enough to cover all the router-base screw holes. Place the plastic over the base, mark and drill the screw holes, and then mount the subbase on the router. Chuck a 1/4-in.-dia. bit in the router, and plunge through the subbase to mark its center. After removing the subbase, drill a 1/4-in.-dia. hole in the center of the baseplate blank, place it on the subbase, and insert a 1/4-in.-dia. rod through the center holes to align the subbase and baseplate. A dab of hot-melt glue or double-sided tape will hold the subbase in position while you drill the mounting-screw holes through the baseplate.

To cut the clearance hole in the baseplate, I chucked my largest bit (it must be sharp) into the router and mounted the router to the baseplate. In most cases, the screws that secure the subbase to the router will not be long enough to fasten the router to the thicker baseplate. For longer screws, I recommend socket flat-head cap screws because heads of both Phillips head or slotted screws are easily stripped, making them difficult to remove. Next, I placed the baseplate in the table recess with the router above the table and cranked down the height adjustment to advance the cutter steadily through the baseplate. Variable-speed routers should be set to their slowest speed for this operation. If the bit is not designed for plunge cuts, the center of the baseplate must first be pierced with a smaller plunging bit.

To support workpieces when using smaller bits, I made a variety of inserts with center-hole diameters about 1/8 in. larger than each bit's diameter. First, I routed a 1/4-in.-wide by 1/8-in.-deep rabbet around the clearance hole in the baseplate with a bearing-guided rabbeting bit. Then, using a circle-cutting jig I designed for my router, I cut several inserts and routed mating rabbets on the inserts, again with a bearing-guided rabbeting bit. (A similar circle-cutting jig is available from Woodhaven, 5323 W. Kimberly Road, Davenport, Ia. 52806.) I also made an insert with no hole to prevent chips and dust from falling into the router when it is not in use. To keep the inserts from rotating, I drilled a 1/4-in.-dia. hole at the edge of the bit clearance hole in the baseplate, epoxied a short piece of 1/4-in.-dia. brass rod into the hole, and cut a matching notch into the edge of each insert.

The fence

In its simplest form, a router-table fence is a straightedge for guiding the workpiece past the router bit. The utility of the fence can be increased greatly with a few minor modifications, such as a recess for bit clearance, a cutout on the bottom of the fence for chip ejection and a ⅛-in.-wide chamfer on the bottom corner of the face to prevent chips from building up between the fence and workpiece. A guard mounted over the cutter will help protect the operator's hands and eyes. The fence shown in figure 2 on p. 9 will meet most users' requirements. It has a thinner profile on each end for clamping to the table, a cutter guard for safety, movable faces to adjust the opening for different-size bits and an unobstructed chip-ejection chute. The outfeed fence can also be shimmed for jointing operations.

To ensure stability, I glued together the main body of the fence from plywood, as shown in figure 2. I used phenolic for the adjustable faces because of its durability and low-friction surface; however, plywood would also work well for these parts. The large, flat heads of toilet flange bolts fit nicely into the rabbeted slots that I routed in the adjustable faces. I also routed a ⅛-in.-wide chamfer around the front edges of the phenolic faces to make it easier to slide workpieces across the faces and to prevent dust buildup at the base of the fence. A clear polycarbonate guard screwed to the top of the fence over the cutter provides good visibility and greater impact resistance than acrylic. When using the router table for edge-jointing, I insert a shim of stiff paper or plastic laminate to offset the outfeed fence by the amount I want to remove in one pass. Slots cut in the shims allow them to slide into place without the face of the outfeed fence having to be removed completely. Also, for supporting stock on edge, high vertical faces can be mounted on the fence in place of the adjustable faces.

As you can see in the photo on p. 11, I like the fence oriented front to back across the short dimension of the top. This orientation allows for shorter fences and fixtures and for easier

Space-saving router tables

by Charley Robinson

Not every shop has room for a large, permanent router table. And while the portability of the knockdown table described in the main article makes it great for on-site work, the router table also may take up more floor space than some of us are willing to allocate. When I was ready to add a router table to my shop, I decided to use a surface that was already taking up space—my tablesaw's extension table (see the photo below). I mounted my router on a clear polycarbonate baseplate for visibility during freehand operations. Then, I cut a recess in my tablesaw's extension table and used the same drop-in technique discussed in the main article. Not only did

this save shop space, but I ended up with a large surface to support longer workpieces. Also, without extra effort, I had an extremely accurate and easily adjustable fence. To protect the laminated face of my rip fence when using it with the router, I clamp on an auxiliary fence with a hole bored in the middle for bit clearance.

Because it was difficult to reach the router's on/off switch, I mounted an electrical box with two outlets, both controlled by the same switch, beneath my extension table. After dropping the router into the table, I lock the router's switch in the "on" position, plug the router into the switched outlet and then plug my shop vacuum into

the other outlet. This way, I control the router and the vacuum with one switch. The disadvantage of this outlet setup is the danger of forgetting to unlock the router from the "on" position when removing it from the table for freehand use. To make sure the router doesn't start up unexpectedly when it's plugged into a live outlet, I always unlock the switch immediately upon removing the router from the table.

A folding router table: Another idea for woodworkers with limited shop space is to mount the router to a folding table that can be quickly set up when needed and then folded compactly for storage. The sturdy, stowable router table shown in figure 3 on the facing page was sent in by David Finck, a professional woodworker in Reader, W.V. His torsion-box top is extremely strong and stable, and because the router is mounted to the underside of the top plywood skin, Finck sacrifices only ¼ in. of a router bit's maximum depth of cut. A pair of legs are hinged to one side of the table and can be locked in the open position with notched, diagonal braces, which pivot to allow the table to be folded for storage. On the side opposite the legs is a mounting block that clamps into a workbench's face vise, as shown in figure 3, to hold the table securely. The wide open base provides easy access to the on/off switch and the router chuck for bit changes.

Although construction is straightforward, as shown in figure 3, Finck offers several construction hints. The plywood block that reinforces the center of the table should be about 2 in. larger than the router base, and the cutout should allow ¹⁄₃₂-in. clearance between the block and the router base. If your router base is rec-

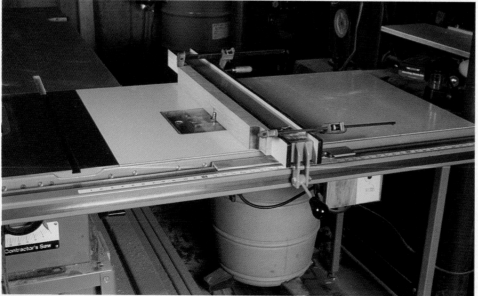

Mounting a router in a tablesaw extension table offers a large work surface, with no additional loss of floor space, and an extremely accurate fence. Attaching an electrical box with two switched outlets to the front of the extension table provides safe and convenient control of the router and the shop vacuum.

fence adjustments. The shorter fence also makes it easier to work with slightly bowed stock, and since I have a two-router table, I can set up separate fences for two operations. Although any C-clamp can be used to secure the fence to the table, I prefer Vise-Grip locking C-clamps with swivel pads. The lock/release action of these clamps makes it quick and easy to reposition the fence or to remove the fence to gain access to the router. Because the fence will always be parallel to the bit in any horizontal orientation, I can make accurate and fine adjustments by simply tapping one end of the fence.

Chip collection

I designed my fence for efficient chip clearance even without a dust-collection system in operation. But the router makes a lot of chips, and most of the time I run it with a shop vacuum to collect the mess before it gets blown all over my shop.

My chip-collection system, shown in figure 2 on p. 9 and in the photo at left on p. 11, consists of two main parts: a U-shaped chip chute that extends from the fence over to the other baseplate cut-out in my router table; and a plywood table insert with a hole cut through it into which a vacuum-hose connector is glued. The chip chute was first bandsawn from two pieces of ¾-in.-thick birch plywood that had been laminated together, and then the chute was topped with a sheet of clear polycarbonate. Adhesive-backed foam weather stripping forms an air seal between the chip chute and the fence and tabletop. When chip collection is needed, I just place the chute in position, connect the vacuum hose and turn on the vacuum; the pressure created by the vacuum holds the chip chute in place. I routed a rabbet around the vacuum connector hole in the plywood table insert, and made a plug to fill the hole when the vacuum is not in use. □

Ed Walker is executive director of the Triangle Area Woodworkers Club (Raleigh, N.C.), conducts router seminars, and manufactures and markets router tables in Apex, N.C.

Fig. 3: A stowable router table

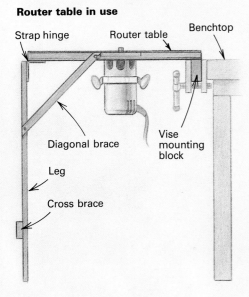

Router table in use

Strap hinge · Router table · Benchtop

Diagonal brace

Leg

Cross brace

Vise mounting block

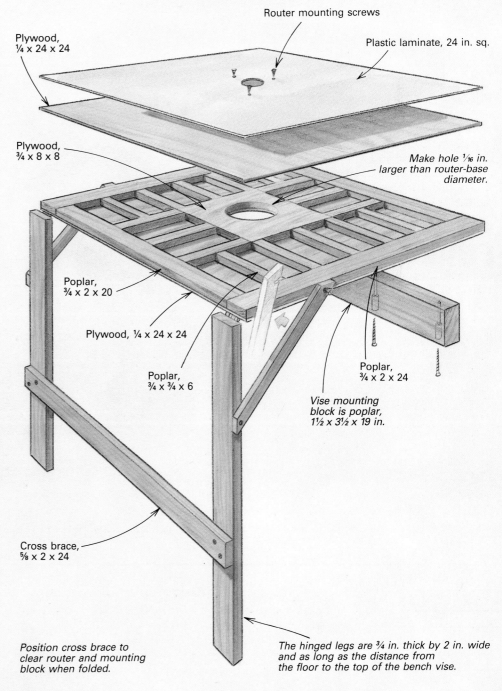

Router mounting screws

Plywood, ¼ x 24 x 24

Plastic laminate, 24 in. sq.

Plywood, ¾ x 8 x 8

Make hole ¹⁄₁₆ in. larger than router-base diameter.

Poplar, ¾ x 2 x 20

Plywood, ¼ x 24 x 24

Poplar, ¾ x ¾ x 6

Poplar, ¾ x 2 x 24

Vise mounting block is poplar, 1½ x 3½ x 19 in.

Cross brace, ⅝ x 2 x 24

tangular, orient the router cutout so that the controls will be facing forward. Finck also cautions you to position the router cutout to avoid interference between the router and your bench-vise handle. The wider stock around the edges of the torsion-box core provide a solid area for attaching the hinges and vise mounting block and for clamping fences to the table. Finck also suggests that the legs be made slightly long and then trimmed to length after the table is completed; this way, the table can be made level when it's clamped in position in a bench vise. When assembling the table, position the cross brace, legs and vise mounting block so that they won't interfere with each other when the table is folded. For a fence, Finck uses a 1¾-in.-thick by 2½-in.-wide piece of jointed-and-squared hardwood with an opening for chip and bit clearance. □

Charley Robinson is an assistant editor at FWW.

Position cross brace to clear router and mounting block when folded.

The hinged legs are ¾ in. thick by 2 in. wide and as long as the distance from the floor to the top of the bench vise.

Shop-Built Pin Router

Delicate carving with a precision machine

by Hans Sporbeck

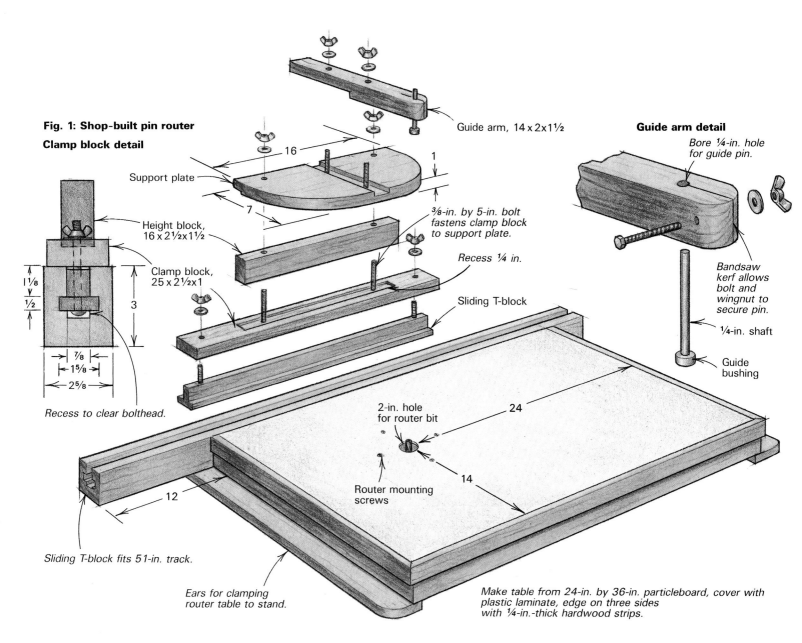

Fig. 1: Shop-built pin router

Clamp block detail

Support plate

Height block,
16 x 2½x1½

Clamp block,
25 x 2½x1

1⅛

½

3

⅞

1⅝

2⅝

Recess to clear bolthead.

16

7

1

Guide arm, 14 x 2x1½

⅜-in. by 5-in. bolt
fastens clamp block
to support plate.

Recess ¼ in.

Sliding T-block

Sliding T-block fits 51-in. track.

Ears for clamping
router table to stand.

2-in. hole
for router bit

24

Router mounting
screws

14

12

Guide arm detail

*Bore ¼-in. hole
for guide pin.*

*Bandsaw
kerf allows
bolt and
wingnut to
secure pin.*

¼-in. shaft

Guide
bushing

*Make table from 24-in. by 36-in. particleboard, cover with
plastic laminate, edge on three sides
with ¼-in.-thick hardwood strips.*

I have always enjoyed solving the problems that accompany each new woodworking project. The thrill is in figuring out how to build a piece, modifying tools and making jigs to produce the piece efficiently, then having everything come out right. Many of my projects involve carving, such as hollowing trays and cutting geometric patterns and decorative recesses on the lids of boxes and platters. Since hand carving is often too tedious and time-consuming, even for a hobbyist, I began looking for a better way. The pin routers I'd read about seemed ideal for my work, so I decided to build one onto my router table.

My router table was designed by Wally Kunkel. I built it because it has a large work surface, is more solidly built than many metal versions being sold and has a versatile fence that slides in a T-shaped track.

This track is ideal for mounting a pin router arm. Since the router table worked so well and I didn't want to lose it completely, I designed the pin router so I wouldn't have to alter the basic table, and could quickly switch from pin router to router table. My router arm could also be modified to fit other router tables.

Before you build this pin router, you need to know how the machine operates. Commercial models are usually overarm routers (see photo, p. 16). A spindle chuck that can hold a bit up to ½ in. in diameter is mounted at the top of a C-shaped frame, which extends over a movable table. In the middle of the table, centered directly under the bit, is a guide pin, which gives the tool its name. The table can be raised or lowered with a foot pedal, and has a stop to regulate the depth of cut.

An overarm router can do everything a shaper or router can. Used with templates, it can also do much of the contour and pierced cutting normally done with a bandsaw or jigsaw. The machine's versatility is due to a combination of factors—the pin itself that guides and steadies the work while it's being cut; the almost endless variety of available router bit sizes, shapes and styles, many of them with pilots that guide the work the way the pin does. In addition, you can clamp straight and shaped fences to the table to guide the work. Once you get used to the machine, you can also do quite a bit of work freehand.

Unlike a commercial machine with its cutter mounted over the table, my setup has the cutter underneath the work, just like a regular router table, and the guide pin is suspended over the work and cutter. This means that you can't see the bit when you're hollowing out a tray or cutting a rabbet, but this hasn't been a problem. In fact, I feel it's a safer way of working. Regardless of its diameter, the cutter is always centered directly beneath the pin, as shown in figure 1, so you always know where you're cutting. Because the cutter and pin are aligned in this way and the cutting edge is so narrow, the bit doesn't tend to grab the work.

You can build the pin router attachment shown in the drawing with any hardwood. Assembly is pretty straightforward, as long as you're careful to align all the bolt holes. I taped the clamp board to the T-shaped slide and with my drill press, bored the holes shown through all three pieces at once. Remember to recess the bottom of the T-slide for the bolt heads. After the bolts are inserted and the T-slide fitted into the router table track, the clamp block is added and the whole assembly tightened with wing nuts, thus locking the slide into place.

The clamp block also connects the pin guide assembly to the slide. I routed a ¼-in. recess in the clamp block, then squared the corners to fit the height block shown. This 1¼-in. block sets the pin at a good working height for my ¼-in.-shank bits, but you may need larger blocks if you have longer bits. Before shaping the support plate, I cut a 7-in. by 16-in. rectangle, then rabbeted one long edge, as shown, to fit the height block. I curved the front of the support plate mainly for looks—make it any shape that pleases you. To hold alignments for the bolt holes, again tape or clamp the three pieces together and drill the holes shown. At this time you could also drill the two holes needed for bolting the support plate and guide arm, and recess the bolt holes on the bottom of the support plate and clamp block.

After I assembled the unit, I visually lined it up over a ¼-in. straight bit chucked in the router. The straight bit is the same diameter as the shanks of the guide pins I use, so the alignment has to be accurate. Next, I raised the router to score the bottom of the straight arm, removed the arm and used my drill press to bore a ¼-in. hole through the score mark. At the same time, I bored a hole next to and perpendicular to the pin hole. After bandsawing from the front of the arm to the hole, as shown in the guide arm detail, and gently rounding the arm's front end, I added a bolt, washer and wingnut to secure the pin. The sawkerf gives the arm enough flexibility to make an efficient clamp. Whenever I want to realign the router and pin, I locate the arm so I can drop a ¼-in. rod through the guide pin hole and into the router's collet. Then I tighten the T-clamp to lock the arm in place.

My table is built from 2x4s, with the crosspieces fit into half-laps cut in the uprights. I just clamp the table to the base so I can disassemble the unit when it's not being used. The table height is a matter of personal preference—mine's about waist high, with the router table surface 36½ in. from the floor. I also wrapped the

Unlike commercial models, Sporbeck's shop-built pin router has an overarm guide pin and the cutter is mounted beneath the table. The plastic wrapped around the router base keeps chips and sawdust from flying all over the shop. To clean up, just open the sheet and vacuum away the waste.

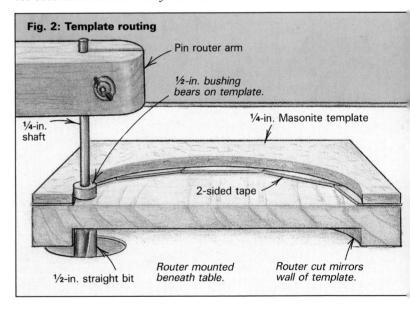

Fig. 2: Template routing

Pin router arm

½-in. bushing bears on template.

¼-in. shaft

¼-in. Masonite template

2-sided tape

½-in. straight bit

Router mounted beneath table.

Router cut mirrors wall of template.

whole base in clear plastic, as shown in the photo above, to confine most of the chips and sawdust under the table, where they can easily be picked up with a shop vacuum.

Most of the time I make a ¼-in.-thick Masonite template for the design I want to cut (figure 2), then fasten the template to the stock with double-faced tape (Scotch 400 Crepe line Double Coated tape, #021200-07131, manufactured by Industrial Specialties Division of 3M, St. Paul, Minn. 55144). I cut out the templates on an old 20-in. Delta jigsaw. Rather than messing with threading the blade through holes bored into the inside pattern areas, I cut the templates with a fine-cut sabersaw blade mounted in the lower collet of the saw. The blade is stiff enough to make an accurate cut on the thin Masonite. Usually

Joinery with a pin router

by Kelly Mehler

The pin router is one of the most versatile tools in my shop—it can do many cutting and shaping jobs by itself, and it complements the tablesaw, drill press and other tools I use. The router is particularly handy for finishing parts rough cut on the bandsaw or tablesaw. Using quick-release clamps or tacks, I fasten the rough-cut piece to a shaped template. By running the template against the guide pin, as shown in the photo at right, the router bit will plane the rough edges smooth and cut the stock to the shape of the template. If you replace the straight bit with a cove or roundover bit, you can mold the edge of the piece without changing templates.

Some of the router jigs can be used on more than one machine, a big production aid. The jig shown in figure 3, for example, is used with both the pin router and the drill press to mortise and bore ladder-back chair posts. The top of the jig has a V-shaped trough to support the post, and the bottom is Masonite with routed areas for slot locations. I clamp the post in the jig, fit a ¼-in. guide pin into the first slot and rout the rocker slot with a ½-in. spiral upcut bit. After taking the jig to the drill press, I bore the side rung holes, rotate the post 100° and bore the holes for the back rungs. Finally, I go back to the router and fit the ¼-in. guide pin into the bottom slots and rout mortises for the chair slots with a ¼-in. straight bit.

I use the router most often to cut mortises and tenons, a common joint on the custom furniture I build. Instead of the guide pin, I clamp the fence shown in the drawing to the table. After sizing the pieces, I cut the mortises freehand with a

To shape a tray, Mehler tacks the piece to the template, then cuts the edges while running the template against the router's guide pin, left. To check if the bit is mortising the center of the stock, he holds the wood against the fence and scores it with the bit, above. After flipping the piece end-for-end, he scores another mark. The two marks should coincide.

⅜-in. straight bit. For mortises the same width as the cutter, I adjust the fence by eye so the bit will cut in the center of the workpiece. To check it, I score the wood slightly with the bit, then flip it end-for-end and score again with the other face against the fence. If everything lines up, the two circular score marks coincide as they do in the photo, above right.

To cut a mortise wider than the bit, I locate the fence to set the thickness of the mortise wall, then cut to depth on that side before flipping the piece and cutting to depth on the other side. Any waste in the middle can be removed freehand. The depth of cut is controlled by a stop on the table mechanism. Generally I set it so the depth will be ⅝ of the width of the piece being mortised. When cutting, I seldom take off more

the cut is smooth enough that I don't need to sand the cut edge. Because of the size of the router table and the length of the pin router arm, the templates can be fairly large. The arm gives you 10 in. of work space between the router collet and the fence, so you can rout pieces up to 20 in. in diameter.

The pin router attachment is easy to use. I center the template over the bit, then bring the pin down and start cutting. The ½-in.-thick guide bushing on the pin only has to bear on a narrow section on the template, but I adjust it to reach the full depth of the template. When the bit is set to take a light ⅛-in. to 3⁄16-in. cut, you can hold the workpiece on the pin without making contact with the cutter. I turn on the router, slide the workpiece until the guide pin bears against the template, and plunge the work down onto the spinning cutter. The bushing will be bearing on at least the top 1⁄16 in. to ⅛ in. of the template, which is more than enough for guiding the cut. I follow the outline of the template on the first pass, moving the piece so that it's always going into the rotation of the cutter. Once I've outlined the pattern, I move the entire assembly back-and-forth, working from left to right, until I've cleared the waste in the center. I tend to take fairly light cuts, especially in the final stages when I'm trying to get a very

When cutting a recess on a box lid, Sporbeck follows a Masonite template fastened to the workpiece with double-faced tape.

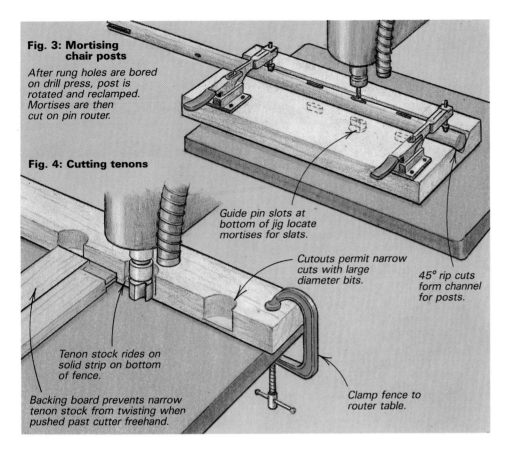

Fig. 3: Mortising chair posts

After rung holes are bored on drill press, post is rotated and reclamped. Mortises are then cut on pin router.

Fig. 4: Cutting tenons

Guide pin slots at bottom of jig locate mortises for slats.

Cutouts permit narrow cuts with large diameter bits.

45° rip cuts form channel for posts.

Tenon stock rides on solid strip on bottom of fence.

Backing board prevents narrow tenon stock from twisting when pushed past cutter freehand.

Clamp fence to router table.

than ⅛ in. to ¼ in. per pass, to avoid heating and dulling the bit.

I rout the tenons freehand after setting the fence and cutter depth by trial and error. The fence has a solid edge at the bottom, beneath the large openings that fit around the bit. By holding the end of the tenon stock against the solid section, as shown in the drawing, I can run the end past a 1½-in. straight bit. After making

the first pass to cut the tenon shoulders, I hit the edges with a hand sanding block to remove any fuzz that might throw the cut off. The backing board behind the piece prevents tear out and stabilizes narrow pieces. I round the tenon edges with sandpaper until they fit the round ends of the mortises.

The pin router can follow both simple and intricate patterns. To shape a pull on

a drawer front, I use a template with the shape of the pull cut into its base. When this shape bears against the pin, the cutter will form an exact duplicate shape in the work clamped on top of the jig. I often use a dovetail bit when shaping the handpull of a drawer front to create a pleasant undercut groove. If the router's normal guide pins are too large to fit into an intricate pattern, I substitute a tiny wooden plug that can follow delicate curves. Tiny router bits (Manhattan Supply Corp., 151 Sunnyside Blvd., Plainview, N.Y. 11803 has ¹⁄₁₆-in. end-mill router bits with ⅛-in. shafts) are especially useful for restoration work. To repair damaged fretwork, for example, I'll glue the old piece together and tack it to a piece of stock. By running the guide pin in the original fretwork, I can cut an exact duplicate without making a new pattern and sawing out the fretwork.

The pin router can do anything a router can do. It's great for breaking or rounding over edges, making molding, chamfering, and cutting any type of rabbet. With a straight bit, you can use it to mortise hinges into cabinet stiles. I even use it to round over spindle stock before turning. It's faster than sawing off the waste or turning from the square. Used freehand, it can cut letters. I use it to cut steps in chair blanks, removing most of the waste before I begin carving. The pin router is good for almost any type of joint. About the only joints I regularly cut by hand are dovetails. The machine will cut them, but I prefer the hand-cut look, and besides, I find cutting dovetails to be pretty relaxing. □

Kelly Mehler operates the Treefinery Woodshop and Gallery in Berea, Ky.

fine surface that won't require much sanding. My Craftsman 1½-HP router has a rack-and-pinion adjustment, making it fairly easy to raise the cutter with just a turn of the height-adjustment knob. As for any type of routing, sharp bits are important. Carbide bits hold up best. A more powerful ½-in.-shank router might work even better, and minimize the chance of bits being broken when cutting tough hardwoods.

My guide pins have ¼-in. shafts, the same diameter as the router bit shafts, but the actual bushing surfaces range in diameter from ⅛ in. to 1 in. I made the ⅛-in. pin by turning down one end of a ¼-in. drill rod. For the other guide pin I purchased drill rods in diameters from ⁵⁄₁₆ in. to 1 in., in ¹⁄₁₆-in. increments. I mounted each rod in a 3-jaw chuck on my lathe and bored a ¼-in. hole through the center. Next I bandsawed each rod into ½-in.-thick discs. I then slide whatever bushing I want onto the ¼-in. guide pin.

The size of the bushing is important. Most of the time I use one that's the same diameter as the router bit. To cut straight-walled partitions, I use a ¼-in. bit and ¼-in. pin. Since the guide and the cutter are the same size, the router will cut an opening that is an exact mirror image of the template. This saves me the trouble of figuring out how much undersize I have to make the

templates, as you often have to do when using various diameter pilots and bushings with a router, or making different templates to accommodate different size bits.

You can achieve some nice effects by varying the size of the bit and bushing. For example, I often cut patterns using a ⅜-in. bit with a ½-in. guide pin, which makes the routed opening ⅛ in. smaller than the template. Next, I use a ½-in. cove bit with the ½-in. pin. This cut removes the final ⅛ in. of material, making the opening the same size as the template, and pleasantly curves the walls of the recess. You could also use the same template to cut a rabbet along the edge of the recess, for a lid, for example, by using a bit wider than the pin. If you cut the recess with a ¼-in. bit, for example, you might make a shallow cut around the edge with a ⅜-in. bit to cut a ¹⁄₁₆-in. rabbet. The effects you can create by varying the size of the guide pin and the size and style of bit are almost endless. This is one of the nice things about pin routing. You get speed and precision, and still have lots of freedom to work in those custom touches that set off any project. □

Hans Sporbeck lives in Pewaukee, Wisc., and is a maintenance supervisor for an aerospace firm in Milwaukee.

A Shop-Built Panel Router

Tearout-free dadoes in large sheet stock

by Steven Grever

Fig. 1: Panel router

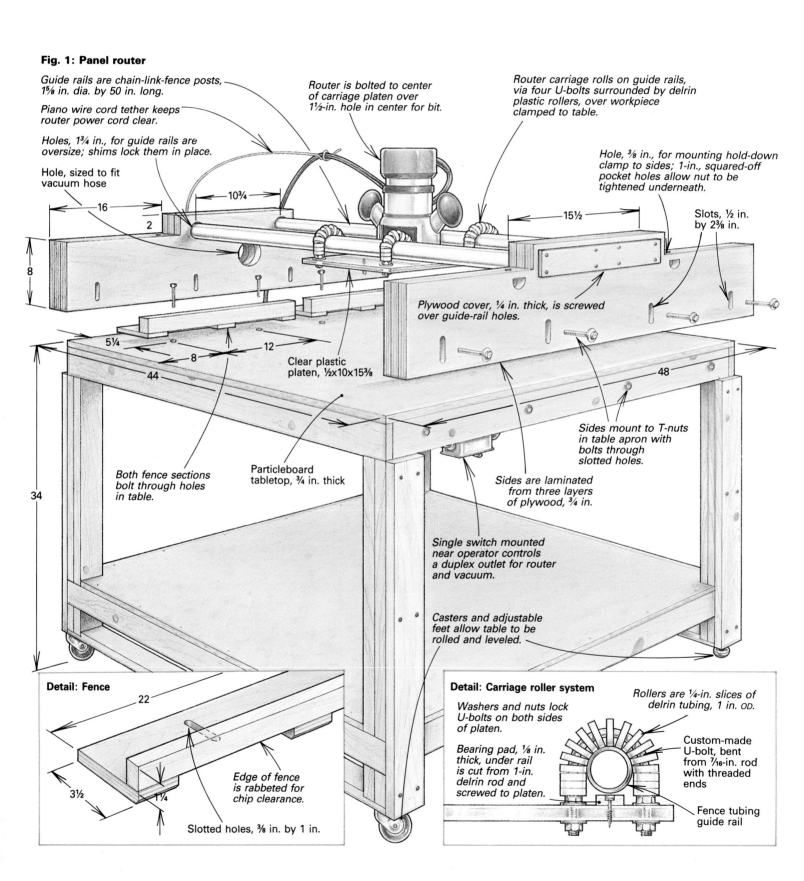

Guide rails are chain-link-fence posts, 1⅝ in. dia. by 50 in. long.

Piano wire cord tether keeps router power cord clear.

Holes, 1¾ in., for guide rails are oversize; shims lock them in place.

Hole, sized to fit vacuum hose

Router is bolted to center of carriage platen over 1½-in. hole in center for bit.

Router carriage rolls on guide rails, via four U-bolts surrounded by delrin plastic rollers, over workpiece clamped to table.

Hole, ⅜ in., for mounting hold-down clamp to sides; 1-in., squared-off pocket holes allow nut to be tightened underneath.

Slots, ½ in. by 2⅜ in.

16   10¾   2   8

Plywood cover, ¼ in. thick, is screwed over guide-rail holes.

15½

Clear plastic platen, ½x10x15⅜

5¼   8   12   44

48

Both fence sections bolt through holes in table.

Particleboard tabletop, ¾ in. thick

Sides mount to T-nuts in table apron with bolts through slotted holes.

Sides are laminated from three layers of plywood, ¾ in.

34

Single switch mounted near operator controls a duplex outlet for router and vacuum.

Casters and adjustable feet allow table to be rolled and leveled.

Detail: Fence

22

3½   1¼

Edge of fence is rabbeted for chip clearance.

Slotted holes, ⅜ in. by 1 in.

Detail: Carriage roller system

Washers and nuts lock U-bolts on both sides of platen.

Bearing pad, ⅛ in. thick, under rail is cut from 1-in. delrin rod and screwed to platen.

Rollers are ¼-in. slices of delrin tubing, 1 in. OD.

Custom-made U-bolt, bent from ⁷⁄₁₆-in. rod with threaded ends

Fence tubing guide rail

Photos: Sandor Nagyszalanczy; drawings: David Dann

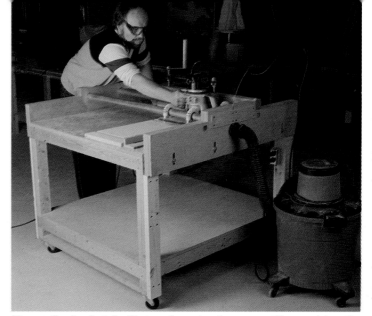

The author's shop-built panel router is a versatile machine for grooving or rabbeting delicate sheet materials without chipping them. Here, Grever cuts dadoes in melamine using a standard router mounted on the machine's sliding carriage.

W hile contorting to squeeze myself into the back corner of a melamine cabinet to touch up some chip-outs, I told myself there must be a better way to cut this stuff than on a tablesaw. The problem with melamine, I explained to my fussy customer, is that one piece will cut perfectly while the next will chip at the edges. My explanation fell on deaf ears. "Just get in there and touch it up if you want to get paid," my client dictated.

Once the ordeal was over and the check was in hand, I sat down to work out a small-shop system that would eliminate chipping when cutting or shaping sensitive sheet materials, like melamine or thin-face-veneered plywood. I had previously routed clean, crisp dadoes and rabbets in these materials, but moving the router from cut to cut and maintaining accuracy was difficult and time-consuming. What I needed was something like a panel saw, which would support the workpiece while the blade moved through the cut. But unlike a normal panel saw, the device I envisioned would employ a router and operate *horizontally* rather than vertically.

When I designed my device, I borrowed some ideas from commercial panel saws, which had the motor-blade assembly fastened to a plate suspended from two parallel guide rails. This setup was efficient, without being overly complicated to build. It also yielded several other advantages: most parts could be fabricated from wood or purchased locally; the router mount permitted easy installation or removal, so this versatile power tool wasn't permanently lost to one operation; the depth of cut could be controlled with the router's height-adjustment mechanism; and the device could be sized to accommodate a 24-in. panel, the largest size I was likely to encounter.

The panel router I ended up building is shown in the photo above and in figure 1 on the facing page. But even after working out a plausible design that incorporated the features mentioned above, I had to refine several details to make my machine function smoothly and accurately. I'll tell you how I solved these problems so you can avoid the same pitfalls if you decide to build your own panel router. Figures 1 and 2 illustrate the parts and sizes I used, but you may wish to make your machine larger or smaller. In any case, you'll need to build a router carriage and guide system, so I'll start with those components.

The router carriage – The heart of my machine is a movable carriage, which supports a standard router. Four U-bolts, each ringed with numerous plastic rollers, are attached to a clear plastic platen to allow the carriage to ride back and forth on two parallel guide rails suspended over a table on which the workpiece is clamped. I decided to use two 50-in. lengths of 1⅛-in.-dia. chain-link-fence post for the guide rails. I used a piece of tubing made of delrin plastic (available from a plastic-supply house) with a 1 in. OD and a ⁷⁄₁₆-in. bore, which I sliced into rings for the rollers. With those two components on hand, I calculated the size of the U-bolts needed for a snug fit between the rollers and guide rails. Unfortunately, I couldn't find the 2³⁄₁₆-in.-dia. U-bolts I needed, and so I headed to a local sheet-metal shop, which made me a pair of U-bolts from ⁷⁄₁₆-in. steel rod shaped with a wire bender and a jig block. My design called for the U-bolts to fasten to the platen with nuts and washers on both sides. This meant threading the legs of each U-bolt to 1¼ in. deep. I wish I had done this before the rod was bent because there wasn't enough room to rotate a regular die-holder handle between the legs of the U-bolt. Instead, I had to cut the threads with the die held in a pair of lock-jaw pliers; a much more tedious job.

I was now ready to make the platen. Polycarbonate plastic seemed just the ticket; besides being strong enough to support the router, the clear material increased visibility under the carriage. I cut out a rectangle 10 in. wide by 15⅜ in. long from ½-in.-thick

stock, and marked the U-bolt mounting holes, aligning them to match the 10¾ in. spacing of the guide rails. Next, I positioned my router over the exact center of the platen and oriented the grips in line with the guide rails. That way the grips could be used to pull the carriage back and forth. After marking the grips' orientation, I marked the location of the screws used to hold the regular plastic base to the router and outlined the tool's center opening. I used the drill press to bore all the holes, including a 1½-in. hole in the center of the platen, which is large enough to accommodate any bit I planned to use. Lastly, at the points directly under the center of each U-bolt, I drilled holes and screwed on solid delrin plastic discs, which serve as rub pads between the guide rails and the platen (shown in the detail in figure 1 and in the left photo on the following page).

I took the rollers I had previously sliced from delrin tubing and enlarged their center holes to ²⁹⁄₆₄ in., to allow the discs to rotate freely on the arched portion of the ⁷⁄₁₆-in.-thick U-bolt stock. After covering the unthreaded portion of each U-bolt with rollers, I added washers and nuts, as shown in the detail in figure 1, and attached the U-bolts to the platen. Next, the guide rails were coated with molybdenum disulfide (a dry lubricant available from your local bearing-supply house) and inserted through the U-bolts. I adjusted the tension on the nuts on the underside of the platen until the rail glided through each U-bolt pair freely, yet without excess play.

Building the table – To support the guide rail-carriage assembly, as well as the workpieces the machine would cut, I constructed a stout 44-in. by 48-in. pine table with a ¾-in.-thick particleboard top. No fancy joinery was needed: I used drywall screws to join the table's apron and legs and reinforced the joints with corner blocks and cross supports, for added strength and stability. Casters on two legs make this large table mobile, and adjustable feet on the other two allow the table to be leveled on an uneven floor.

Next, I cut out three layers of ¾x10x47 birch plywood for each of the side supports that hold the guide rails. Before gluing up the layers, I bandsawed a step in each piece, as shown in figure 1. After trimming and cleaning up the laminated sides, I drilled a number of holes as shown. Two oversize holes, 1¾ in. dia., were bored in each side for the guide rails. The extra ⅛ in. around each rail end provides enough play for adjusting the pieces to the same height and parallel to each other. The ends are then locked in place by shims, made from plastic laminate scraps, forced in

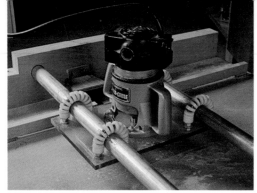

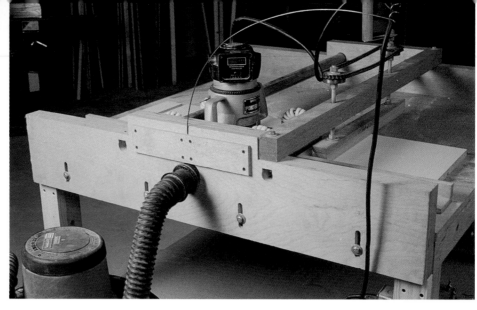

Above: *The router carriage is made from clear polycarbonate, held by four U-bolts ringed with plastic rollers cut from delrin tubing.* **Right:** *The laminated-plywood sides support the steel tubes that guide the router carriage and the beam for the hold-down clamp. Slotted holes allow the sides to move up and down, and one side has a hole for vacuum hose connection.*

around the rails and capped with a cover plate made from ¼-in. plywood. Bolts attach the sides to T-nuts in the table apron through four slotted holes (see the photo above, right). The slotted holes allow the height and tilt of the guide rails to be set so that the carriage will ride at exactly the same distance above the workpiece all the way across the table. Two ⅜-in. holes drilled in the upper edge of each side provide places to attach the panel router's hold-down clamp (made later). A ¾-in.-dia. hole is bored through the side beneath each of these mounting holes and then squared off with a chisel, to create a pocket for the hold-down bolt's locknut.

To hold workpieces square to the router's path of cut, I mounted an adjustable fence to the table. The basic fence is assembled from two pieces: a base and an upright section glued on at a 90° angle. Rabbets in the lower edge of the fence provide clearance for dust or chips, so they don't prevent the workpiece from butting up flush to the fence. For greater flexibility in adjusting cuts, I divided the fence into two sections, like a shaper fence. Bolts fitted through slotted holes in each fence section attach through holes in the table, bolted from underneath. With this arrangement, you can set each fence half independently; by offsetting them, you can edge-trim with the router.

To deal with the cloud of dust that routers produce, I made a funnel-shaped chute out of some scrap ⅜-in. plywood, and glued and screwed it to the side support and table just behind the gap in the fences. A hole bored through that side provides a socket for a shop-vacuum or dust-collector hose (size the hole as needed to fit your vacuum setup).

Wiring and the cord—For safer operation, the router is turned on and off with an easy-to-reach remote switch mounted on the frame of the table. This switch (a regular household on/off switch rated to handle 15 amps) controls a duplex outlet box mounted to the rear of the table. Both the router and the shop vacuum are plugged into this outlet and the power switch on each machine is left on, allowing the operator to start and stop both units simultaneously.

To keep the router's power cord from running afoul of the work or the carriage, I made a cord tether from a length of ⁷⁄₃₂-in.-dia. piano wire. I discovered this wire in a hardware store and found it was strong enough to support the cord, yet springy enough to flex as the router carriage moved. One end of the wire is held in place by screws under the ¼-in. plywood cover on the side support. A short section on the other end coils around the cord, leaving enough slack for the carriage to travel across the table.

The hold-down—My panel router needed some kind of mechanical hold-down, since hand pressure alone can't keep a workpiece

from creeping during a cut. Further, if a panel is cupped or twisted, the depth of a dado cut will change along the length of the cut—not a desirable condition. Therefore, I made the hold-down clamp shown in figure 2 and the left photo on the facing page. Its construction is sturdy, yet its chain-driven action makes it quick to use. The clamp consists of an upper beam that bolts to the side supports and spans the width of the table. The beam holds two threaded rods that ride in captured nuts and that are topped with gears linked together via a chain loop. A crank atop one rod turns both rods simultaneously to lift or lower the clamping bar evenly.

To make the hold-down, I machined the upper beam from ⁸⁄₄ oak, 1⅞ in. wide by 48¼ in. long, and drilled bolt holes on the ends of the beam to align with the mounting holes in the sides. For the raising-lowering mechanism, I bought two 3-in.-dia. chain gears, with ½-in. bore, and 40 in. of #35 chain (which fits the gear teeth) from a bearing company. The gears were mounted on two ½-in.-dia. threaded rods, one 9 in. long and the other (for the clamp's crank) 10½ in. long, held in place with nuts and lock washers above and below the gears. Placing the rods about 16 in. apart, I assembled a loop of chain over the gears and then separated the rods until the chain was moderately taut. After marking each rod's center on the beam, I drilled two ½-in. holes through the beam and counterbored halfway through from below with a ⁹⁄₁₆-in. drill. I then embedded two ½-in.-dia. by 1-in.-long nuts into the countersunk holes, pinning them permanently in place with sheet-metal screws.

Attached to the bottom of the threaded rods is a clamping bar. I made the bar from two pieces of yellow poplar, which is soft enough not to mar the workpiece. The ⅝x2x24 upper piece was drilled through with ½-in. holes on the same centers as the threaded rods. The top of the lower 1x2x24 piece was drilled partially through with two 1-in.-dia. holes, located on the same centers as before. These latter holes provided pockets for a ½-in. nut and washer on each rod end. Nuts and washers were then installed about 1 in. onto the ends of the threaded rods, and the upper half of the clamp bar was slipped on. A washer and nut were then installed, tightened only slightly, and locked onto each rod with a ⅛-in. tension pin driven through a hole drilled in the nut (shown in figure 2). After checking that the rods turned smoothly, I glued on the lower piece of the clamping bar. Finally, I installed an L-shaped hand crank, made from some flat iron and a length of 1½-in.-dia. dowel, on top of the threaded rod on the side nearest the panel router's fence.

Stop blocks—To increase the versatility of my panel router, I made a pair of hinged stop blocks that clamp to the guide rails

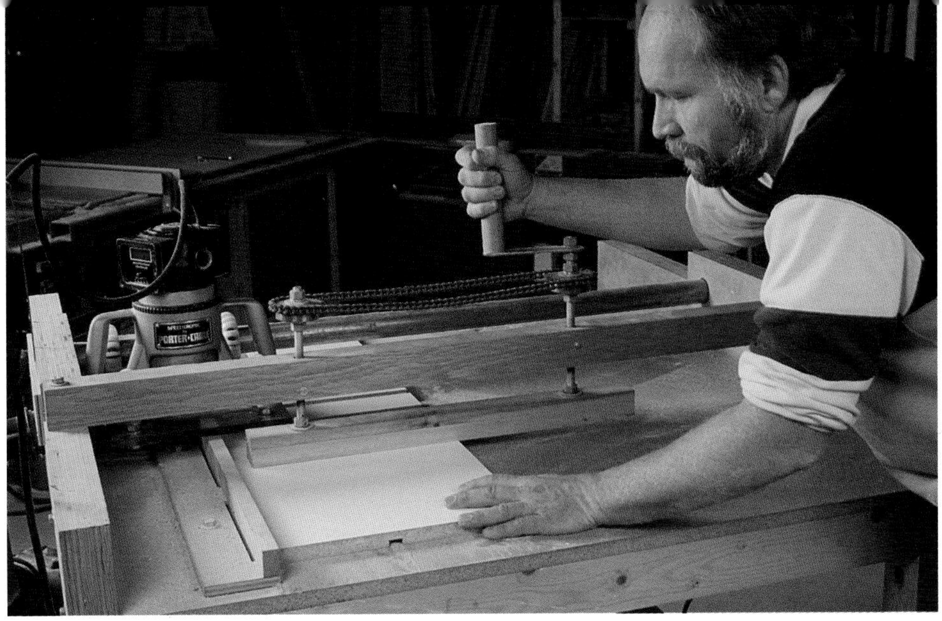

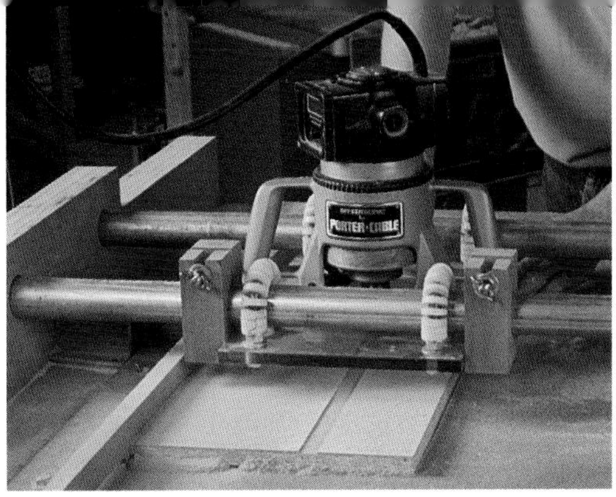

Left: *To keep sheet goods steady during routing, the author built a special hold-down clamp; two threaded rods, connected by gears and chain, raise or lower a clamping bar via a crank on top.* ***Above:*** *By locking the router carriage in place with two wing-nut-tightened stop blocks, the author can run sheet materials through the panel router for lengthwise cuts.*

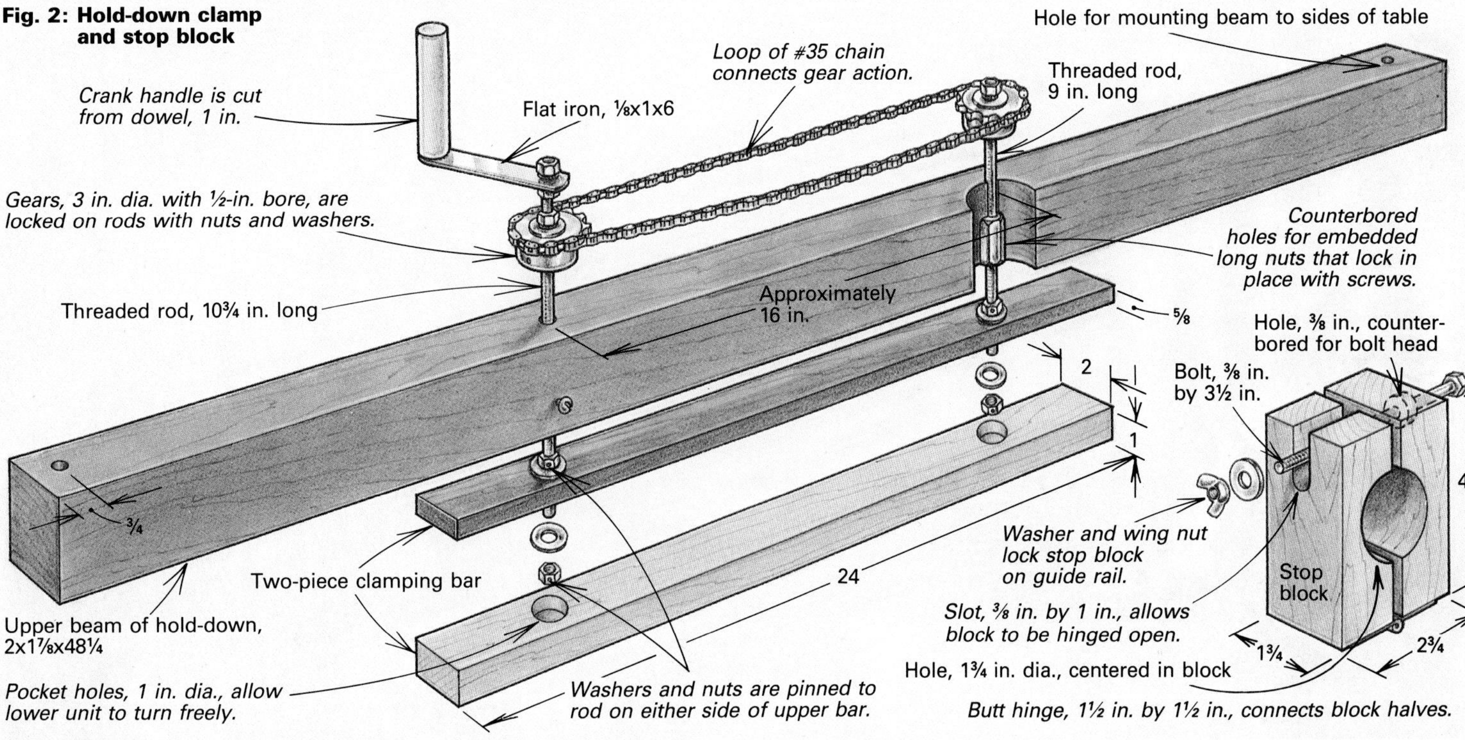

Hole for mounting beam to sides of table
Loop of #35 chain connects gear action.
Threaded rod, 9 in. long
Crank handle is cut from dowel, 1 in.
Flat iron, ⅛x1x6
Gears, 3 in. dia. with ½-in. bore, are locked on rods with nuts and washers.
Counterbored holes for embedded long nuts that lock in place with screws.
Threaded rod, 10¾ in. long
Approximately 16 in.
⅝
Hole, ⅜ in., counter-bored for bolt head
2
Bolt, ⅜ in. by 3½ in.
1
4¼
¾
Washer and wing nut lock stop block on guide rail.
Two-piece clamping bar
24
Stop block
Upper beam of hold-down, 2x1⅞x48¼
Slot, ⅜ in. by 1 in., allows block to be hinged open.
1¾
2¾
Hole, 1¾ in. dia., centered in block
Pocket holes, 1 in. dia., allow lower unit to turn freely.
Washers and nuts are pinned to rod on either side of upper bar.
Butt hinge, 1½ in. by 1½ in., connects block halves.

Fig. 2: Hold-down clamp and stop block

easily. Each block is hinged in the middle and tightened with a wing nut. By using one or two stop blocks, I can make stopped dadoes or run sheet goods along the panel router fence, for lengthwise cuts, as described below.

To make the stop blocks, I started with four yellow poplar pieces, each 2x2⅝x3¾. I bored each with two holes, one 1¾ in. dia. and the other ⅜ in. dia., located as shown in figure 2. Next, I used a ½-in. drill to counterbore each ⅜-in. hole from one end to ⅜ in. deep. Each block was then ripped down the center of its 2⅝-in. face into two halves. I made the ⅜-in. hole on the non-counterbored side into a slot by sawing out the waste on the bandsaw. I embedded the head of a ⅜-in.-dia. by 3-in.-long hex-head bolt and lock washer into the counterbored hole, gluing the bolt head in place with quick-setting epoxy. Once the epoxy had set, I screwed a small butt hinge to the side opposite the slot, connecting the block halves. The finished stop blocks open to slip around a guide rail and lock in place with wing nuts backed by washers fitted on the bolts.

Since using the panel router in my shop, I have found it more useful than I had anticipated. Of course, the device cuts dadoes across cabinet sides, for shelves or dividers, to perfection. But by locking the position of the router carriage on the guide rails using a pair of stop blocks on either side, workpieces can be rabbeted or grooved lengthwise, as shown in the photo above, right. The panel router can also cut stopped dadoes with one or both stops locked to the guide rail, limiting the travel of the carriage. You can also start and stop a cut in the middle of a panel by lowering the bit into the workpiece. This is possible with my regular router, but a plunge router would be much better. My panel router can also work as a pin router if you lock the carriage and fit a dowel guide pin directly below the bit. A thin pattern attached to the bottom of the workpiece follows the guide pin as the bit cuts the matching shape on the top side. You do have to be very careful, because there is not much room beneath the carriage for handling small workpieces. But more important than all these extra benefits, I have discovered that my panel router works melamine without any chipping. And that means no more angry customers telling me to touch up chipped areas inside cabinets. □

Steven Grever is a woodworker living in Madison, Wisc.

Surfacing Stock with a Router

How a simple fixture can true up wide boards

by Tim Hanson

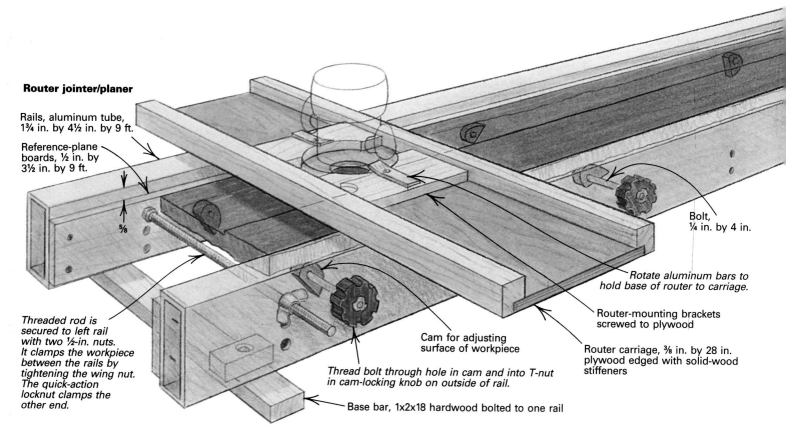

Router jointer/planer

Rails, aluminum tube, 1¾ in. by 4½ in. by 9 ft.

Reference-plane boards, ½ in. by 3½ in. by 9 ft.

⅝

Threaded rod is secured to left rail with two ½-in. nuts. It clamps the workpiece between the rails by tightening the wing nut. The quick-action locknut clamps the other end.

Thread bolt through hole in cam and into T-nut in cam-locking knob on outside of rail.

Cam for adjusting surface of workpiece

Base bar, 1x2x18 hardwood bolted to one rail

Bolt, ¼ in. by 4 in.

Rotate aluminum bars to hold base of router to carriage.

Router-mounting brackets screwed to plywood

Router carriage, ⅜ in. by 28 in. plywood edged with solid-wood stiffeners

Did you ever get a good deal on a load of lumber, only to notice while unloading it at home that the rough boards were all twisted, bowed or cupped? Then, as the stack of 8- and 12-in.-wide boards began to dwarf your narrow jointer, and it became clear that it would take forever to process the lumber, did the flush of a great deal give way to disappointment? I know the feeling. I put off using 500 bd. ft. of roughsawn walnut for more than two years because of the limitations of my 5-in.-wide combination jointer/planer.

Finally, I decided to set up a router to flatten the boards. I mounted my router on a bridge that would slide on my workbench while straddling one of the rough boards clamped to the bench. Oh, I got a smooth face, but when I removed the clamps, the bow and twist were still there. I needed to hold the board without clamping out its twists or bends, then pass the router over the board in a straight, flat plane—and I needed to know where that plane was in relation to the board. The router jointer/planer in the drawing above solved these problems better than I hoped. It consists of two aluminum rails with "reference-plane" boards screwed to their inside faces, six cams with locking knobs for aligning the workpiece's top surface with the reference plane boards, some all-thread rod to clamp the rails to the workpiece and a carriage for my 1½-HP Black & Decker router. For "planing" with the router, I use a 1¼-in.-dia. carbide mortising bit with a ¼-in.-dia. shank made by W.K.W. Wisconsin. The bit is available from Edwin B. Mueller Co. Inc., 3940 S. Keystone Ave., Indianapolis, Ind. 46277; (317) 783-2040.

How to surface stock—The two 9-ft. rails are the backbone of the rig. They provide a flat and true plane for the router carriage to slide on. The rough or twisted workpiece is supported between the rails on the adjustable wood cams. By adjusting the cams, you can raise or lower one end, or even one corner of the workpiece until its entire top surface is level with or higher than the reference-plane boards. The reference-plane boards are also used to set the depth of the router bit, therefore defining the plane in which the cutter will pass over the surface of the workpiece. After the top surface of the workpiece is set, the rails are "clamped" to the edges of the workpiece with an all-thread rod at each end of the rails. Then the carriage-mounted router is switched on and slid along the rails, "planing" the board flat.

The cutting passes are made in a continuous motion and at a moderate speed along the grain of the wood from one end of the board to the other. The cutter should be in motion at all times to avoid scorching a circle into the work. To thickness-plane the flattened board, set a combination square for the desired thickness and use it to set all six cams the proper dimension from the tops of the reference-plane boards. Lay the workpiece on the cams, flattened side down. When the router carriage is passed over the board, the result will be a flat, planed board.

I can surface both sides of a 1-ft. by 8-ft. board in a matter of minutes. Short boards, only 6 in. or 8 in. long, can be surfaced just as easily. I wouldn't cut a ¼-in.-deep pass with a planer, yet I think nothing of making such heavy cuts with one pass of the rout-

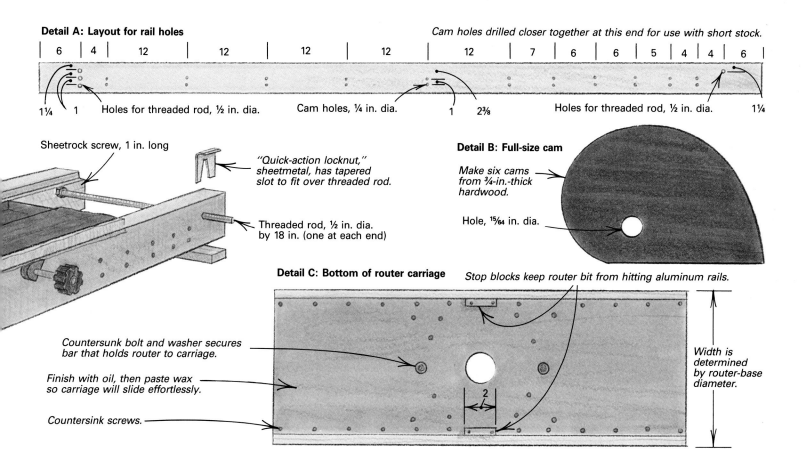

Detail A: Layout for rail holes

Cam holes drilled closer together at this end for use with short stock.

| 6 | 4 | 12 | 12 | 12 | 12 | 12 | 7 | 6 | 6 | 5 | 4 | 4 | 6 |

1¼   1   Holes for threaded rod, ½ in. dia.   Cam holes, ¼ in. dia.   1   2⅜   Holes for threaded rod, ½ in. dia.   1¼

Sheetrock screw, 1 in. long

"Quick-action locknut," sheetmetal, has tapered slot to fit over threaded rod.

Threaded rod, ½ in. dia. by 18 in. (one at each end)

Detail B: Full-size cam

Make six cams from ¾-in.-thick hardwood.

Hole, ¹⁵⁄₆₄ in. dia.

Detail C: Bottom of router carriage

Stop blocks keep router bit from hitting aluminum rails.

Countersunk bolt and washer secures bar that holds router to carriage.

Finish with oil, then paste wax so carriage will slide effortlessly.

Countersink screws.

2

Width is determined by router-base diameter.

er. If I want a super-fine finish, I raise the cutter ¹⁄₆₄ in. above the reference plane for the first cut, then lower the cutter to just clear the plane and make the final cut. I end up with a smoother finish than the planer gives me, with no little waves in the surface. In addition, the shearing action of the router bit leaves a nice finish on curly maple with no chip-out. Even if you have a thickness planer, this rig will come in handy as a 12-in.-wide jointer for flattening one side of a wide board in preparation for planing.

Jointing edges—I've had the router jointer/planer for about three months, and I'm still finding new tricks it can do. By removing the cams and clamping the rails to both faces of a board, you can "joint" edges for a straight glue joint. Using the same method, you can plane the faces of a 12-in. by 12-in. timber, or any other piece too thick to fit through a normal planer. Going to the other extreme, I've planed stock to ³⁄₃₂ in. thick for my son's dulcimer. First, I surfaced two sides of a ¾-in.-thick board and resawed it in half on the bandsaw. Then, with double-faced tape, I stuck the finished side of the resawn board to the finished side of a thicker board and used the rig to plane the resawn board to ³⁄₃₂ in. thick. No other tool in my shop would have handled such thin stock.

Building the fixture—The aluminum rails are light, rigid and perfectly straight. I got them free of charge from the owner of a glass company who salvaged them from a remodeled storefront. New, they would cost about $80. Drill the holes for the cams and the threaded rods, as shown in detail A of the drawing above, in one rail with a drill press. Then clamp the two rails together and use the holes in the first rail as guides for boring into the second rail.

After all the holes are drilled, attach the reference-plane boards to the rails. Make sure both boards are straight and true, then clamp them to the insides of the rails using a ⅝-in. spacer to check their distance from the tops of the rails. Don't forget, you want to end up with a left and right rail. Attach the boards to the aluminum rails with 1-in. drywall screws by drilling slightly under-

size pilot holes through the wood and the aluminum. This way the screws will act like sheet-metal screws and will cut their own threads in the ⅛-in.-thick side wall of the rails. After the reference-plane boards are secured, drill the holes in the rails on through the boards with a portable electric drill.

The cams, shown in detail B of the drawing above, and the cam locking-knobs are bandsawn from ¾-in.-thick hardwood. A ¼-in.-dia. bolt is threaded through a ¹⁵⁄₆₄-in.-dia. hole in each of the cams. The bolts pass through the rails and thread into T-nuts in the center of each knob. To make a knob, draw a 2-in.-dia. circle on the wood and then draw diameters to divide the circle into eight equal parts. Drill a ⁵⁄₁₆-in.-dia. hole at each point where the diameters cross the circle, then bandsaw out the original circle. Sand the rough edges and you have a nice knob with good finger grips.

The two walnut "base bars," shown above, provide a flat surface for the rails to sit on and ensure that both rails are aligned in the same plane. The bars are attached to a single rail with one bolt so they can pivot "closed" when not in use.

The all-thread rods are secured to one of the rails with a nut on each side of the rail. A wing nut on one of the rods and a shop-made, sheet-metal, "quick-action locknut" on the other clamp the rails to the workpiece.

Build the router carriage as shown in the drawing and in detail C above. Glue and screw the solid-wood stiffeners and the mounting brackets to the plywood. The router is held in place by two aluminum bars bolted to the carriage. Two small blocks screwed to the underside of the carriage restrict its sideways movement so the router bit can't contact the aluminum rails (see detail C). I finished all the wood with two coats of Watco Danish Oil and waxed the bottom of the carriage so it slides easily along the rails. □

Tim Hanson is a retired general contractor who still enjoys woodworking as a hobby in his shop in Indianapolis, Ind.

Fig. 1: Mortise jig

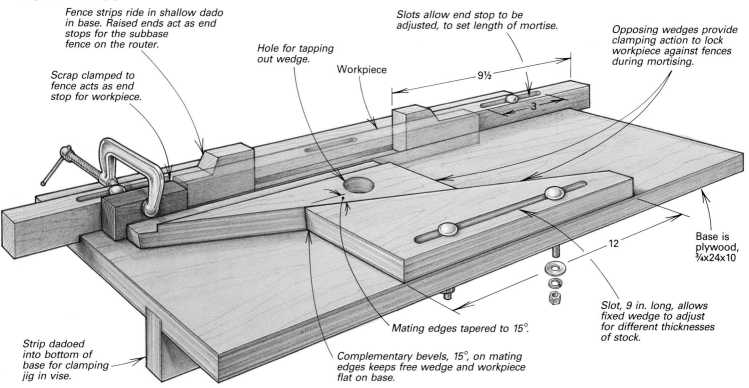

Fence strips ride in shallow dado in base. Raised ends act as end stops for the subbase fence on the router.

Scrap clamped to fence acts as end stop for workpiece.

Hole for tapping out wedge.

Slots allow end stop to be adjusted, to set length of mortise.

Workpiece

Opposing wedges provide clamping action to lock workpiece against fences during mortising.

9½

3

12

Base is plywood, ¾x24x10

Strip dadoed into bottom of base for clamping jig in vise.

Complementary bevels, 15°, on mating edges keeps free wedge and workpiece flat on base.

Mating edges tapered to 15°.

Slot, 9 in. long, allows fixed wedge to adjust for different thicknesses of stock.

Machine-Made Mortises and Tenons
Production techniques for high-quality joinery

by Mark Duginske

Craftsmen have been joining pieces of wood together for centuries, always looking for a better way to do it. Our ancestors had to depend on interlocking joints for strength because their glues were not reliable. Dovetails were preferred for carcases; mortise-and-tenon joints for frames. Today these joints are still favorites for high-quality work, but cost-conscious workers need economical ways to make them. Modern router jigs efficiently turn out miles of dovetails, but there's no comparable, low-cost machine for mortise-and-tenon production. So I decided to develop my own system for making mortises and tenons quickly and efficiently with shopmade jigs and standard machines found in most woodshops.

The mortise-and-tenon joint is ideal for frames of desks, chests of drawers, bookcases and cabinets of all kinds. Once a well-fit mortise-and-tenon joint is glued together, the mechanical contact and the large surface area of the mating faces make it very strong. Mortises and tenons are also great for joining stretchers to chair and stool legs, since the tenons' shoulders make the joint particularly resistant to racking. The joint's only real weakness is that the tenon can be pulled straight out of the mortise fairly easily, but this can be controlled by good gluing and, in demanding situations, a locking pin.

My joinery system is specifically designed for production with machines. A plunge router, fitted with an end-mill type bit and a special base, works in conjunction with a holding-and-referencing jig to cut slot-type mortises. The tenons are cut with both the tablesaw and bandsaw: shoulders are crosscut on a tablesaw, and then cheeks are ripped on a bandsaw equipped with an adjustable tenon fence. Finally, the tenons' square corners are chamfered to fit snugly in the rounded corners of the mortise (see the left photo on the facing page). One advantage of my three-machine system is that some setups can be fine-tuned independently of others. This allows you to go back and repeat a step, say if you accidentally mess up a cut.

Preparing the stock—The first step of my machine system is to rip all the frame stock to width and plane it to the same thickness. To ensure consistency and accuracy, every piece needs to be exactly the same thickness; otherwise it will be difficult to fit the tenons later. Also, make sure your planer's knives are parallel to the bed, or take the final pass over the same area of the bed. Next, cut all frame members to length, remembering to leave extra length on stiles or rails that will receive tenons. Be sure to cut a few extra

Photos by author except where noted; drawings: David Dann

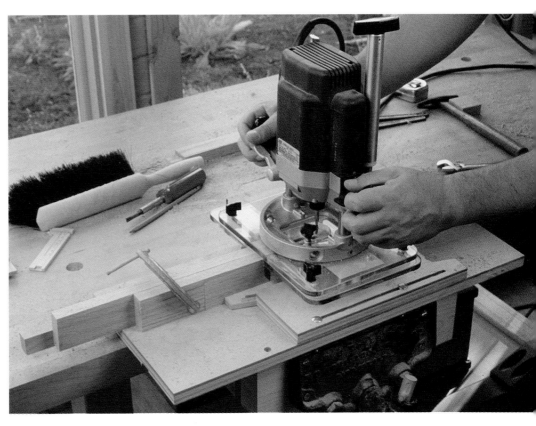

The author's system for cutting mortises and tenons, shown above, is based on three common shop machines: mortises are cut with a special plunge-routing fixture and tenons are cut accurately and efficiently with bandsaw and tablesaw setups. Shown at right, Duginske's shop-made mortise jig uses a pair of opposing wedges to firmly support the frame member on edge as the slot mortise is routed. The adjustable fence also features a set of stops, which limit router travel and hence the length of the mortise.

pieces of stock, which are later used to set up the jigs.

Traditionally, mortise-and-tenon joints are proportioned so the thickness of the tenon equals one-third the thickness of the stock; for instance, a ¼-in.-thick tenon would be right for ¾-in. stock. Likewise, the deeper the mortise, the stronger the joint because of the increased contact area between the two pieces. Usually on 2-in.-wide stock, I make the mortises 1⅜ in. deep. Later, I cut the tenons 1¼ in. long, which leaves a ⅛-in. clearance at the bottom of the mortise. In this case, members with tenons on both ends need to have an extra 2½ in. in length. On a narrow, 1-in.-wide frame, I would use a ⅞-in.-deep mortise and a ¾-in.-long tenon.

Cutting mortises—My machine method follows the same order that is traditionally used for handmade joints: I make the mortise first, which is cut with the plunge router and end mill, and then cut the tenon to fit into the mortise. Since most routers are a little top-heavy, and this makes them hard to control, I replace the standard router base with a special auxiliary base fitted with two adjustable fences. These fences fit snugly on either side of the workpiece during mortising, to align the cut on the thickness of the stock and to stabilize the router atop the edge of the workpiece, allowing it to only move forward and backward. Although I have made bases out of wood, I now use a clear, plastic base and fence system made by Woodhaven, 5323 W. Kimberly Road, Davenport, Ia. 52806; (319) 391-2386. The clear base makes it easy to see alignment marks on the workpiece.

The mortise jig, shown in the right photo above and figure 1 on the facing page, holds the workpiece steady during routing and provides stops for limiting the cut of the router. It can be assembled in about an hour from pieces of scrapwood and a few nuts and bolts. The jig consists of a ¾-in.-thick plywood base with a strip dadoed into the underside for clamping in a bench vise. A shallow dado in the top of the base holds two fences, and their inside ends serve as stops for the router base fence. Once the stops are set, the fences lock to the base with bolts riding in slotted holes. Two plywood wedges, each tapered and beveled at a 15° angle, secure the workpiece during mortising. One wedge is fixed, bolted to

the base via a slot, and the other wedge is free-moving. The tapered edges are driven against one another by tapping the free wedge with a hammer, forcing the workpiece against the fence. A hole in the free wedge provides a spot to tap, for separating the work after mortising. An end stop—a scrap the same width as the workpiece—is clamped or screwed to the router stop, to locate the end of the workpiece in relationship to the position of the router. Thus the distance between the mortise and end of the workpiece can be accurately set, for cutting corner joints. Only those frame members with mortises in the center need to be marked and positioned before mortising. In this case, I mark out the two ends of the mortise, put the router against one stop and then move the stock so one of the layout marks is aligned with the bit. After clamping the stock, I move the other stop to align the router bit with the second layout mark.

For efficiency, I follow a definite sequence in setting up the router and jig for mortising. First, I center the mortise, and then set the depth of cut of the router's bit; finally, the fence stops for the length of the mortise are set. The mortises must be exactly centered on the stock; it may take a little extra time setting up the fences on the router base, but you'll save time later when the tenons are made and fitted. The best way to check the position of the mortises is to make a plunge cut on one edge of a scrap piece, turn the piece over and make another plunge cut on the other side. When the cuts line up, the mortise is centered.

The router bit I use for mortising is a double-flute, "up-cut" end mill. This bit cuts on both the sides and the bottom, making a clean, slotted mortise. Flutes on an up-cut bit are similar to a drill bit: They pull the waste up and out of the cut. Although end mills are capable of taking up to a ⅜-in.-deep cut per pass, you'll get the best results with many small passes, perhaps taking ⅛ in. or less per pass. Move the router back and forth with a slow rhythmic motion and plunge slightly deeper on each pass until you reach the desired depth. Avoid heavy cuts: Overtaxing the bit can produce chatter or vibration that will leave the sides of the mortise irregular and rough and possibly cause bit slippage, which can rapidly wear the collet. The latter can not only cause too-deep mortises, but, if the bit slips completely out of the collet, it can be dangerous. Keep an eye on this by placing an ink mark on the bit and the collet; if the marks move during mortising, the bit is slipping and it may be time to order a new collet. Also, a sharp bit has much less of a tendency to vibrate than a dull one. If you do a lot of mortising, you might consider using solid carbide bits instead of high-speed steel bits.

If you're using a variable-speed plunge router, you should set it to run at about 12,000 RPM. The slower speed, combined with taking light passes, is best for smooth, clean mortises—especially with a small bit, such as ¼ in. dia., or with a particularly hard wood, such as maple. You should experiment on scrap stock before deciding on the best router speed.

The length of the mortise is now set by adjusting the mortise jig's stops. With my system, the mortise must be cut ¼ in. shorter than the width of the tenon stock because of the way the tenons are trimmed later. In this case, the stock is 2 in. wide, so the mortise is 1¾ in. long. Once the stops are adjusted, you're ready to run your batch of mortises. When machining wider stock, such as chair or table legs, the router can slide directly on the edge of a single member. But when mortising narrower stock, such as ¾-in. face frames, it's best to clamp two members side by side for a wider, more stable base for the router, to prevent it from tipping. After you've mortised all the necessary workpieces, mortise two extra scrap pieces for setting up subsequent operations.

Sawing the tenons—The tenons are made in three cutting stages. First, a shallow kerf is crosscut all the way around the end of the workpiece, to define the tenon shoulder. Second, the cheeks of the tenon, as well as the edges, are cut off. Finally, the edges of the tenon itself are chamfered to fit the round-cornered mortise. The shoulder cuts are made using the miter gauge on the tablesaw. I prefer to use a sharp crosscut or combination blade, which yields a crisp cut without tearout. The saw's rip fence is used as a stop for setting the length of the tenon, which is determined by the distance between the fence and the left edge of the blade. As a rule, you should not use the fence and the miter gauge together, but in

this situation you don't have to worry about a cut-off piece binding between the blade and fence. To assure a perfect tenon shoulder all the way around, square the miter gauge to the blade and set the fence parallel to the blade. Further, it's important for the face of the fence to be square to the table; otherwise, when you rotate the stock for the various cuts, the wood will contact different parts of the fence and the shoulder cuts won't match all the way around.

All four shoulder cuts are made with the blade at the same height, which is set as follows. Crosscut one of the extra mortised pieces through its mortise, place it next to the blade and set the blade to be about ⅟₃₂-in. higher than the wall thickness (see the left photo below). Rotate the blade back and forth to make sure you are setting the saw height with the tooth at top dead center.

After all the shoulders are cut, I cut the tenon cheeks on the bandsaw, which yields some distinct advantages over a tablesaw. First, the bandsaw blade's narrower kerf makes taking this power-hungry end-grain cut easier. Second, the cheeks are cut with the stock horizontal on the table; with a tenon jig, the stock sticks straight up, and the length of stock you can tenon is limited. Also, frame pieces don't need to be clamped to a jig, which saves time when cutting dozens of tenons. For accurate, repetitive cuts on the bandsaw, use a rip fence. If your saw doesn't have one, you can make the special rip fence, shown in figure 2 on the facing page, from wood scraps and carriage bolts. The face of this fence bolts to a subfence with wing nuts, which allows me to insert paper shims for fine-tuning the fence-to-blade distance and, hence, the thickness of the tenon. The subfence is bolted to a crosspiece that references to the edge of the bandsaw table, and it's attached to the table with a clamp. The crosspiece allows the angle of the fence to be fine-tuned for accommodating blade lead, the tendency of the blade to pull slightly one way or another during the cut. An adjustable stop, bolted to the fence through a slotted hole, allows you to set the depth of the tenon cuts. Although it doesn't make a great deal of difference what bandsaw blade you use, a ¼-in. four or six teeth-per-inch (TPI) blade works well. The bandsaw must be properly adjusted for this technique to work. To prevent the blade from fluctuating sideways, the guides are actually placed in contact with

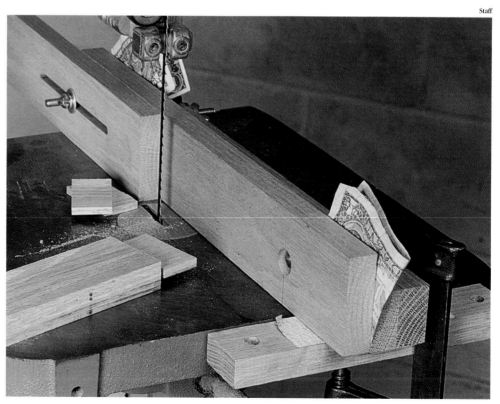

Above: A scrap piece of frame stock that's been mortised and cut through serves as a gauge for setting up the tablesaw blade for the crosscut that defines the tenon shoulder. The frame members are guided through the cut by the saw's miter gauge, while the fence acts as an end stop. Right: The tenon cheeks are bandsawn because it's easier to hold the stock horizontally during the cut, rather than vertically as with a tablesaw tenon jig. The tenon fence position, and hence the thickness of the tenon, is fine-tuned with dollar-bill shims.

the blade. I use cool blocks, which are non-metal replacement guide blocks containing a dry lubricant (available from Garrett Wade Co., Inc., 161 Ave. of the Americas, New York, N.Y. 10013; 800-221-2942) to decrease the friction created by metal-to-metal contact.

Set up the fence on the bandsaw, as shown in the right photo on the facing page, with the tenon between the blade and the fence, so as the cheeks are cut, the waste doesn't get trapped between blade and fence. Now use the scrap mortise as a gauge to set the fence-to-blade distance in the same way as you set the depth of the shoulder cuts earlier. With the mortise scrap against the fence, the blade should cut the first sample tenon about 1/64-in. oversize. Adjust the fence closer to the blade by inserting paper shims (I often use dollar bills for shims, because each one is 0.004 in. thick) between the fence halves and make another cut. Remember that the amount you move the fence will be doubled because you're taking that amount off each side of the tenon. Also, use a new piece of scrap for each new adjustment; if you use the previously cut piece, the bandsaw blade will deflect and you will not get a true reading. Ideally, the tenon should fit into the mortise with about 0.004 in. extra on each side, which is the thickness of a layer of glue.

After the face cheeks are done, trim the edge cheeks of the tenon back to the shoulder. This requires the fence to be reset so that the blade will take slightly more than 1/8 in. off each edge of the tenon. To do the trimming, follow the same procedure as with cutting the face cheeks, described previously. Remove material until the tenon is about 1/16 in. narrower than the mortise. In the case of a 1¾-in. mortise, the tenon will be 1¹¹/₁₆ in. This space enables me to fit the tenons by chamfering the corners rather than fully rounding the tenon.

Fitting the joint with bevel cuts—Since the tenon corners are square and the mortise corners round, the tenon won't fit until either the mortise corners are chiseled square or the tenons are rounded. After years of experimentation, I've decided that it's easiest to chamfer the tenons. The chamfers allow a small space between the flat surface of the tenon and round surface of the mortise, and ensure a perfectly mating joint because the space allows glue squeeze-out. If there is too much glue in the mortise, the space

releases the hydraulic pressure, allowing air or glue to escape. Chamfering can be accomplished by hand with a rasp, but it's better done on the bandsaw, especially if you need lots of tenons for a large job. Set the bandsaw table to 45° and adjust the fence so that it cuts off a small portion of the tenon's square edge. You may want to take the corners off a scrap tenon by hand and trial-fit it into a mortise, to get an idea of how much material has to be trimmed. Once set, chamfer all pairs of opposite edges on each tenon, and then tilt the table 45° the other way and repeat the cuts.

If you've been careful, you should have a close but not-too-tight fit between the mortise and the tenon. If the joint is too loose, the inside contact between the two pieces—so important for strength—is insufficient. If the joint is too tight, you may actually crack the frame members during glue-up or starve the joint of glue and leave it weak.

Gluing up—After all the mortises and tenons are cut, I usually test-fit the frames together. If I'm making face frames, as for kitchen cabinets, I like to reduce the thickness of the mortised members (usually the stiles) so that the tenoned members (the rails) on the front side of the frame are slightly proud (less than 1/64 in.). This makes it easier to plane the frames around the joints perfectly flush without cutting across the grain.

When I'm ready to glue up, I prepare all the clamps and clamp pads I'll need and clear a flat surface to work on. I apply glue to the tenons with a flux brush (available at a hardware store) with the bristles cut at a 45° angle. I then apply yellow glue into each mortise using a cotton-tip swab. When you clamp the frame, make sure the pressure is even at the joints. When all clamps are in place and tightened, check the flatness of the frame with a straightedge, measure the diagonals for frame squareness and clamp across to pull the frame true if necessary. Clean up squeeze-out with a sharp plane or chisel after the glue has dried for a couple of hours—not overnight. If the glue dries overnight, it becomes brittle and hard on sharp tools. □

Mark Duginske is a Wausau, Wis., author, instructor and woodworker. His latest book, Bandsaw Handbook, *was published recently by Sterling Publishing Co., 387 Park Ave. S., New York. N.Y. 10016.*

Fig. 2: Adjustable tenon fence

Fence, 16½x2x¾

Shims inserted between subfence and fence fine-tune fence-to-blade distance, to adjust thickness of tenon.

6

Slot in stop strip allows it to slide back and forth, for adjusting depth of tenon cheek cuts.

Holes in blade side of fence counterbored, so carriage bolt heads are below face of fence.

Sandpaper glued on top of crosspiece keeps fence angle from shifting.

Pivot bolt attaches subfence to crosspiece and allows slight angle changes of fence to account for blade lead problems.

Subfence, 1½x1½x14

Crosspiece, ¾x1½x8, references to edge of bandsaw table.

All-Purpose Joinery With the Router

A joint-cutting fixture that operates in three planes

by Claude E. Graham III

Back when King Tut's craftsmen were dulling their bronze chisels chopping out mortises in solid ebony, I imagine they dreamed of gadgets that would make joint cutting easier. Three millenia later, woodworkers are still seeking the all-purpose joinery device, and their quest seems to have spawned one-half dozen, do-everything router machines. One of these is the Multi-Router (see photo below), the invention of South Carolina industrialist and woodworker John Ducate, who borrowed a few tricks from metalworking machinery to expand his router's repertoire.

I first saw the machine while browsing at Highland Hardware in Atlanta, Ga. Even on first examination, it was easy to tell that the

Below: Like the metalworking machinery that inspired its design, the Multi-Router's joint-cutting accuracy comes from a two-axis worktable that slides on Thomson linear-motion bearings.

Multi-Router is a cleverly designed, well-made machine that addresses the router's fundamental weakness: how to hold the work (or, conversely, move the machine) precisely enough to cut accurate joints. Ducate's solution was to adapt to woodworking the kind of X-Y-Z axis milling system found on metalworking milling machinery. Here's how it works. The wood is clamped to a horizontal table that moves in and out (X-axis) and side to side (Y-axis) in relation to the bit. The router of your choice is mounted to a vertical table that moves up and down in relation to the horizontal table, providing a Z-axis. Although this movement seems complicated, it's kept under precise control by a pantograph-like ball-bearing stylus that follows a template fastened to the horizontal table. There's a series of templates for the various-type joints the machine is capable of cutting.

In its sales literature, JDS Co., which Ducate founded to make and market his machine, claims the Multi-Router will quickly cut mortises and tenons, box joints, dovetails and more. Since I wanted to explore all of the Multi-Router's capabilities, I ordered the basic machine ($1,495), the optional air-clamp hold-downs ($255), a metal stand ($88) and a collection of over a dozen templates (ranging in price from $13.50 to $18.50 each), for a total price of over $2,000, not including truck shipping or the router.

Setting up—Assembling the machine with basic hand tools is straightforward. The Multi-Router's X-Y- and Z-tables, which slide easily on hardened-steel rods, come factory mounted and have Thomson linear-motion bearings, which, as far as I can tell, won't clog with sawdust. The heart of this contraption is the router. For this, says JDS, you're on your own. The Z-axis plate is factory drilled for a range of router bases or it can be custom drilled as necessary. A gas cylinder connected to the plate counterbalances the weight of the router. I decided to go whole hog and slap in my 3-HP Porter-Cable Speedtronic, but it was too big to fit. An old Rockwell #6902 router worked fine. Given a choice of any router, I'd recommend one with at least 1¾ HP and ½-in. shank capacity. Unless you have a spare router, buy an extra router base to leave on the Multi-Router so you can alternate the router between bases.

The Multi-Router's operating instructions are, to put it kindly, vague. They consist mostly of photographs with numbered captions and labels for the machine's various parts. JDS says a better manual is in the works. Most of the Multi-Router's setups begin with a pencil line marked on the stock in the center of the joint to be cut. This mark should align with a fine index line scribed on the Z-axis table, providing a point of reference for all cuts. Simple enough. Unfortunately, the Multi-Router I received had the line machined ⅛ in. off center. I sent the machine back and JDS fixed it in short order, without cost or complaint.

Five days later, I tried my first joint: a mortise, which the Multi-

From *Fine Woodworking* magazine (September 1989) 78:62-63

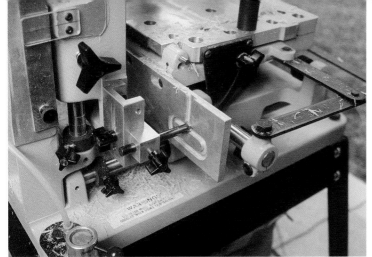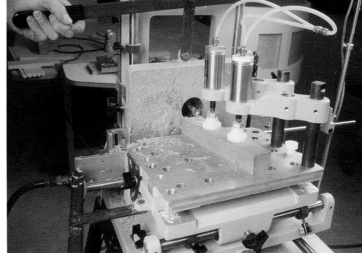

Left: To make a tenon, the wood is first clamped to the worktable, and then moved past the bit by a ball-bearing-tipped stylus that traces the template's profile, transferring its shape to the work. Right: A pair of optional air-actuated clamps holds the work firmly to the sliding table.

Router excels at making. The instructions included a long-winded photo essay on mortising; instead of reading them, I simply marked the mortise length on the stock, and then used my marks to set up the stops that control the cuts in all three axes. A pair of hand-screw hold-downs on the stock machine secure the work to the horizontal table, which is riddled with mounting holes for the hold-downs. While the optional air-powered clamps mount like the standard ones, their clamping action is powered by an air compressor and controlled by a foot pedal that allows the workpiece to be clamped and unclamped effortlessly. Once everything is adjusted and ready, the workpiece is plunged into the spinning bit using the X-axis lever, while the Y-axis lever simultaneously moves the table side to side to clear the waste. It's a very precise, controlled operation that takes less time to do than it takes to read about.

Tenon templates—To make tenons and all other joints except mortises, the Multi-Router requires an array of milled aluminum templates, each of which precisely matches the joint's shape. All together there are 14 conventional tenons and four round tenon templates. The first step is to select the template closest to the size tenon you want and mount it, along with the proper-diameter bit, on the machine. The bit size you'll need is stamped on the template. A steel rule on the operator's side of the machine indicates how deep the Z-axis cut will be and thus aids in centering the tenon in the stock thickness. A couple of thumbscrews set the ball-bearing stylus so it will accurately follow a template's profile. As with mortising, setting stops on the X-axis rails controls the depth of the cut and thus the length of the tenon (see the photos above). This is a four- or five-minute task that gets easier with practice.

When all this is done, the actual tenon cutting is over in no time. With the Z-handle, you insert the stylus into the template then move the Y-handle back and forth, and presto, the bit faithfully follows the template and produces a perfect tenon. Duplicate tenons can be cut by positioning the stock against a shopmade fence or by using the provided plastic locator pins that fit into holes bored in the table. Round tenons, on the ends of either square or round stock, are just as easily made. One of the Multi-Router's strongest features is that the worktable tilts between 0° and 45°, which means making angled tenons is a snap. This would be very welcome in a chair shop where oddball joinery is more the rule than the exception.

As a tenoner, the Multi-Router has a few drawbacks, but careful setup is required for good results. Also, because the stylus is trapped by the template, the router may fail to clear the waste if the stock is much larger than the tenon. In this case, you can retract the stylus and use the Y- and Z-axis control to freehand the waste, or you can just trim it off on the tablesaw. Some of the tenon templates I received were slightly undersize, but a little bit

of filing cured the problem. If the bits are slightly oversize from the factory or undersize from repeated sharpening, the tenon will be too loose or too tight. To compensate for inaccurate bits, JDS sells a special, adjustable tenon template that has three inserts of minutely different sizes, which allow for fine-tuning the tenon.

Box joints and dovetails—Making box joints and dovetails requires separate templates. The setup is not quite as involved for box joints as for tenons because the cut needn't be centered in the stock thickness. I cut a few practice joints in oak and found that, exclusive of set-up time, it took about 30 seconds to cut a clean, tight box joint in 5-in.-wide boards. The Multi-Router will box-join parts up to 8 in. wide; by relocating the stock on the table, however, infinite widths are possible, provided boards that extend beyond the table are supported. One limiting factor is that the width of the box-joined parts has to be an even increment of the bit diameter; otherwise you'll end up with odd-looking, fractional fingers.

Dovetailing on the Multi-Router is limited to either ½-in.- or ¾-in.-thick stock; to cut the tails, you need a 14° dovetail bit for each thickness. Two templates are required, one for the pins and one for tails, and as with the box joints, the stock widths are limited to even increments of the bit width and template spacing. You fine-tune the fit by changing the position of the stylus holder; this is a tedious process, but it's worth it for a stack of dovetails. In addition, a set of templates is available for making mitered dovetails.

Conclusions—I think the Multi-Router is a demanding machine to use. It requires much eyeball-alignment for such things as bit clearances and depth settings, and it requires a lot of knob-twirling (it has 12 separate adjustments) to set it up. Dealing with its various quirks sometimes made me feel more like a machinist's mate third class than a woodworker. But then quirks go with the territory when a single machine is expected to perform so many functions. JDS has put much effort into a machine that is surely useful to both weekend amateurs and small production shops. Still, at a base price of $1,495, some thought should be given to the Multi-Router's cost versus your anticipated use. Personally, the box-joint and dovetail capacities of the Multi-Router are too limited for my furniture-building needs, especially given the lengthy set-up time. But any woodworker in need of a slot mortiser and tenoner will find the Multi-Router up to the job; its additional capabilities—especially making compound-angle tenons—might be considered a no-cost bonus. □

Claude Graham III manages furniture production at Arc International Inc. in Jacksonville, Fla. The Multi-Router can be purchased directly from JDS Co., 800 Dutch Square Blvd., Suite 200, Columbia, S.C. 29210; (800) 382-2637.

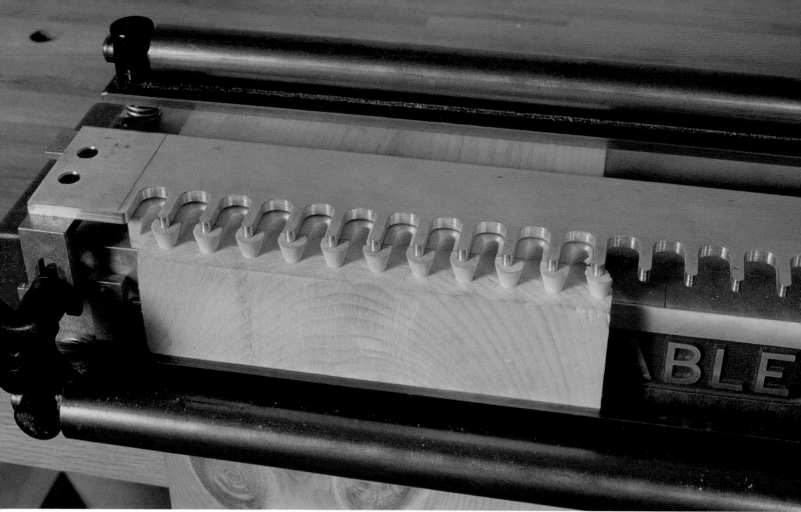

Like most dovetail jigs, Porter-Cable's Omnijig makes milling half-blind dovetails easy. The pins and tails have been cut simultaneously with a ¹/₂-in. dovetail bit. Side stops orient the pin board and tailboard to ensure correct alignment when the boards are assembled.

Comparing Dovetail Jigs
Versatile fixtures for cutting classic joints

by Alan Platt

I'm fond of sawing and chopping dovetail joints by hand for drawers and carcases. I like the personal touch that these joints, with their minor variations and, yes, small imperfections, give a piece. Cutting pins and tails is relaxing for me because I don't have to pump out lots of drawers or meet production schedules. If I did, I'd be looking for a jig that would cut the joints quickly and economically, without sacrificing that distinctive dovetail look. You could come up with your own jigs and fixtures to do the job, but fortunately there are many dovetail jigs on the market that offer a variety of desirable features, and for a good price.

For an investment of less than $100, you can purchase a jig and templates that will reliably turn out tight-fitting, half-blind, rabbeted or flush dovetails or box joints. These systems are fast, but don't allow the design variations possible with hand-cut joints. Pins and tails will have fixed, uniform spacings and the shape of the joint

components must match the stock router bit used to cut them. The photo above shows a typical router-based commercial jig for cutting half-blind dovetails. Joints resembling hand-cut dovetails, complete with variable-size and/or variable-space pins, can be cut on some models fitted with special templates. However, these inexpensive models generally cannot mill through dovetails, and you'll have to invest at least $300 to buy a more versatile jig.

All of the dovetail jigs I examined are based on the same idea: The pins and tails are milled with a router guided by a template. Construction of the fixtures ranges from extensive use of plastic and phenolic parts in the least-expensive models to heftier aluminum castings and steel components in the more-expensive models. In evaluating the jigs, I assembled, fine-tuned and tried them out according to the manufacturers' instruction manuals, which were generally clearly written. A typical assembly requires no

From *Fine Woodworking* magazine (September 1989) 78:46-50

special tools and takes just a few moments. With each jig, I joined enough pine boards to fine-tune the performance of each jig and produce several tight-fitting joints. I was surprised to discover that the inexpensive jigs performed as well as the costlier models. All of the fixtures I evaluated, once they had been adjusted properly, turned out quality joints quickly, but some models were much easier and faster to use. Therefore, apart from cost, your choice of jig should be based on the particular variety of joints you make and the amount of work you do. The chart on p. 33 lists information about the jigs that will help you compare them, and it explains the types of joints possible with each jig. You should check these details carefully, especially if your prime interest is through dovetails because not many of the jigs will cut this joint.

How jigs work—Most of the inexpensive jigs work the same way: A template guides a bushing on the router base and a dovetail-shape router bit cuts the tails and pins at the same time. Half-blind, flush or offset dovetails can be cut this way. The pin board is clamped, inside surface up, to the top of the jig's base so it butts perpendicular to the end of the tailboard, which is clamped vertically to the front of the jig. In turn, the jig is clamped to the edge of the workbench. The template overlays the pin board and tailboard and clamps to the base of the fixture.

Adjustable stops are used to align the edges of the boards to each other and to the template fingers. The fit of the tails in their sockets is adjusted by making small changes in the router bit depth. Increasing the depth of cut widens the tails and tightens their fit with the pins. Conversely, when the tails fit too tightly, the bit depth is decreased. The template can be independently adjusted to control the length of the sockets in the pin board and to make sure that they mate perfectly with the tails. If the sockets are too shallow, the template is moved back; if they're too deep, the template is moved forward until the fit is perfect. A few trial cuts on scrap pieces are sufficient to fine-tune the fixture and router. The major drawback of this type of jig is its inability to cut through dovetails. Jigs that cut through dovetails are more elaborate and use two templates, one for the pins and one for the tails. In addition to the usual dovetail-shape bit for the tails, a straight bit must be used to cut the pins.

Router requirements—For joint cutting, most jig manufacturers recommend at least a ¾-HP or 1-HP router. That's good advice, particularly if you work with hardwoods, such as oak or cherry. Because dovetails have tapered sides and are wider at one end than at the other, there is no way they can be milled in stages; the cut must be made in a single pass. Even relatively small, ¼-in. dovetails require a hefty cut, which can load down routers with less power; larger dovetails require even more power. Some of the manufacturers, such as Leigh and Keller, supply bits with ⅜-in.- or ½-in.-dia. shafts that fit only one-plus horsepower routers.

Except for the Keller and Wolfcraft models, the jigs I evaluated rely on a guide bushing attached to the router baseplate to guide the router. The bushing follows the edge of the template and prevents the router bit, centered in the bore of the bushing, from contacting the template. Unfortunately, the lack of standardization in router bases means that the available guide bushings won't fit every router. For example, Sears' guide bushings fit only Sears' routers. Porter-Cable's guide bushings, on the other hand, are compatible with several domestic- and foreign-made routers. Before investing in one of the dovetail jigs, determine if your router can be equipped with guide bushings that will be compatible with the fixture's templates. It's also a good idea to purchase the router

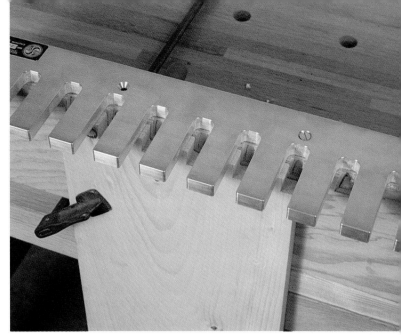

Cutting through dovetails requires using two templates. In the photo above, the Keller #2400 template has been used to mill the tails with a dovetail-shape bit, and in the photo below, the pins have been milled with a straight bit. The text describes the procedure in more detail. Note the templates are fastened to backing blocks, which align the stock to the templates and prevent tearout as the router exits the stock. Keller makes three models for cutting through dovetails in ¼-in.- to 1¼-in.-thick wood.

bits recommended by the jig manufacturer. These will have longer-than-usual shafts, which are necessary for the bit to extend through the bore of the guide bushing and clear its shoulder.

Jigs that cut uniformly spaced pins and tails—The lowest-price jigs are look-alike models, one of which is supplied by Sears, Roebuck & Co. (Chicago, Ill. 60684; 312-875-2500; catalog #2570) and the other by Vermont American (Lincolnton, N.C. 28092; 704-735-7464; model #23460), shown in the top, left photo on the next page. They handle boards up to 1½₆ in. thick and 8 in. wide. U-shape clamps, made from steel channel stock, hold the work firmly to each jig's base, but everything else is plastic. The jigs are furnished with two templates for milling ¼-in. and ½-in. flush or rabbeted, half-blind dovetails.

Sears and Vermont American also sell an additional template for

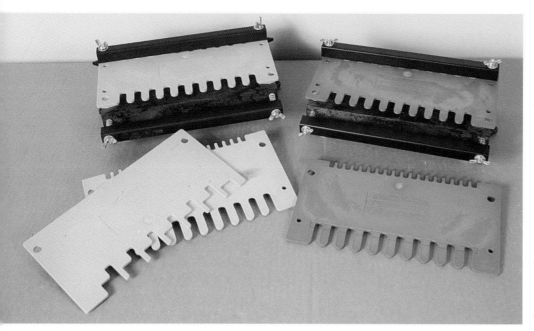

Left: The Sears jig (catalog #2570), left, and Vermont American jig (model #23460), right, are virtually the same. Capable of handling pieces up to 8 in. wide, these are the smallest jigs available; their light construction is more than adequate for dovetailing small drawers and boxes. Sears sells an optional template for milling hand-cut style dovetails.

Below: Wolfcraft's fixture is unique. Its specially designed baseplate attaches to the router and has a built-in adjustable stop to control the depth of the pin sockets. The pins and tails are cut using the pattern milled into the top and front side of the template, which clamps to the work. A small guide is used to align the jig with previously cut pin sockets so the jig can be indexed along workpieces of any width.

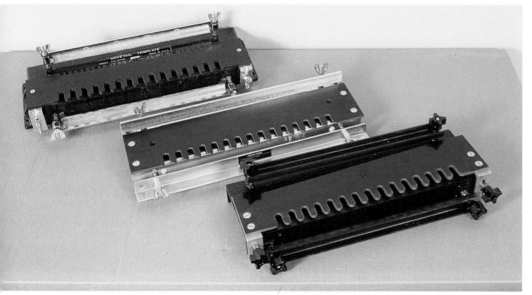

From top to bottom, the Sears model #2579, Porter-Cable model #5008 and Black & Decker model #C52331 can mill half-blind dovetails in pieces up to 12 in. wide.

cutting ½-in., widely spaced, hand-cut style dovetails. Molded into each template are directions for setting up the jig; although they're a little hard to read, they eliminate the need to keep the instruction manual handy. The templates are held in place by clamp bolts at the back of each jig's base. Small tabs, which are seated in the template, can be rotated to adjust the template's position, in or out, to set the depth of the tail sockets. Four-position stop blocks at each end of the base eliminate guesswork in aligning the pin board and tailboard. Although I didn't find any difficulty in producing snug-fitting joints, these lightly constructed jigs might not stand up well if subjected to heavy use.

Sears also supplies a larger fixture (catalog #2579), shown in the bottom, left photo above, that can handle 12-in. wide boards. This jig is also plastic, but more solid than the company's smaller model. This jig's two clamping bars are L-shape steel sections fastened with wing nuts. The standard two-sided template allows you to mill ¼-in. and ½-in. flush or rabbeted, half-blind dovetails. Instead of using tabs, the template position is adjusted by moving the template-bracket stop nuts, located at the front of the jig's base, in or out. Different settings for the side alignment stops are available, depending on whether flush or rabbeted joints are being cut.

The Porter-Cable jig (Box 2468, Jackson, Tenn. 38302; 901-668-8600; model #5008) and the Black & Decker jig (626 Hanover Pike, Hampstead, Md. 21074; 301-239-5000; model #C52331), both shown in the bottom, left photo above, offer the same 12-in.-wide capacity as the Sears #2579, but instead of being plastic, the jigs are all metal with phenolic templates. These two jigs differ from each other in minor ways, but performed equivalently. I like the large knobs on the Black & Decker jig, which are quicker and easier to use than the wing nuts on the Porter-Cable jig, but I prefer the built-in side alignment stops on the Porter-Cable jig as opposed to the removable stops on the Black & Decker jig; these small parts could easily be lost.

The jig made by Wolfcraft (1520 W. Ardmore Ave., Itasca, Ill. 60143; 312-773-4777; model #4250) operates differently than the ones I have already discussed, but it too produces excellent dovetail and box joints. As shown in the bottom, right photo above, the Wolfcraft's L-shape template is an aluminum casting with built-in screw clamps that secure the pin board and tailboard to a flat work surface. To use this jig, the tail sockets are routed first using the pattern in the template's vertical leg. Then, the jig is used to cut the tails, following the pattern cast in the template's horizontal

Dovetail jigs							
Manufacturer and model number	List price	Maximum wood thickness (in inches)	Maximum wood width (in inches)	Guide bushings (diameter in inches)	Straight bits (diameter in inches)	Dovetail bits (diameter in inches)	Templates (see key below)
Black & Decker #C52331	$232	1	12	S-$\frac{7}{16}$ A-$\frac{5}{16}$	***	S-$\frac{1}{2}$, $\frac{1}{4}$	S-#1 A-#2
Keller #1600	$169	$\frac{3}{4}$	6*	not required**	S-$\frac{1}{2}$	S-$\frac{7}{16}$	S-#9
Keller #2400	$269	$1\frac{1}{8}$	24*	not required**	S-$\frac{3}{4}$	S-$\frac{5}{8}$	S-#9
Keller #3600	$365	$1\frac{1}{4}$	36*	not required**	S-$\frac{3}{4}$	S-1	S-#10
Leigh #D-1258R	$339	$1\frac{1}{4}$	24	$\frac{7}{16}$, $\frac{5}{8}$ (available from router manufacturer)	S-$\frac{5}{16}$ A-$\frac{7}{16}$, $\frac{1}{2}$	S-$\frac{1}{2}$ A-$\frac{3}{8}$, $\frac{7}{16}$, $\frac{13}{16}$	S-Adjustable template cuts joints 1 thru 10
Porter-Cable #5008	$ 95	1	12	S-$\frac{5}{8}$ A-$\frac{5}{16}$	***	S-$\frac{1}{2}$ A-$\frac{1}{4}$	S-#1 A-#2
Porter-Cable Omnijig #5116	$299	1	16	S-$\frac{5}{8}$ A-$\frac{5}{16}$	A-$\frac{1}{2}$, $\frac{1}{4}$, $\frac{3}{4}$	S-$\frac{1}{2}$ A-$\frac{1}{4}$, $\frac{3}{4}$	S-#1 A-#2, 3, 4, 5 6, 7, 8, 9
Sears #2579	$ 49	$1\frac{1}{16}$	12	A-$\frac{5}{16}$, $\frac{7}{16}$, $\frac{5}{8}$	A-$\frac{1}{2}$, $\frac{1}{4}$	A-$\frac{1}{2}$, $\frac{1}{4}$	S-#1, 2 A-#5, 6
Sears #2570	$ 39	$1\frac{1}{16}$	8	A-$\frac{5}{16}$, $\frac{7}{16}$, $\frac{5}{8}$	***	A-$\frac{1}{2}$, $\frac{1}{4}$	S-#1, 2 A-#7
Vermont American 23460	$ 29	$1\frac{1}{16}$	8	A-$\frac{5}{16}$, $\frac{7}{16}$, $\frac{5}{8}$	***	A-$\frac{1}{2}$, $\frac{1}{4}$	S-#1, 2 A-#7
Wolfcraft #4250	$ 50	1	6*	not required**	A-$1\frac{1}{2}$	A-$\frac{1}{2}$	S-#1, 6

S = Standard, A = Accessory
* = Jig can be repositioned to eliminate width restriction
** = Bearing-mounted bit, bushing not required
*** = Not applicable

Templates:
1. ½-in. half-blind, flush or rabbeted dovetail
2. ¼-in. half-blind, flush or rabbeted dovetail
3. ½-in. sliding dovetail
4. Adjustable through dovetail
5. ½-in. box joint
6. ¼-in. box joint
7. ½-in. "hand-cut" dovetail
8. ¼-in. through dovetail
9. ½-in. through dovetail
10. ¾-in. through dovetail

leg to guide the router. A scrap piece, underlying the work, prevents tearout. In both cases, the depth of cut is controlled by an adjustable stop block built into the special router baseplate that is supplied with the jig. While the baseplate is drilled to fit many routers, check if it fits yours before you purchase this jig. The joint tightness is controlled by adjusting the router bit depth, as with the jigs already discussed. Although this template is only 6 in. wide, it will work on wider boards by moving the template and using the spacing guide to align the first slot in the template with the last cut of the previous setup.

Jigs for through dovetails – Keller (Keller & Co., 1327 I St., Petaluma, Cal. 94952; 707-763-9336; model #1600, #2400, #3600) is the only manufacturer I know that makes jigs specifically for routing through dovetails. The Keller templates, shown in the photo at right, are designed solely for through dovetails, and I found them uncomplicated and easy to use. The ruggedly constructed, ½-in.-thick, machined aluminum templates aren't inexpensive, but you may want all three models to work on a full range of wood thicknesses (see chart above).

Each model comes with two templates, one for cutting pins

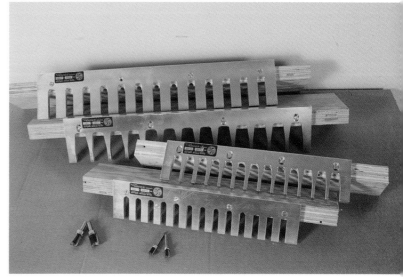

The Keller jigs are the only ones designed specifically for cutting through dovetails. The templates are simple to use and there is no limitation to the width of wood that can be milled. Shown are the pin and tail templates for model #1600, bottom, and #2400, top.

and the other for cutting tails, as well as router bits that have pilot bearings mounted on the shanks above the cutters, eliminating the need for guide bushings. The smallest bits have ¼-in.-dia. shanks; the largest, ½-in.-dia. shanks. Each template is screwed to wooden backing blocks (not supplied), and then the workpiece is clamped to the backing blocks, which prevent wood tearout as the router bit exits the cut.

Working with the templates is straightforward. The tails are cut first using the dovetail bit. Then, one or two of the tail locations are transferred to the pin board in the same manner as if you were making hand-cut dovetails. During production runs, stop blocks can be clamped to the backing blocks to eliminate any need for transferring marks, and to make it even simpler to align the pin board to the pin template. After the pin board is clamped, the pins are cut with the straight bit. The photos on p. 31 show the Keller model #2400 set up to cut the pins and tails. There's no restriction on the width of the wood: You just have to reposition the template and continue routing. If you're setting up the templates for the first time, cut a trial joint in scrap pieces to check the fit. You can adjust the fit of the joint in either of two ways: by changing the router bit depth or adjusting the pin template location. The pin template has slots for the mounting screws to allow this adjustment.

Shortly after I evaluated these jigs, Keller introduced revised versions of its templates for both the #1600 and #2400 models, which are now models #1601 and #2401. Keller is also supplying additional router bits with these templates, as well as for the unchanged model #3600 template, which increases the range of wood thickness these templates can accommodate.

Versatile hybrids—The Porter-Cable Omnijig #5116 and the model #D-1258R jig from Leigh Industries Ltd. (Box 357, Port Coquitlam, B.C., Canada V3C 4K6; 604-464-2700) offer a versatility that goes well beyond any of the other fixtures on the market. Porter-Cable's Omnijig, shown in the top photo at left, is adjusted and used the same way as the company's model #5008 described earlier, but it has a lot more going for it. For starters, its base is a heavy, ⅝-in.-thick aluminum casting, and all of the templates are machined from rigid, ¼-in.-thick aluminum stock. The Omnijig is also bigger than the #5008 and can accommodate boards up to 16 in. wide. An even larger model that can accommodate 24-in.-wide boards is also available. Best of all, I like the Omnijig's fast-action, lever-operated clamping system, which rotates eccentrically mounted 1¼-in.-dia. steel bars that uniformly clamp the width of the workpieces.

The Omnijig comes with a template for cutting ½-in. half-blind dovetails; but what really makes the jig versatile, are the many templates available as accessories, including ¼-in. half-blind dovetails, ½-in. rabbeted or flush box joints, ½-in. hand-cut style dovetails (varying sizes of pins and tails), ¼-in. and ½-in. tapered sliding dovetails, and adjustable-position, ½-in. and ¾-in. through dovetails. The half-blind dovetails are made with a single bit that cuts the pin board and tailboard at the same time, as described earlier. Hand-cut style and sliding dovetails each require two templates, and the pins and tails are milled in separate passes, but with the same dovetail bit. This is a well-made tool that will withstand heavy use; I found it easy to set up and simple to use.

The Leigh jig comes with a single, 12-element, adjustable template. I was amazed that this jig, shown in the bottom photo at left, could make so many joints. You can arrange the template elements in any pattern you like to cut through dovetails, end-on-end joints, box joints, angled dovetails, sliding dovetails, and half-blind, flush or rabbeted dovetails. It's the only jig capable of making both variable-width and variable-spaced dovetails. However, it is time-consuming to set up the jig because you must position and fasten each of the 12 elements individually. But that, of course, is the price to be paid for the jig's versatility. Like the Omnijig, this jig has a heavy, cast-aluminum base and the template elements are precision-machined aluminum castings. Although it worked well, I didn't care for the way the Leigh clamped the workpiece in place: You must tighten or loosen up to six knobs, two each on the top clamp, front clamp and template, each time the jig is used. Leigh's instruction manual is exceptionally well written and the company sells an instructional video for $29.95.

The well-built Omnijig owes its versatility to the several templates available for cutting fixed-space dovetails, finger joints, sliding dovetails and variable-spaced dovetails (not shown).

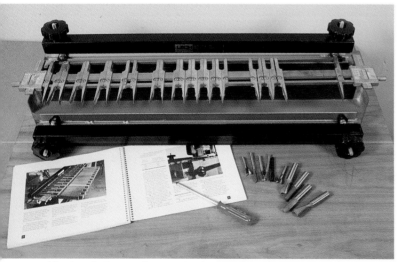

The Leigh jig employs a single template for all dovetailing operations. Pin width and spacing is set by adjusting each of the template's 12 elements; the corresponding tails, cut using the opposite side of the template, are set at the same time. Flipping the template end for end allows box joints to be similarly milled.

Alan Platt is an Assistant Editor at FWW.

Mortising Machine

A shop-built combination of router and precision sliding table

by Samuel Butler

A mortising machine can be an economical, precise alternative to hand work in any custom furniture shop. Sam Butler built his machine, above, with a stock router and an Inca sliding table. The rack on the base is for storing bits and cutters.

The speed and accuracy of a horizontal milling machine make it an important mortising tool for anyone who builds a lot of furniture. Commercially available machines can cost more than $2,000, but, for about $270, I combined my Bosch 2¼-HP router and a stock Inca mortising table to come up with the sturdy home-built model shown above. Equipped with a standard double-fluted cutter (see p. 37), the router is fast and powerful enough to make short work of most mortises, unlike many moderately priced mortisers, which are notoriously slow.

The key to my machine's versatility is the Inca table, which can move back and forth enough to make a 4-in.-long mortise. A handwheel and threaded-rod system also lets me move the table up and down enough to cut a 2½-in.-wide mortise without unclamping or shimming the wood in any way. The two nylon cam clamps supplied with the table are capable of gripping wood up to 4 in. thick. The table also has several precisely scored lines running perpendicular to its long edges. These marks are ideal for lining up workpieces or cutter bits. If the score marks aren't in the right position for lining up a cut, it's very easy to make temporary pencil marks on the aluminum table. As an added bonus, the sliding table tilts up to 90°, making it handy for cutting angled mortises for chair parts.

Despite the router's power, I don't hog large cuts in one pass. I seldom cut more than ¼ in. deep in a single pass, although I'm sure the machine could handle heavier cuts. I think this produces a neater mortise without straining the router or excessively heating the cutter. Actually, the lighter cuts don't take very long. Once the wood is clamped in place, you can adjust the Inca's horizontal stops, which work very much like the margin tabs on a manual typewriter, to control the length of the mortise. The depth of cut is set with a simple stop and setscrew arrangement. By working the machine's two control levers, one to move the table from side to side and one to slide the table in, you can make gradually deepening passes from horizontal stop to horizontal stop until you hit the depth stop. To widen the cut, you use the handwheel to raise or lower the table. Each turn of the handwheel moves the table about ¹⁄₁₆ in.

The cutters I use most often for mortising are Onsrud ⅜-in. and ½-in. double-fluted bits (part number 48-150 348 and 40-139 ½ AAK, available from C.R. Onsrud Inc., P.O. Box 416, Highway 21 South, Troutman, N.C. 28166). Because these cutters are shaped just like drill bits, the machine cuts mortises with round corners. Instead of squaring the corners with a chisel, I prefer to leave them round and shape the mating tenons. The machine could be rigged to cut tenons, but I find it easier to cut them on a tablesaw, then round the edges with a rasp and sandpaper. A jig for cutting the tenons with a hand-held router is shown on p. 39.

To hold the router assembly at a comfortable work height, I

Shop-built mortiser

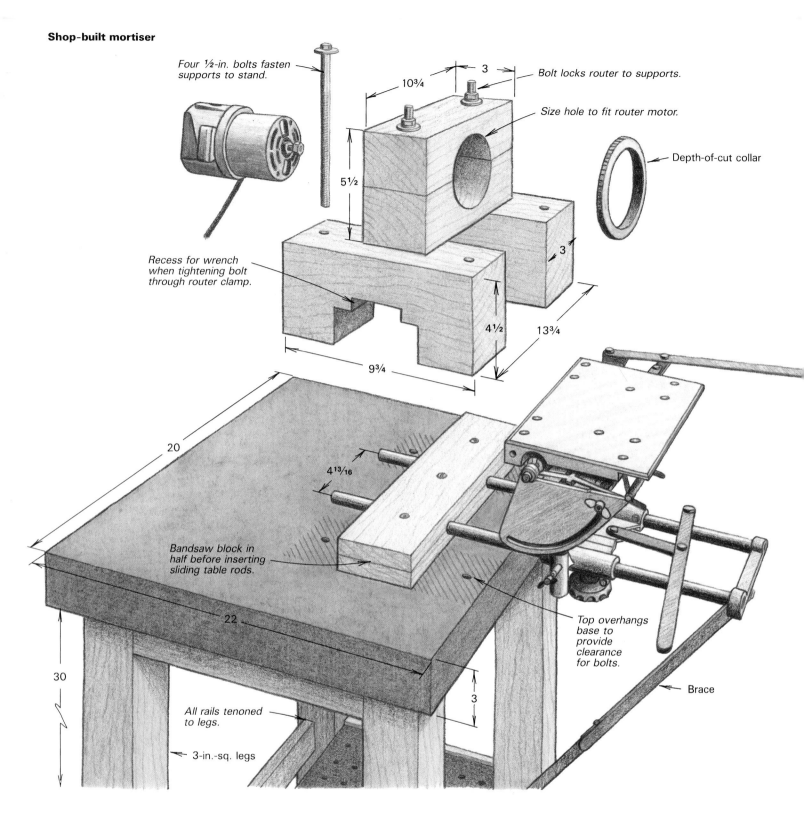

Four ½-in. bolts fasten supports to stand.

Bolt locks router to supports.

Size hole to fit router motor.

Depth-of-cut collar

10¾

3

5½

3

Recess for wrench when tightening bolt through router clamp.

4½

13¾

9¾

20

4¹³⁄₁₆

Bandsaw block in half before inserting sliding table rods.

22

Top overhangs base to provide clearance for bolts.

Brace

30

All rails tenoned to legs.

3

3-in.-sq. legs

built a stand with 3-in.-square hardwood legs and a 3-in.-thick top made by laminating four pieces of particleboard. I covered the top with a piece of wear-resistant, easily cleaned Formica. The design of the stand shown in the drawing is not important, as long as it's sturdy and heavy enough to minimize vibration, and to allow large pieces (like bed frames) to be mortised without tipping the machine over. I made my stand about 30 in. high, which puts the sliding table slightly above the level of my wrists when my arms are hanging by my sides. This height is especially important when working with long pieces. For a bed rail, for example, I clamp the end to be mortised on the table, reach over and support the wood with one hand while operating the table levers with my other hand.

After building the stand (using mortise-and-tenon joints), I cut two pairs of mahogany blocks, as shown, to secure the router to the laminated top. The Bosch router is ideal for horizontal mounting because the cylindrical motor unit can be removed from its housing and clamped in a bandsawn block of wood. Since the electrical cord is independent of the housing, the router doesn't have to be rewired. Just plug it into a switch-controlled receptacle after the motor is clamped to the table. You could use any router with a removable housing, but I'd recommend you pick one with at least a 1½-HP motor.

To bolt the sliding table to the stand, I improvised a simple wooden clamp to accept the two metal support rods that come with the Inca table. Once the rods are sandwiched between the two halves of the wooden clamp, the whole assembly is bolted directly to the table. You must be very careful when making this clamp. Since the clamp also provides tracks for sliding the table in and out, the two rod holes must be parallel to each other. Otherwise, the rods will twist when they are forced into the blocks and the table assembly won't move freely back and forth, making it difficult to vary the depth of cut or align the machine. I made the clamp from a piece of hardwood 1¾ in. by 3¾ in. by 13¾ in. long. Accurately square up the block before you bore two ¾-in. holes centered 4¹³⁄₁₆ in. apart. Again, accuracy is important, so make sure you bore the holes with a properly aligned drill press. Next, resaw the drilled block in half and clamp it around the rods. The bandsaw kerf removes enough wood to allow the two halves to clamp the table supports snugly when the block is bolted to the table. Before tightening the bolts all the way, square up the wooden block with the front of the table and position the table so that 14 in. of each rod hangs over the front edge of the stand. This will give you enough room to vary the depth of cut from a fraction of an inch up to about 3 in. without extending the table precariously from the stand. Inca also provides a metal table brace that goes from the end of the rods to the base of the stand. I think the rods and wooden clamp system

Bits for horizontal milling

by Rich Preiss

To get the best results from horizontal mortising or milling equipment, you need high-quality, well-designed bits. I've found two basic types of cutters, shown in the photo below, to be suitable: the mortise drill, which is patterned for wood, and the machinists' end mill, which is designed for metalworking but has many advantages for the woodworker.

Mortise drills resemble extra-long router bits. They are available in at least three types. The simplest one has a single, straight flute with occasional serrations on the long cutting edges to help chip clearance. The second type, the mortise miller, has a straight cutting edge and an additional row of deeply cut teeth that promote quick chip ejection, which leads to faster and cleaner mortises. The double-edge spiral cutter looks like an end mill but is designed for routing wood. Its flat cutting nose and spiral flute make for quick, smooth plunges and rapid chip ejection. These short cutters are ideal for mortising with a plunge router.

Two types of metal-cutting end mills work extremely well for mortising wood. Two-flute, center-cutting spiral mills provide the best combination for plunging and clean cutting. They leave smooth-walled mortises and eject waste rapidly. If you select double-ended cutters, you'll have twice as long between sharpenings for less than the cost of two separate cutters. For you carbide fanatics, end mills are available in carbide, including straight-flute router mills designed for metal. The carbide greatly extends cutter life in hardwoods or abrasive materials.

Over time, end mills have greatly outnumbered my mortising-style drills for many reasons. For one thing, end mills are more readily available in a greater variety of sizes at a significantly lower cost. The performance of end mills versus even the specialized mortise miller bits is virtually the same, although plunges are not quite as smooth due to the lesser rake angle of the nose's cutting edges. When sharpening is needed, end mills don't require the more exotic specialty grinding needed for the toothed-type or carbide cutters. In Charlotte, N.C., where I live, sharpening an undamaged, dull end mill costs $3. Carbide sharpening normally costs about twice as much. End mills, especially the smaller diameters, tend to come in shorter lengths than comparable diameter mortising drills, but this hasn't been a problem because narrow mortises are generally shallow. Because end mills are available in larger sizes, your ability to cut wider mortises in one pass is limited more by the chuck size of your machine than by the cutter selection. □

Rich Preiss supervises the architectural woodworking shop at the University of North Carolina at Charlotte.

A mortising drill (1) resembles a router bit with one or two notches in its long cutting edges for chip clearance. The mortise miller (2) has a long cutting edge and a row of chip-clearing teeth. The double-edge spiral cutter (3) has a flat nose and deep flutes for quick plunging and clearing. Two-flute spiral mills, flat (4) or round nose (7), plunge well and cut smoothly. Double-end cutters extend time between sharpening. Four-flute end mills (5) produce the smoothest cuts, but feed more hesitantly. Bits for aluminum (6) work well with abrasive hardwoods.

Sources of supply

Double-edge spiral cutters are available from Woodworker's Supply of New Mexico, 5604 Alameda, N.E., Albuquerque, NM 87113 and Garrett Wade, 161 Ave. of the Americas, New York, NY 10013. Mortise drills and miller bits are available from Garrett Wade.

Double-flute end mills and solid-carbide mills are available from Manhattan Industrial Supply, 151 Sunnyside Blvd., Plainview, NY 11803 and C.R. Onsrud, P.O. Box 416, Troutman, N.C. 28166.

are adequately strong without the brace, but since it came with the table I figured I might as well install it.

The dimensions of the blocks used to clamp the router motor to the stand are shown in the diagram. These dimensions allow for the 4 in. height adjustment of the table. Size the router hole to fit the motor of the machine you will be using. Again, band-sawing the block in half will give you enough clearance for snug clamping when the router is bolted to the table. When you remove the motor from its housing, also remove the depth-of-cut collar from the router. Flip the collar over so that the flat side, the side the router usually rides on, faces the motor. After inserting the motor in the wood clamping blocks, thread the collar back onto the base of the motor, as shown in the top left photo. The flat side of the collar makes a strong flange that prevents the router motor from being pushed back through the blocks under the strain of mortising.

You will notice from the drawing that ½-in. bolts secure the table clamp and the two router supports to the table. Another set of ½-in. bolts secure the router and hold it to the two supports. I bored ⅝-in. holes for all these bolts. The oversize holes allow enough free play to shift the router assembly slightly to align the motor shaft perpendicular to the table. When making this alignment, place a long bit in the router collet, move the table forward on its tracks and pivot the router/block assembly so that the router bit is exactly parallel to the lines Inca has scribed into the table surface, as shown in the photo at left. Caution: the bit is for alignment only. Don't use a drill bit in a router; the bits can't withstand a router's high RPMs. Since these lines are exactly perpendicular to the edge of the table, the router and the table will be aligned. Tighten the bolts and begin cutting mortises.

I like the speed and quality of this mortiser, and I'm also pleased that I did not have to give up a router to get a mortising machine. Once the mortising is done, the router can easily be removed from the blocks and used in its own housing for standard router work. □

Butler reversed the base on his Bosch router to make a flange that prevents the router from being pushed through its support blocks. To align the mortiser, he loosens the clamp bolts and twists the blocks until a long drill bit lines up with the scribe marks on the table (not safe for actual mortising).

Samuel Butler builds custom furniture in Kennebunkport, Maine. Inca mortising tables are available from Garrett Wade, 161 Avenue of the Americas, New York, NY 10013.

A commercial mortiser for small shops

If you don't want to build a mortising machine, a new tool called the Easy Mortise might be a low-cost solution for your shop. The machine shown on the facing page is a router stand married to a sliding table. Mount any 1-HP or larger router to the $398 stand, and you're ready to work.

Without the router, the Easy Mortise weighs 40 lb., hefty enough to operate without being clamped down. The 22-in.-long by 19-in.-wide by 16-in.-high machine is constructed of ⅛-in.-thick sheet metal, which is rigid enough to support the router and the workpiece without twisting. The router is bolted to a vertical plate that is raised or lowered with a threaded rod controlled by an easy-to-use palm-size plastic knob. After setting the router height, you tighten two more plastic knobs to lock the plate and the router in position.

Wood to be mortised is clamped on the machine's sliding table, which is large enough to easily accommodate a large board. My favorite aspect of the Easy Mortise is the 20-in. universal-joint control arm, which moves the table both into and across the router bit in one motion. The table moves on ball-bearing wheels that track on sheet metal ways beneath the table. Stop washers for the table movement are tightened onto a ⅛-in. steel rod with a thumbscrew. The rod is attached to the machine at only one end, making a wobbly, but adequate mechanism. Initially, I thought the wobble might be a problem, but all the joints I cut were true and accurate. Even so, a manufacturer's representative told me that new models will have attachments at both ends of the rod.

I didn't find much use for the pointer gauge and ruler mounted on the table front. The pointer didn't logically line up with the router bit, so I found myself referencing the cuts from marks I drew on the stock. This was somewhat awkward because the vertical router mounting plate makes it difficult to see where the router bit actually contacts the stock.

A lever-action mechanism holds the stock to the table and can be adjusted for different thicknesses by moving a series of nuts up or down on a threaded rod. At the end of the hold-down arm is a heavy rub-

Router tenoning jig

by David Marshall

I have developed a simple router jig that will cut "perfect" tenons at the rate of around 60 an hour. All you need are two pieces of plywood, three offcuts from the stock to be tenoned, and about 15 minutes assembly time.

Two offcuts are used to support the router base during the cut and form a channel to align your workpiece, as shown. A third piece is a stop to set the length of the tenon. When you build the jig, put paper between the workpiece and the two offcuts, so you'll be able to move the tenon stock easily. Clamp the three pieces together and nail the offcuts to the baseboard from underneath.

Cut the tenon with any sharp, parallel-sided, straight router cutter $\frac{3}{8}$ in. or $\frac{1}{2}$ in. in diameter. Insert the bit and adjust the router's depth-of-cut mechanism until the bit just begins to cut. Insert the workpiece in the guides, put the router on the jig and rotate the cutter by hand until it grazes the shoulder line. Then place a square against the edge of the guide and the router base and mark across the guides with a knife.

Step on the clamp cord to back the fence down, push the router across the jig and adjust the depth of cut. On the return cut, remove the waste at the end of the tenon. From there, work toward the fence as you cut away the waste. If the shoulder cut isn't exactly right, shim the stop block with paper or veneer, or pare the block thinner. To complete the tenon, flip the stock over and repeat the process. □

David Marshall is a woodworker in Gwynedd, North Wales.

Making the jig

1. Nail offcuts in position on plywood base.

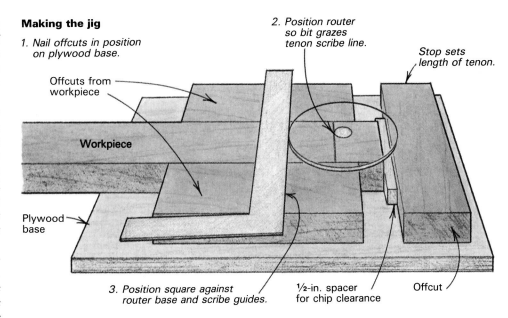

2. Position router so bit grazes tenon scribe line.

Stop sets length of tenon.

Offcuts from workpiece

Workpiece

Plywood base

3. Position square against router base and scribe guides.

½-in. spacer for chip clearance

Offcut

Using the jig

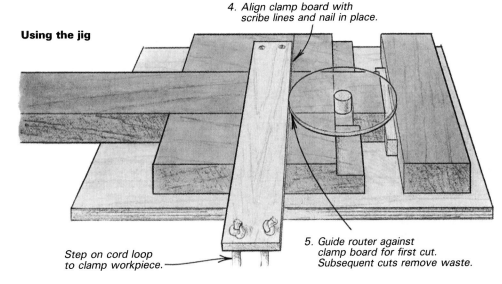

4. Align clamp board with scribe lines and nail in place.

Step on cord loop to clamp workpiece.

5. Guide router against clamp board for first cut. Subsequent cuts remove waste.

---

ber stop (like an industrial doorstop) that deflects onto the stock when the handle is lowered. Flanges protrude at the front of the table and on one side of the rear. When the stock is butted against these flanges, it's referenced either parallel to the router plate for mortising, or perpendicular for tenoning. You can cut accurate tenons if you set up a jig and stop block to cut the shoulders at the same depth. The mortise is the guide for setting the bit to cut the tenon cheek to be just above the height of the lower mortise wall, then the stock is set to overhang the table and the bottom cheek is shaved off with the cutter. The piece can be flipped over, realigned against the stop jig you built and the other side cut, or the bit can be raised and re-aligned against the mortise for the top cut.

I found the Easy Mortise to be a reasonable value. Unlike some inexpensive machines, the control knobs on the Easy Mor-

On the Easy Mortise machine, a single lever moves the sliding table in and out, as well as from side to side.

tise are large enough to grab hold of. The rubber pads the machine sits on keep vibration to a minimum, though I would bolt the machine to the table so long stock won't cause it to tilt. A heavier-gauge sheet metal would beef-up the machine, but if you're willing to take light passes and not bang the bit into the end of the mortise, the Easy Mortise won't flex excessively. On the negative side, I thought the hold-down mechanism was fickle when adjusting for thickness and it won't accept stock thicker than 2½ in.

All in all, the Easy Mortise, which is distributed by N.J. Cote Enterprises, P.O. Box 182, Cooper's Mills, Maine 04341, can do good work once you align it and devise stop references to suit your needs. The manual provided with the machine also showed some interesting ways to cut reeds and flutes and make shutters, but I didn't try any of those operations. —S.R.B.

Don Strong, left, cuts a sliding dovetail on the Joint-Matic, a router joinery machine he invented and manufactures in his garage machine shop. He subcontracts foundry work, then does final assembly himself. A similar small-scale manufacturing setup turns out the Wirth Machine, a sophisticated joinery tool developed by former aerospace engineer John Wirth, right.

Two New Joinery Machines
And a look at their backyard beginnings

by Paul Bertorelli

"Look here," says Don Strong, reaching into a plastic milk crate heaped high with small, gray iron castings, "this is the kind of problem you run into building your own machines." Pointing with a pencil, Strong shows me how sloppy pattern work mislocated a dimple needed to center a machinists' bit. At Delta or Powermatic, they'd probably toss the lot back into the furnace, then dispatch a stiff memo to the pattern foreman. Not Strong. He's devised a positioning jig for his drill press so the hole can be bored true, correcting the mistake.

Remedial engineering is all in a day's work for Strong, who in his garage workshop manufactures a machine called the Joint-Matic, a router-based joinery tool he invented nine years ago. The casting we are inspecting, a bracket for the Joint-Matic's cutter guard, is one of six that go into each machine. Recasting them would be costly and might delay shipment of the new ma-

chines, neither of which Strong's budding business can afford. So, to keep things rolling, Strong improvises.

He's ideally positioned to do so. As chief designer, manufacturing supervisor, quality control inspector and customer relations rep of Strong Tool Design, he's a one-man show, with a little help from his wife Bonnie, who handles the books. Strong is part of a tiny network of cottage-industry manufacturers sprung up during the past 10 years to service—and in part create—a demand for woodworking tools that the bigger companies don't make. He and John Wirth, another small-fry tool manufacturer I visited for this report, are true inventor-entrepreneurs, inveterate machine tinkers who've channeled their compulsive thingmaking into the manufacture of genuinely new tools. Wirth's machine, which bears its inventor's name, cuts many of same joints that the Joint-Matic will, but operates differently enough to provide an interest-

The Joint-Matic makes quick work of the sliding dovetails used in this leg-and-apron table joint with corner bracket. A compound miter gauge available as an option positions the bracket to cut the angled pins.

ing look at how a tool design can be approached in distinct ways.

Strong's Joint-Matic represents the direct approach. It was born out of the peculiar ingenuity of a woodworker accustomed to modifying machines to do what some workers might accomplish by handtools. "I had been building a little set of shelves...nothing really fancy, but it seemed a shame just to dado the corners," recalls Strong. He had in mind a sliding dovetail, an excellent carcase joint but a nuisance to cut by hand or machine. His Shopsmith and a new router offered a solution. If he could cobble up a bracket to hold the router, he could feed the work on the Shopsmith's horizontal table past the bit, cutting first the dovetail's socket, then the pin. After much trial and error, Strong got the arrangement down well enough to suggest commercial potential and two more weeks of night-time work refined it enough to produce the Joint-Matic prototype. The production machine looks a bit crude at first glance, but a shrewd design rationale lurks beneath its coarse exterior.

Essentially, Strong took the idea of a router table—an upright cutter past which the wood is fed via fence or miter gauge—and flipped it 90°. The Joint-Matic has two metal tables, one horizontal and one vertical. The vertical table, which holds the router, rides on two steel ways, allowing it to travel up and down, thus positioning the router bit relative to the work instead of the other way around, as with a router table. Wood is fed free-hand past the bit on the horizontal table or gripped in a tablesaw miter gauge that rides in a groove milled in the table surface. Borrowing a trick from metal-working machinery, Strong added a pair of steel lead screws synchronized by a bicycle chain and sprocket to crank the vertical table up and down.

Strong's design has notable advantages over a router table. For one, the lead screws have 16 threads per inch so they move the table (and bit) up or down $\frac{1}{16}$ in. per turn, where it stays put. Fine adjustments are made by cranking the screws through a portion of a turn. This is far better than fumbling with an imprecise shop-made fence and it gives the Joint-Matic remarkable accuracy, expanding its repertoire of joints. Using the miter gauge or an optional compound gauge for angled parts, you can grip the wood positively and feed it without slipping or skewing. The Joint-Matic solves one other router table shortcoming, as well: the router is mounted horizontally to one side of the cutting face instead of vertically beneath the cut so it doesn't suck sawdust into its guts, ruining the bearings and armature.

Originally, Strong had no intention of building the Joint-Matic himself. "I knew I had a great idea and that a lot of them could sell," says Strong, "but I thought I could make more money at it if I sold it to someone else." Strong offered his invention to Sears, Black and Decker, and Porter-Cable, all of whom turned it down as having too little sales potential. Rather than see the project wither, Strong began producing the Joint-Matic on his own, financing its development with income from his job as a millwright at an auto plant. "Every time I'd get $1,000 ahead, the money would go to pay for something...one week it might be patterns for castings, the next week it was the patent lawyer." By the time the Joint-Matic was ready for demonstration, Strong had spent more than $100,000.

To keep costs down, Strong used as many off-the-shelf parts as he could. The lead screws and table tracks, for instance, are standard industrial-hardware items. The sprocket and bicycle chain come from a Belsaw planer's depth-setting mechanism. Strong has castings poured at three foundries and subcontracts most of the machining and assembly work. Final inspection, testing, and shipping is done in his garage machine shop. The Joint-Matic

retails for $778, which includes a Bosch 1¾-HP router. Two options, a stamped-steel base and a compound miter gauge, cost $79 and $119.95, respectively. Strong sells a universal mounting plate so another router will work, so long as it has at least 1¾ HP and a ⅜-in. or ½-in. collet.

I experimented with the Joint-Matic for a couple of days, and I found that it's easy to set up and that it generally performs as advertised, without much fuss. It will cut basic carcase and frame joints like the mortise-and-tenon, box joints, several kinds of dovetails plus grooving and dadoing operations that yield various drawer corner joints. I think it's best at sliding dovetails, though. I usually don't bother with this joint for the same reasons that led Strong to invent the Joint-Matic. But his machine makes fast and nearly foolproof work of it. To make the socket, you chuck a dovetail bit in the router, set it to the desired depth, then position the bit by cranking the lead screws. The wood—say the side of a small carcase—is held upright on the horizontal table, fed into the bit and backed out once the socket is long enough. To cut the pin, you feed the wood held flat on the horizontal table, assisted by the miter gauge if the board is narrow.

Now the lead screws do their stuff. By referencing the initial bit setting from the same surface, usually the top face of the stock, you can accurately keep track of the bit's position by counting turns. If, for example, the wide end of the pin is to measure ½ in. and be centered in ¾-in.-thick stock, you simply crank the cutter down two turns (⅛ in.) and make one pass. Flipping the board edge for edge for the second pass automatically centers the pin. I got pins to fit perfectly by cutting them a little fat first, then trimming with partial turns of the crank. Increments as small as $\frac{1}{16}$ of a turn are practical, and move the bit about 0.003 in. At those tolerances, and because the Joint-Matic references off two surfaces, good results come only with accurately milled and square stock.

Mortising on the Joint-Matic is like mortising on a router table. You set the router to the desired mortise depth, center the bit in the stock thickness by counting turns, then plunge the wood onto the spinning bit, feeding it against the rotation as you go. Using spiral end mills (regular flute cutters don't seem to plunge as well), I got controlled, clean mortises on the Joint-Matic. The Bosch router has power enough to cut ⅜-in. wide mortises to about 1¼-in. deep in one or two passes. Anything wider or deeper gets a bit hairy. A ½-in. bit I tried grabbed and chattered unless I nibbled away at the mortise by tedious step cutting, which seemed more trouble than it's worth. Tenoning is done with the same bit set at the same depth. Using the miter gauge, the end of the stock is fed into the bit, cutting one cheek and one shoulder simultaneously. Flipping the board does the other half, centering

Wood to be mortised on the Joint-Matic is plunged onto the bit then advanced against rotation. Mortises up to 1¼-in. deep and ⅜-in. wide are practical. Tenoning is done by feeding stock with the aid of a miter gauge, cutting cheek and shoulder simultaneously. Flipping the stock edge for edge automatically centers the tenon in stock thickness.

the tenon. Again, I found it easiest to make a test tenon overlarge then trim to a perfect fit by tweaking the lead screw crank.

Through dovetailing is not the Joint-Matic's strong suit. If I hadn't actually done it, I wouldn't think it possible to cut both pins and tails, but Strong has devised a method that involves chasing one dovetail cut with another made at 90° to the first. At the end of all this, you're left to clean up the pins with a chisel, making me wonder why I hadn't started with a chisel in the first place. Half-blind dovetailing is more rewarding, the results looking like the round-bottomed jobs a Sears router-dovetailer produces. You can vary the pin-tail spacing, if you remember the correct number of cranks for each drawer front or side. On a carcase full of drawers, I'd prefer to use the Joint-Matic in the box-joint mode, at which it beats any of the tablesaw or router jigs I've used before.

Overall, I liked the Joint-Matic. Its forthright design reminds me of a mid-'60s station wagon: homely, but no hidden vices and rugged enough to last into the next century. The Joint-Matic's capacities and price are well-suited to an amateur woodworker's needs and, by dint of a first-rate owner's manual, anyone comfortable with a router should get good work out of it.

John Wirth's joinery machine, on the other hand, is an edge-of-technology counterpoint to the Joint-Matic's dowdiness. Where Strong's machine has a crank and bicycle chain, Wirth's has a complement of templates, gizmos and adjusters that make it a machine junkie's dream come true. In a way, the Wirth Machine's complexity reflects the background of its inventor. During the 1960s, Wirth worked as an engineer for McDonnell Aircraft, developing and testing airplane electronics systems in New Mexico. The climate appealed to Wirth so he settled there, founding Woodworker's Supply of New Mexico in 1972. His joinery machine is as much a result of his habitual need to engineer, as it is new product for Woodworker's Supply.

Wirth's experience parallels Strong's. He tried to interest Delta in a prototype at a time when that company's former parent, Rockwell, was selling its stationary power tool division and wasn't in a new-product mood. Powermatic nibbled too, but later declined to buy the design. Wirth ultimately invested some $70,000 of his own to put his machine into production. Like Strong, Wirth farms out the all-aluminum castings and major machine work. In a well-equipped machine shop in a corner of his retail store and warehouse in Albuquerque, Wirth makes the machine's accessories and does the painting, assembly and fine tuning. The day I visited, six machines in various stages of completion sat on long work tables while he experimented with jigs to produce variable-spaced

dovetails. In its current evolution, the Wirth Machine sells for $2,095, which includes a 1½-HP induction motor stepped up by belt and pulley to spin the bit at 20,000 RPM. A less expensive model, using a router instead of the induction motor, is being developed and is expected to sell for about $800.

Wirth's invention is an intriguing hybrid of a woodworking slot mortiser and a metalworking horizontal mill. It consists of an aluminum sliding table mounted to a base via bearings and a pair of steel tracks. The tracks and bearings allow the table to move along two axes, one perpendicular to the bit (y) and the other toward or away from it (x). Sounds like a slot mortiser so far, but Wirth added a twist. He mounted the cutter on a pivoting-arm arrangement which permits it to move up and down in the z-axis, then connected a template follower on top of the arm. By fastening a template where the follower can get at it, the machine functions as a part-reproducing pantograph.

In principle, the Wirth Machine is fathomable enough, but it requires undivided attention to set up, especially for operations involving the templates. All the basic joints are possible: the mortise-and-tenon, dovetails (except half blind), box joints, plus horizontal boring for doweling and neat, angled mortises for fixed-louver shutters. It'll also reproduce in wood any part capable of being traced by the template follower. If the base is bolted to a stout bench, the Wirth Machine can grasp and joint long stock, providing it's supported with roller stands.

I found the Wirth Machine to be a splendid mortiser, the operation for which it seems best suited. As with a slot mortiser, you first clamp the wood to the table with a fast-action clamp, then center the cut in the stock thickness, which, on the Wirth Machine, is done by locking the bit in its z-axis. Grasping a handle bolted to the table, you plunge the work onto the spinning bit by sliding the table in the x-axis. Moving the table back and forth in the y-axis completes the cut. Adjustable stops limit table travel, controlling the mortise depth and length. The Wirth Machine's cutting action is evener and quieter than you'd expect from a router, and mostly chatter free, chiefly because the induction motor doesn't bog down under load as does a router. By step cutting in three or four passes, I milled ½-in. mortises up to 2-in. deep and probably could have gone deeper with a longer bit. Mortising on this machine feels very safe because manipulating the table keeps your hands well clear of the cutter.

Every mortise deserves a tenon and at that, the Wirth gets involved. Tenoning is done by using the machine's one-to-one pantograph capabilities. Wirth provides Delrin tenon-shaped templates, each corresponding to a specific tenon size. One size, ⅜ in. by 2 in., comes with each machine, others are sold as accessories for $21.50 each. You screw the template onto an aluminum plate mounted on the machine's frame, then adjust the follower—a steel rod with a bearing threaded into one end—to contact the template. To cut the tenon, trace the template's profile with the follower by grasping one handle, which moves the bit up and down, and the other, which moves the table in both axes. This requires coordination not unlike rubbing your head and patting your belly at the same time, but it's not hard to get the hang of it and, while you concentrate on template tracing, the bit chews away all the wood that isn't tenon.

I got acceptable tenons easily enough but had trouble putting them where I wanted them. An index indicates how the template's position relates to what the bit will actually cut, but I found it time-consuming to adjust everything so that the tenon was accurately centered in both the thickness and width of the stock. Trial and error finally got the job done, but test tenons sliced off the end of my ever-shrinking scrap littered the floor under the radial-arm saw. The templates are made slightly undersize to compensate for a bit whose diameter has shrunk after sharpening. To fatten the tenon to a snug fit, you wrap a turn or two of tape around the follower. If it seems ludicrous to trim a $2,000 machine with a 29-cent roll of tape, the method does work and I can't think of a better way to do it. One nice thing about the tenons is that their radiused edges match the mortise, thus solving the nagging dilemma of whether to round the tenon or square the mortise.

Two other templates I tried, for dovetails and for angled shutter-louver mortises, were faster to set up. Both are 12 in. long, but the stock can be repositioned to allow for wide boards or long shutter stiles. The shutter template works particularly well, simplifying what would be a daunting task on a slot mortiser or a router table. Using this template, I was able to produce a 12-in.-long shutter start-to-finish in about 20 minutes.

The Wirth Machine's facility at shuttermaking suggests that its real potential is as a specialized joinery and shaping tool rather than as a general, jack-of-all-joints shop machine. If you want an odd-shaped tenon or one that's angled relative to the board's thickness, the Wirth Machine can accommodate. My joinery tastes are more straightforward, so except for mortising, I wouldn't have the patience to fuss with it unless I needed a dozen or so of one particular joint—which isn't always the case in the amateur's shop. But the sliding table is readily jigged and the template holder can accept all kinds of shop-built templates, making the Wirth Machine ideal for reproducing small or odd-shaped wooden parts, say in a pattern or model shop. An attachment Wirth sells for $325 converts the machine into a duplicator, which can reproduce long three-dimensional objects up to about 8-in. in diameter, a capability that ought to interest gunstock makers.

Wirth believes that's market enough to justify his investment and I for one would like to see him succeed. The major manufacturers introduce new products cautiously and then only if sales in the thousands are predicted. Wirth (and Strong) represent an innovative, less hidebound alternative source of new tools and there ought to be room for them in an expanding market. □

Paul Bertorelli is editor of Fine Woodworking. *For more information, write Woodworker's Supply of New Mexico, 5604 Alameda N.E., Albuquerque, N.M. 87113 or Strong Tool Design, 20425 Beatrice, Livonia, Mich. 48152. We welcome comments from owners of machines described in this report.*

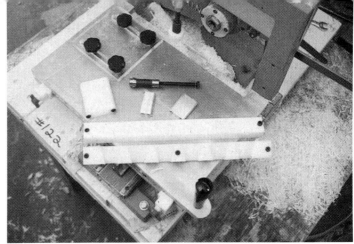

About two dozen templates are available, including those for various sized tenons and for dovetails. The templates are made of a tough plastic called Delrin. The Wirth Machine's collet, top of photo, is drawn into a hollow tapered spindle by a long bolt.

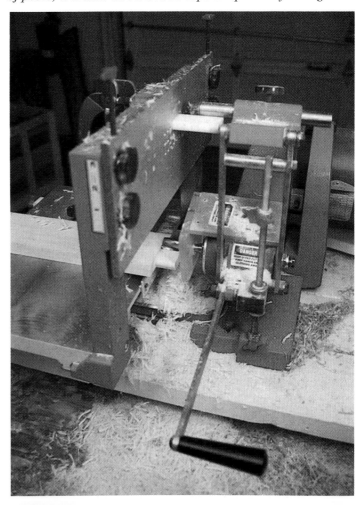

The Wirth Machine set up for tenoning. The template follower, top, traces the template, guiding the bit to reproduce its profile on the end of the stock. As the bit cuts, the wood is held firmly against a plastic plate, setting the shoulder depth.

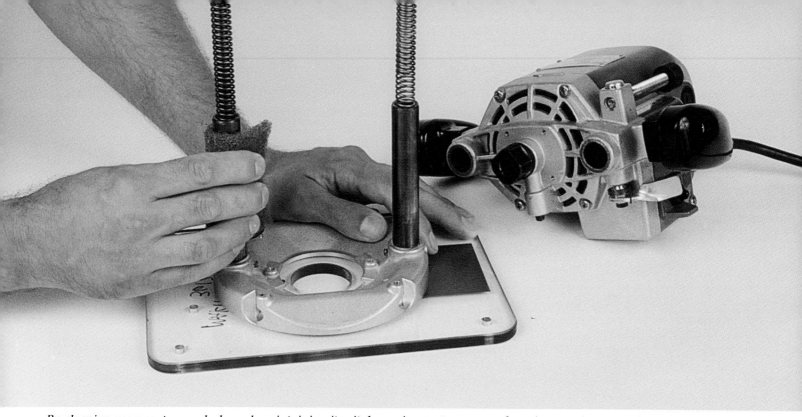

By cleaning your router regularly and maintaining its vital running parts, you can keep it operating at peak performance for many years. Here, a plunge router's motor housing has been removed from its base so that the columns can be cleaned with a plastic abrasive pad.

Tuning Your Router
Maintenance and tips for top performance

by Mark Duginske

When woodworking historians look back at the 20th century, the tool they probably will spotlight is the router. This American invention has invaded all aspects of woodworking: It is the first-recommended power tool for a novice, and it is a workhorse for the professional. But while many woodworkers assume that a router will automatically produce good results—just install the bit and you're ready to go—it's not all that simple. In many respects, the router needs more maintenance and care than any other tool in the shop.

A router has wearing parts, such as the brushes, bearings and collet, that should occasionally be replaced over the life of the tool. Tuning your router means caring for its basic parts and knowing when those key parts need to be replaced. This and a few other tricks will help you get the best performance out of any router, whether it's a bargain-basement cheapie or a top-of-the-line bruiser, as well as help keep repair bills down. I'll tell you exactly what you have to do, but first let's examine the collet: the Achilles' heel of a router and the part that usually needs the most attention.

The collet—The collet is the device that holds the router bit. The inside is straight to fit the bit's shaft, while the outside is tapered

and fits into the cone at the end of the arbor shaft. As the locking nut is tightened, the collet is pushed into the cone and the bit is squeezed tight. The compressive force on the outside of the collet is concentrated on the bit shaft. Unlike the drill chuck, which holds the drill with three points, the collet holds the bit with the entire inside surface.

Not all router collets are created equally and many routing problems can be traced to the design of the collet itself. A router can have a powerful motor and attractive features, but if it has an inferior collet it is still a poor machine. To hold a bit securely, a collet must be flexible; the best collets have many slits in them and are so flexible that you can easily compress them with your fingers (see the left photo on the facing page). Conversely, some simpler collets are very stiff and do not do a good job of gripping the bit. Here is a quick review of several collet designs found on most routers.

With the simplest collets, such as the ones used on many laminate-trimming routers and some Sears models, the actual collet that grips the bit is machined directly onto the end of the arbor (see A in the drawing) and a separate locking nut tightens the collet around the bit. The problem with this design is if the collet wears out or is damaged, the entire arbor must be replaced.

From *Fine Woodworking* magazine (January 1991) 86:56-59

Router collet designs

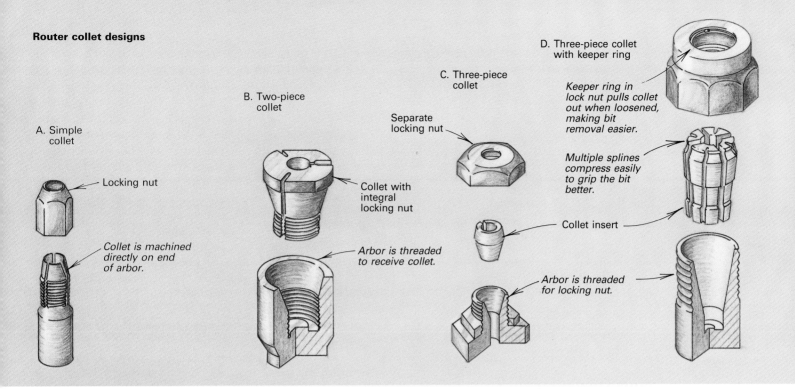

A. Simple collet — Locking nut — Collet is machined directly on end of arbor.

B. Two-piece collet — Collet with integral locking nut — Arbor is threaded to receive collet.

C. Three-piece collet — Separate locking nut — Collet insert — Arbor is threaded for locking nut.

D. Three-piece collet with keeper ring — Keeper ring in lock nut pulls collet out when loosened, making bit removal easier. Multiple splines compress easily to grip the bit better.

In order for a three-piece collet to get a good grip on the shank of a router bit, it must compress into its socket on the router arbor when the locking nut is tightened. **Left:** *Multiple-spline collets like the one here are very flexible and compress easily to grip a bit firmly.* **Center:** *To keep rust, pitch and grime from causing prob-lems, a router collet should be kept clean inside and out. Using a fine-bristle brass brush to clean the collet's bore makes that job a snap. Pitch and dirt produced during routing can also foul the collet socket in the router's arbor* **(right),** *as well as threads that hold the collet's locking nut.*

A two-piece system, such as that used on many Japanese-made routers and certain Porter-Cable and older Rockwell models, has a separate collet that screws into the end of the arbor (see B in the drawing). As the nut atop this collet is tightened, the arbor's tapered socket presses the collet's cone-shaped body, tightening the collet around the bit. But there are two problems with this design: Two-piece collets (even those models with multiple slits) tend to be stiff and don't grip the bit very well. Second, the collet cone and arbor socket surfaces can abrade and gall (explained below), making the collet difficult to tighten and loosen.

With a three-piece collet (see C in the drawing), the arbor, collet and locking nut are separate pieces; the collet fits into the cone on the arbor and is tightened by a separate locking nut. This design allows the collet insert to come out when the nut is loosened, making it easier to remove the bit. The most advanced collets (see D in the drawing) have a "keeper" ring on the nut that engages the collet, pulling it out when the nut is loosened. These last two types of collets are typically made of polished spring steel and have multiple slits, giving them great bit-holding power, even on bits with slightly undersize shafts. Routers made by Milwaukee and Elu, as well as the Makita 3612 and the Ryobi 600 series, feature these types of collets.

Collet use and maintenance — In order to get the best performance out of whatever style collet your router has, you must take care to use it correctly and to maintain it. To tighten a router collet properly, insert the bit until about $\frac{1}{8}$ in. of space is left between the end of the shaft and the bottom of the collet/arbor. If the shaft is not long enough to go that deep, set the bit so that the cutting portion is about $\frac{1}{8}$ in. above the top of the collet. Then tighten the locking nut, taking care not to fasten the collet onto the bit's fillet—the raised area just below the cutting portion of the bit—as this prevents the collet from tightening properly and allows the bit to slip. If you suspect any slipping, use a marking pen to indicate the same position on the bit shank and collet (like timing marks on an auto engine); if the marks shift when you use the router, the bit is moving in the collet.

Even a properly used collet may perform poorly if it is not well maintained. Dirt, rust, sawdust and pitch decrease a collet's ability both to grip and release the bit. A number of problems can be traced directly to a poorly maintained collet, including bit slippage, bit or collet freezing, excess vibration, bit bending or breakage, and even excessive bit runout (when the bit is not turning concentrically).

To ensure your collet is working properly, keep as smooth and clean a surface as possible on both the inside and the outside of

Drawing: Aaron Azevedo

When a collet fails to keep a bit from slipping during a cut, galling can occur, which is shown here as the shallow grooves in the shaft of the bit. Fortunately, these can be filed off to restore the shaft.

A simple method for determining the concentricity of the collet employs a bar clamped to the base and a special pointed bit called a "know bit" (demonstrated here by Brad Witt of Woodhaven). A feeler gauge indicates the amount of runout.

the collet, the collet socket in the arbor and bit shaft. The outside of the collet and the collet socket can be cleaned with steel wool, an abrasive pad or a fine-bristle brass brush. The best solution for cleaning the inside is to use a fine-bristle round brass brush like the one in the center photo on the previous page. (I bought mine from Woodhaven, 5323 W. Kimberly Road, Davenport, Ia. 52806; 800-344-6657.) Rust is much harder to remove than pitch or dirt and may take some extra effort. But no matter how badly the surface is rusted, resist the temptation to use sandpaper (even the finest grade), as the resulting scratches can decrease the collet's grip. Some people use rubbing compound to clean the collet and bits, but that leaves a fine film that must be removed with a dry cloth.

Don't make a habit of leaving the bit in the router after you have finished using it: release the bit and clean both the bit and the collet, as pitch and dirt can accelerate the rusting process. If you store the router in a humid area, remove the collet and place it in a plastic bag, to protect it from rusting. If your shop is very humid, you may want to put a fine layer of oil on the cone; but make sure you wipe it down thoroughly *before you use the router*.

Collet wear and replacement—Although proper maintenance will prolong the life of the collet, all collets eventually wear out and need to be replaced, perhaps even several times over the life of the router. One of the most common forms of collet wear is called "bell mouthing." This is when the collet wears more at the top and bottom than in the middle, leaving less contact area to hold the bit. The symptoms of bell mouthing include bit slippage and excessive bit runout. A slipping bit can cause galling on the bit shank, the inside surface of the collet or both. Galling is caused by the friction of two non-lubricated metal surfaces rubbing against one another and results in deformation of the parts, such as grooves or ridges (see the top photo at left). If the galling is deep or extensive, the bit, as well as the collet, may be ruined. Other clues that indicate your collet may need replacing include excess vibration during routing and problems removing router bits.

If you are unsure of whether or not you may need to replace your collet, there are two ways to check for collet wear: one is to feel whether the bit moves in the collet and the other is to check for runout. I suggest using both tests and if either is positive I would replace the collet. First, take a brand new, long straight bit and hand-tighten it in the router. Try to wiggle the end; if you detect movement, replace the collet. Next, check for runout by chucking up a precision rod, such as a drill rod or a "know bit," which is a very accurately machined rod with a point on the end for setting up equipment (available from Woodhaven). Then use a dial indicator to measure the concentricity of the rod an inch up from the collet. If the runout is more than 0.005 in., replace the collet. You can also use the dial indicator to check the tapered collet socket in the arbor: it should be concentric within 0.001 in. If it's much farther out, the arbor might be bent—a condition that probably means it's time to buy a new router.

If you don't have a dial indicator, here's a low-tech method for testing runout. Clamp one end of a narrow bar of wood or Plexiglas to the router's base with the edge pressing lightly against the bit about an inch up from the collet (see the bottom photo at left). Now rotate the arbor; if there is runout, the bit will push the bar away. The amount of runout can be measured with a feeler gauge between the bit and the bar. As with the previous method, 0.005-in. runout means replace the collet.

Bearings—Another area of the router that requires occasional maintenance and replacement is the bearings. Because they rotate at such high speeds, router bearings wear much faster than most other motor bearings. Fortunately, there are a number of things that you can do to prolong bearing life. Surprisingly, router bearings last longest when they are under load. The worst thing you can do to your router is let the motor run when it is not cutting. This is called "run on," and during this process those smooth little bearings pound themselves into a mess. This can happen very quickly: in a matter of days in a production shop. The problem is especially prevalent with a router mounted in a table since there's a tendency to leave it on constantly when you're cutting a run of something like molding. One solution is to use a foot switch, which turns on the router only when you stand on it. Other ways to prolong bearing life include using slower RPM settings on a variable-speed router (when they're appropriate for the particular cutting operation). Also, the "soft start" feature found on some routers can reduce bearing wear by not exposing them to sudden start-up torque.

Eventually your router bearings will need to be replaced. Bad bearings will howl when they are ruined, but don't wait to hear a loud noise before replacing them; if you wait too long you could ruin other vital components that are more expensive to replace. Heat is a good early indicator of worn bearings: The router should never get too hot to touch. You can sometimes tell if the bearings are worn by rotating the arbor by hand. It should feel smooth; if it binds or if there is a rough spot, that's a telltale sign of bearing damage. Also, try to move the arbor back and forth and up and down. If you detect any movement here, it's probably time to replace your bearings.

When it's time for replacement, have the manufacturer's service center do the work (unless you are handy and can tackle the job yourself). Otherwise, a good bearing house can do the job (check the yellow pages under "bearing supply"). If possible, ask the service technician to install a higher grade of bearing than the ones that came in the router. I went through a number of bearing changes with one of my routers, and I always used the manufacturer's replacements. When I switched to a better grade of bearings, they outlasted the originals by a factor of three or four.

Other router parts that need occasional replacement are the motor brushes, found under the small removable caps on either side of the motor housing. These should be replaced every 50 hours of use, or sooner if they exhibit wear. You can change them yourself with the proper replacement brushes obtained from your dealer.

Router bits—Router bits also need care and maintenance for best performance and prolonged life. Not surprisingly, the quality of the bit you purchase is paramount to how well it will run and how long it will last. Good bits will last longer and work better, but most importantly, their shafts will be consistent in size, usually only varying by plus or minus 0.002 in. I once bought a bargain bit that was 0.005 in. undersize and it slipped in the collet like crazy. It is probably a good idea to measure the shafts of new bits when you get them and reject them if they are too far off.

After every routing job, you should clean the bit before putting it away. The surface of the shaft should be as clean and smooth as new. If the shaft is tarnished or rusted, clean it with steel wool or an abrasive pad, and then buff it with a metal polish such as Simichrome Polish (available from Woodhaven). Another option is to buff the shaft with rouge on a buffing wheel. The buffing wheel may be the last hope for a bit that is badly rusted or tarnished. Also, check the bit's shaft for galling; if it isn't too deep, you can usually clean it up with a small file. If a bit continues to gall and is your only bit that consistently slips in your router, throw it away. One of the easiest ways to ruin a collet is to use a damaged bit.

Another key to top router performance is to always keep the bit's cutting edges clean and sharp. Pitch or baked-on residue will prevent the chip from exiting the cut and this will increase the

To keep your router bits running smoothly and to make them easier to get in and out of the collet, clean and polish the shank with steel wool or an abrasive pad. No need to tell you which bit in the picture has been polished.

deterioration of the cutting edge. If you use wood such as pine or cherry, scrape the cutter frequently and/or clean it with a pitch-and gum-removing product (sold at hardware stores), oven cleaner or ammonia. Titanium nitride bits (those gold-colored ones) have a special coating that prolongs edge life by increasing the lubricity of the bit so that deposits do not stick as readily.

A bit with a dull edge will rapidly deteriorate at a router's high speeds. Therefore, I like to touch up the edges of my bits by hand with a diamond hone (mine is from Garrett Wade Co., 161 Ave. of the Americas, New York, N.Y. 10013; 800-221-2942) before each use. If dullness does get a foothold, you can sharpen all but the most badly chipped bits by hand. High-speed steel (HSS) bits can be sharpened with regular oil or waterstones, while carbide-tip bits require using a diamond hone. Sharpen only the flat inside surface of each flute; never sharpen the bit's actual edge because you may destroy its profile or change its balance. And always clean the bit before sharpening. When the edge becomes dull or chipped, the cutter should be reground, preferably by a good sharpening shop. However, you may find that you can buy a new bit for what it costs to get one sharpened.

Keeping your router clean—Taking good care of the router will prolong the life of vital parts, and it will also make the router more dependable and pleasant to use. To prolong the life of the motor—the heart of the machine—you should clean your router after every use by blowing out the inside with compressed air. Sawdust and chips that aren't blown away can clog air passages and cause overheating or foul the motor's commutator (the part the brushes ride on). To keep your router gliding over the work smoothly, clean and lubricate the base occasionally with a dry lubricant, such as Teflon or graphite. (Avoid silicone sprays, as these can rub off on the work and cause finishing problems.) If you own a plunge router, remove the router itself from the base and clean the columns that allow plunging with an abrasive pad (see the photo on p. 44). Finally rub the columns with a dry lubricant or wax them (avoid grease or any sticky lubricants that will attract dust), and then reassemble the router. Clean your router's working parts whenever needed and remember: an ounce of router maintenance is worth a pound of service center cure. □

Mark Duginske is a woodworker and author living in Wausau, Wisc. He is currently working on a book on advanced machine techniques that will be published by The Taunton Press. All photos by author.

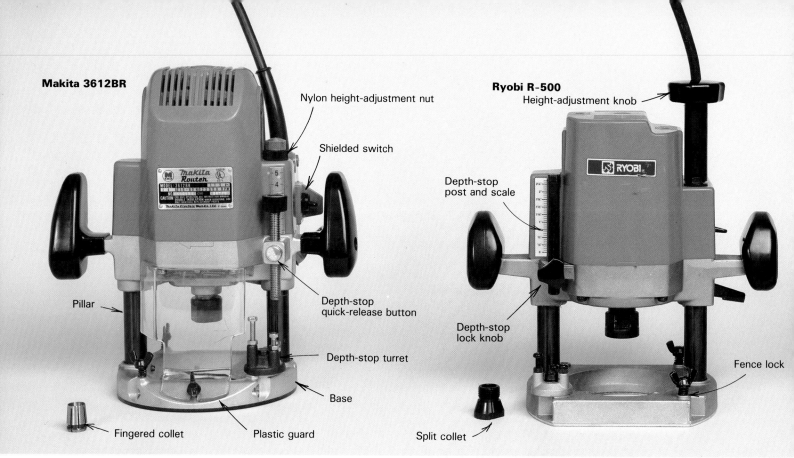

Makita 3612BR

Nylon height-adjustment nut

Shielded switch

Pillar

Depth-stop
quick-release button

Depth-stop turret

Base

Fingered collet

Plastic guard

Ryobi R-500

Height-adjustment knob

Depth-stop
post and scale

Depth-stop
lock knob

Fence lock

Split collet

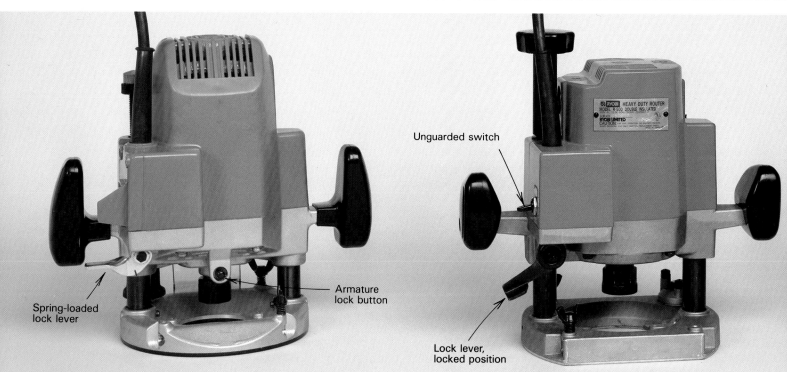

Spring-loaded
lock lever

Armature
lock button

Unguarded switch

Lock lever,
locked position

Husky, versatile plunge routers have become the workhorses of many cabinet shops. The three most popular choices—all imported from Japan—are shown here with their various features labeled. The article explains subtle but significant differences.

Plunge Routers

*A comparison of the top three Japanese imports
and a new machine from Europe*

by Bernard Maas

From *Fine Woodworking* magazine (September 1987) 66:56-60

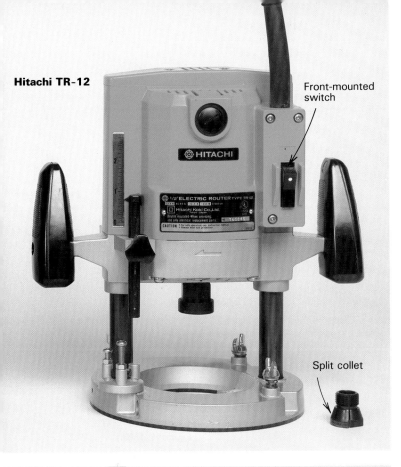

Hitachi TR-12

Front-mounted switch

Split collet

Nuts on rod lock router in fixed position.

ject to vibration, so its greater mass and momentum make for cleaner cuts. Second, the larger surface of a ½-in. shank gives more gripping area to the collet, reducing the chance that a bit will shift position in use. Finally, ½-in.-shank bits are available in a more professional selection of shapes, sizes and lengths.

There are two categories of ½-in.-shank routers: fixed-base and plunge. In this article, I'll try to show why I prefer a plunger to a fixed-base machine, what you should look for in buying a plunge router and what can go wrong with them. I'll concentrate on the top three Japanese machines, which are the plungers most woodworkers consider. But, first, allow me to give just passing mention to some other makes: The big, old Bosch industrial router is, frankly, in need of a redesign—it's a good machine, but outdated. Black & Decker's big Elu (see p. 51) is an outstanding machine, but so new we barely had time to squeeze any mention of it into this issue at all.

Why plunge? The advantage of a plunge router is evident in any joinery/template operation where lots of material must be removed. This includes dadoes, tenons, mortises, grooves and template work. Consider the drawbacks when using a fixed-base machine to start a cut in the middle of a board—it must be tilted and have its bit eased into the work surface. The usual result is kickout, temporary loss of control, ruined lumber and generally unsafe routing. For deep cuts, you have to repeat this business at ever-increasing depth settings—at ever-increasing risk. The plunge router, however, is set over the board and the rotating bit is gently lowered in, much as you'd lower a bit with a drill press. To allow this, the motor rides on two upright pillars and is spring-loaded so it'll retract again when the cut is finished. A lever locks the router body in position at any point on the pillars. This lever is essential to using the machine for plunging (as will be described shortly) and can also be used to convert a plunger into the equivalent of a fixed-base machine.

Most plunge routers employ three built-in, adjustable-height stops, located on a rotating turret. Having these stops can save time in routing work where more than one depth is involved, such as a series of haunched mortises. However, most work requires that only one stop be set—the one for the final depth. Stock removal is accomplished by plunging the bit to take a light cut, then locking the lever and routing. The lever is then unlocked, the bit is plunged a little more, the next increment is routed away and so on. It's easy to develop a rapid-fire rhythm that repeats these steps over and over until the depth stop bottoms out. These tiny, rapid cuts prevent vibration, burning and lugging down. Contrast this with the same operation performed with a fixed-base router where the usual practice is to try to chew off ¾ in. in one or two laborious shots, usually filling the room with smoke as the overtaxed bit tries to remove too much wood at one pass.

Until recently, two plungers dominated the heavyweight market: Hitachi's TR-12, first marketed here about seven years ago, and Makita's 3612BR, a beefed-up version of the company's pioneering 3600 model, which debuted about 13 years ago. These two workhorses are to be found in countless cabinet shops, either as freehand machines or mounted in router tables. Ryobi's R-500 plunge router is a lesser-known newcomer that, in my opinion, has some nice features the others lack. We also tested two other lightweight plunge routers from Ryobi—the R-150 and the tiny R-50. Both of these machines, however, have ¼-in. collets, so their utility is limited. Nonetheless, these lightweights are well-suited for shallow plunging jobs, such as letting in hinges or lock strikes.

The machines were tested in my home workshop and by stu-

Not too long ago, routers were limited to the arsenals of production shops. But after hiding in the wings for nearly forty years, they've come of age. Today, the ¼-in.-shank, fixed-base router is commonplace in basement and garage workshops, and the number of brands and models on the market is truly bewildering. Woodworkers without routers wonder if they should buy low-cost, lightweight machines as a means of finding out what routing is all about, while many ¼-in.-shank router owners I've talked to are impatiently planning to step up to machines that will accept ½-in.-shank bits.

In my opinion, ½-in.-shank bits have clear advantages over the ¼-in. variety. First, the beefier shank is more rigid and less sub-

The lightest, most nimble plunger available is Ryobi's R-50, which weighs in at about five pounds and turns an amazing 29,000 RPM, resulting in smooth (albeit light-duty) cuts.

dents at the university where I teach. We ran a multitude of bits, including carbide and steel, dull and sharp. Our tests were fairly extensive, but nothing exotic: average shop conditions and run-of-the-mill project requirements. All in all, we found that all three heavyweight routers performed about the same. The differences boiled down to subtleties in design and personal preferences.

Studying the specs—The chart below lists factory specifications, with no attempt on my part to remove hype. I wouldn't place too much weight on the manufacturers' claimed horsepower; amperage is a better indication of a router's power. For example, the Makita 3612BR—rated at 14 amps—draws almost two amps more than the Hitachi TR-12 and turns 1,000 RPM faster. Yet distributor ads usually claim 3 HP for both machines (something nobody

would think of claiming for a 14-amp tablesaw motor). The Ryobi R-500 falls in between yet, as a seat-of-the-pants impression, seems to get to speed a little faster than the others. I'd say that all of these routers are comparably and adequately powered for most woodworking jobs.

Retail price can't be believed either—buying a router is like buying tires: nobody ever pays list price. In some advertisements I found the Ryobi at about $150, the Hitachi at about $165 and the Makita at about $175. Price isn't the full story, however—you have to consider standard accessories, too. The Hitachi comes with a full line: a template-guide bushing, a universal-template adapter that accepts Porter-Cable template guides, a router fence, a roller guide and a ½-in.-dia. carbide, two-flute bit. The Ryobi R-500 comes with everything except the universal-template adapter and the bit. But the Makita 3612BR—the most expensive of the three—comes with none of these. If you want a Makita fence, you'll have to shell out about $20 extra (discount price). Another $20 will get you a template guide and a roller guide.

I got each router's weight directly from its manufacturer, and the figures quoted are listed in the chart. Like horsepower, however, manufacturers seem to figure weight differently than I do. The Hitachi TR-12's reported weight of 12.3 lb. pretty closely matched the 12.6 lb. I got using a postal scale—the difference might be just that I included the weight of the cord. The Makita weighed 1 lb. more than claimed, and the Ryobi 1.7 lb. more. Why do manufacturers try to out-hype each other on something that's so easy to check? Weight is a matter of compromise anyway: A light router is less fatiguing to use and somewhat easier to move around, but a heavy router is more stable.

My students all preferred the Ryobi R-500, which, un-hyped, is still a pound or two lighter than the others. This model also has the smallest base, making it very maneuverable. A small base might seem like a disadvantage at times, since a large base is inherently more stable. But it's my practice at the school to fit

Manufacturer specifications

Plunge router model	RPM X 1000	HP	Amps	Collet lock	Collet size	Retail price	Weight in lb.	Base shape	Plunge depth	Accessories included
Black & Decker/Elu 3303	24	1	6.5	N	¼	$235	6	OB	1¹⁵⁄₁₆	SF,UT
Black & Decker/Elu 3304	8-24*	1	6.5/5	N	¼	$285	6.2	OB	1¹⁵⁄₁₆	SF,UT
Black & Decker/Elu 3337	20	2.25	12	N	½	$475	11.25	RF	2⁷⁄₁₆	SF,UT
Black & Decker/Elu 3338	8-20*	2.25	12/10	N	½	$520	11.5	RF	2⁷⁄₁₆	SF,UT
Bosch 90303	22	3.25	15	N	½	$700	19.25	RF	2	CA
Hitachi TR-8	24	NR	6.9	N	¼	$218	6.6	RE	2⅜	SF,TG,UT,CB
Hitachi TR-12	22	NR	12.2	N	½	$338	12.3	RD	2⅞	SF,TG,UT,RG,CA,CB
Makita 3620**	24	1.25	7.8	N	¼	$166	5.7	OB	1⅜	
Makita 3612BR	23	3	14	Y	½	$338	12.5	RD	2½	CA
Makita 3612B	23	3	14	Y	½	$338	12.5	S	2½	CA
Ryobi R-50	29	0.75	3.8	N	¼	$146	5.12	OB	2¼	SF
Ryobi R-150	24	1	6.5	N	¼	$171	5.9	OB	2	SF
Ryobi R-151**	24	1	6.5	N	¼	$187	5.9	OB	2	SF
Ryobi R-500	22	2.25	13.3	N	½	$302	9.7	OB	2⅜	SF,TG,RG,CA
Ryobi R-501**	22	2.25	13.3	N	½	$312	9.7	OB	2⅜	SF,TG,RG,CA

Base shapes: OB: oblong; RE: rectangular; RD: round; S: square; RF: round with flat side
Accessories: SF: straight-guide fence; TG: template guide; UT: universal template adapter; RG: roller guide; CA: collet adapters; CB: carbide bit
* Electronic speed control   ** Switch in handle

new special-purpose subbases to most routers anyway, and these can be made any size.

All three routers have similar plunge mechanisms—twin pillars in the base slide into bushings in the motor housing. If the plunge mechanism is sticky when you unpack a plunge router, don't panic—this is a common problem. If it doesn't stick new, it likely will after it's been in use for a while. Plungers do need some looking after—tolerances are close, and gunk (primarily sawdust and grease) works its way into the bushings. The solution is to undo the nuts or knob atop the adjustment screw and dismount the motor from the base. Be careful not to lose small parts from the locking lever assembly. With a rag or paper towel, wipe off the posts and bushings. Don't use solvents—they may dry out oil-impregnated bushings. Lubricate the mechanism with silicone spray or a light oil and reassemble. If the plunge is still balky, check the posts—slipped wrenches can dent or ding them. Once such rough spots are filed away, easy plunging should be restored.

A sticky plunge is especially troublesome on the upstroke, because the base can lift off the work, unstick and kick out, jarring the work and possibly ruining the cut. The Makita seems more prone to this than the others, requiring the routine maintenance described above more often.

The plunge mechanisms on all three routers work best if the base is fully supported. They also work fine if the base is supported only on the left side. But none of them plunge correctly when only the right side is supported—a condition that must have something to do with the location of the locking lever. The heavier the router, the worse the jamming. But this is a problem you can work around—by using the router so the base is properly supported, and by maintaining even pressure on the handles.

I found that each router has comfortable grips, and that all of them allow the average hand to reach all the controls—switch, locking lever, depth stops—while the machine is running and on the workpiece. The Makita switch is guarded with a projecting flange, but the Ryobi has no guard. I first thought this was dangerous—that the switch was liable to be bumped accidentally—but I found I couldn't make this happen.

Ryobi makes a model R-501 router, which is basically an R-500 router with the switch installed in the handle. I don't like switches in handles—it's too easy to turn the machine on by accident when picking up the router. Hitachi mounts the switch on the front of the machine, so you have to move your thumb from the handle to reach the switch. The motion seems awkward at first, but you get used to it. Some lefties, in fact, work this router from the back, and reach around to flip the switch with their left index finger.

Other considerations—All three routers come with collet adapters for ⅜-in. and ¼-in. bits (Makita plans to discontinue including its ⅜-in. adapter). Ryobi and Hitachi both use the familiar conical, split-nut collets common to most routers. Makita sports a nicely machined collet with fingers, and is the only router with an armature lock that enables you to change bits using just one wrench. Both of these features are nice to have and give Makita an edge.

Ryobi and Hitachi have similar depth-control setups, and I can't say I like either of them very much. The top center photo on p. 48 shows Ryobi's version of the device: a post slides up and down and measures the depth on a scale. The post is locked in position by a skimpy clamp screw with a plastic knob. This is just the sort of arrangement that loves to vibrate loose, and usually does unless pains are taken to really torque it down. But, as I can attest from experience, you can crack the plastic knob by overtightening it. Makita's solution is better—its depth control is a threaded rod that can

A new arrival from Europe

While prototypes of new plungers by Swiss power-tool maker, Elu (with whom Black & Decker recently allied in an effort to upgrade its image), arrived too late to be included in the comparison of the three top-rated Japanese machines, they so far surpassed anything else I tested as to redefine the standards.

Basically, B&D/Elu has two plunge router models: the middleweight 3303 and the heavyweight 3337, both available with slow-start/electronic-speed control. The ¼-in. collet machines incorporate the twist-knob plunge lock of Ryobi's tiny R-50, but use the same old ho-hum stopper-pole depth controls. The monster ½-in. models, however, incorporate precise, zero-reference depth adjustments. Magnifying indicators make this feature absolutely outstanding.

I can live without electronic speed control—it's really designed for cutting materials other than wood. But I'd spend more for it just to get the slow-start feature that squelches shotgun-kickback router starts, making them as gentle as turning on a Norelco shaver. Another powerful plus is the double-action collet that won't drop the bit, no matter how tough the cut. It's a great safety feature that also prevents errant bits from ruining work. Such precision doesn't come cheap—¼-in. and ⅜-in. collets for the ½-in. models cost about $30 each. The bottom line, at discount prices, is that the big plungers will most likely cost more than double the price of a Japanese machine.

Overall, the 3337 offers the smoothest, chatter-free cutting action yet, plus a plunge mechanism you can really count on. Powerful springs ensure positive returns; jamming is a thing of the past. However, this machine requires hefty pressure for plunge spring compression and has a tough-to-twist spring-release plunge lock that can be worked only by large, powerful hands. So unless B&D/Elu remedies this in their current redesign, woodworkers who are slight-of-build or arthritic may miss out on a great machine. —*B.M.*

With a proven track record in Europe, the top-of-the-line Elu variable-speed plunger will now be sold here by Black & Decker.

be turned for fine adjustments; coarse adjustments can be made by pressing a button that releases the threads in the nut so that the threaded rod slides freely. It helps to have three hands, but the arrangement is hefty and will stay put.

Besides the regular locking lever, all three routers have supplemental means to lock the motor in place on the pillars. I like Ryobi's system best: a large plastic knob that sticks up above the router body. You can easily turn the knob up and down to adjust bit projection—just crank the bit out as far as you want it, then lock the lever. For added security when the machine is used for fixed-base work or in a router table, the depth-stop rod can then be locked against one of the stops on the turret.

Hitachi's height-locking system consists of two nuts on a threaded rod. It works well, but requires a metric wrench—something of a nuisance. Another drawback is that these locking nuts fit loosely on the threaded rod. It's a setup that's all right when you have them snugged up to lock the router, but when you want to go back to plunging again, you have to fully unwind the locking nut and jam it against the nut at the top—otherwise, it'll vibrate down when the router runs. You might finish a cut and find that the router won't retract enough to lift the bit from the hole and, with just a little inattention, you might clip the workpiece. Makita's "positive lock" is a nylon nut on a threaded rod. It works on the same principle as Ryobi's, but is much less convenient to reach and turn.

The Makita, incidentally, comes with a plastic safety shield to prevent chips from exiting in the direction of your face—a feature the other two routers lack. The shield is no substitute for safety glasses, however, and in practice it defeated itself—its curved shape caught glare from my workshop lights, and I had to remove it in order to see what I was doing. Nice try, but no points for this one.

With three nearly identical machines, you might wonder about durability. On the Hitachi I bought several years back, the bearings failed during the warranty period due to dust penetration. Rather than losing work time in my shop by sending the router back for evaluation, I just bought new factory parts. The bearings

(shielded, not sealed) soon went again, but when I replaced them with sealed bearings, the problem vanished. Hitachi is somewhat inconsistent in its use of bearings. Sometimes they supply their machines with sealed bearings, sometimes shielded. Apparently, what you get is the luck of the draw. Bearing replacement is not unusual with routers, and bearings are readily available from local suppliers (look under "Bearings" in the Yellow Pages). When it's time to replace your bearings, I suggest that you upgrade the originals (probably grade 4) with grade 7 or higher bearings, at a cost of only about $10 or $15 each.

Dust also did in the switch on my original Hitachi, causing it to arc and burn out. When I replaced the switch, I covered it with a shield of modeling clay, and there have been no further problems. To my knowledge, Hitachi still uses the same switch. As soon as a Hitachi comes into the shop, we pull the cover plate off the switch and seal it as preventive maintenance. This wouldn't be a bad idea with any router.

Suspecting that my problems were pretty typical of all plunge routers, I called a major West Coast repair center, unaffiliated with any specific manufacturer. The manager confirmed that troubles with bearings and switches are the most common complaints. "We always replace bearings with sealed ones," he said. "As far as availability of parts goes, all three are about the same. Once in a while a part may be back-ordered, but that can happen with any tool."

As detailed above, all of these routers have some nice features— sometimes in function, sometimes in price. If you don't have the budget to consider the Elu, I don't think you'd make a mistake with any one of the Japanese machines. Of these, my money is on the Ryobi for several reasons: Its smaller base makes it maneuverable on clamp-crowded workpieces; its easy-to-work adjustment knob brings the cutter into line without wrenches; and its light weight makes it easy to use all day long. This is a very nice combination of features to work with, and the price is right. □

Bernie Maas teaches at Edinboro University of Pennsylvania.

Plunge to destruction

by Jim Cummins

How long does it take to wear out a plunge router? Try four to six hours a day for three weeks, routing about 600 monster mortises for huge loose tenons.

What's the result? Chatter, bearings that sound like cornflakes and a plunge that sticks unpredictably and repeatedly, despite hourly disassembly and cleaning toward the end of the run.

Who would put a machine to such a cruel test? The firm of Waxter and Lee, just north of Annapolis, Maryland.

Here's the story. Peter Waxter and John Lee have a 3,000-sq.-ft. shop that's geared for production work. When the order came in for fifty $4,000 doors, they said, "No problem." They had a shaper for coping and sticking, and an industrial-grade hollow-chisel mortiser for chopping into all the stiles. The rails, howev-

Photo: John Lee

Peter Waxter, flanked by a few mortises, holds the Makita plunger that did the job.

er, required mortises in endgrain—a job for which a hollow-chisel hardly excels— so they shopped for a plunge router.

"If we'd known at the time that Bosch makes a $700 plunge router, we might have been tempted," says John Lee. "But we wanted to get going quickly, so we bought a Makita, figuring it would be a throwaway. Peter did all the routing, then I'd take each rail and run it through the shaper to cope it. All told, we're pleased with the Makita, and plan to rebuild it for general shop work. It held up at least as well as my partner did. When that last mortise was done, he walked out the door and went straight to Hawaii for a two-week rest." □

Jim Cummins is an associate editor at Fine Woodworking.

Complementary Template Routing
Tight-fitting curved joints from a single pattern

by Patrick Warner

Template routing is one of the most powerful methods in the workshop. With homemade medium-density fiberboard (MDF) templates and a router with a bushing or ball-bearing piloted bit, you can quickly rout grooves, chop mortises, recess inlays and shape workpieces. Template routing is repeatable, accurate and capable of handling either straight or curved shapes with ease. You can encounter problems though, when you want to fit two workpieces along an irregular curve. For this jigsaw work, you usually must painstakingly make two templates that precisely match each other, a hassle that limits the usefulness of template routing.

To avoid this predicament, I developed a method I call complementary template routing. Its beauty is that only one master template must be shaped by hand—a router handles all the subsequent steps—and the final fit is perfect. I've used the method for all sorts of curved joinery and inlay. Some applications are shown at right. Best of all, aside from buying a few sealed ball bearings and perhaps a standard router bit or two, no expensive fixtures or custom cutters are needed.

The template-routing process is straightforward: A master template guides a piloted straight bit that plows a path through a piece of particleboard, simultaneously creating complementary work templates. These templates guide the router as it shapes the right and left halves of the workpieces. The two work templates don't nest snugly together, because the bit used to cut the templates apart creates a kerf as wide as the bit. This is where the trick to my method comes in: In making and using the work templates, you must make offset cuts with the router, to shift the final joint line enough to compensate for the kerf and allow the workpieces to mate perfectly. Offset cuts are accomplished by piloting a router bit with a ball bearing that has an outside diameter (OD) larger than the cutting circle of the bit. Figure 1 on the next page shows how my method of template routing can be used to produce a butt joint. By varying the combination of bits and bearings used with the templates, as shown in the chart on p. 55, you can cut several other common joints. Note that in each case, only stock, off-the-shelf straight bits and sealed ball bearings are used. Once you get accustomed to making the offset cuts, you can also figure out bit/bearing combinations for making other joints, as described later in the article. But first, let's go through the steps of making a butt joint.

Making the templates—Before you can make the master template, you must lay out the joint line along which two workpieces will meet, say the leg and the foot of a trestle table. For a butt joint, the pieces can meet along any straight or curvy line, because right and left workpieces can slide down over one another, much like interlocking jigsaw-puzzle pieces do. Sometimes the workpieces aren't clearly a "right-hand" piece and a "left-hand" piece, but I always designate one right and one left, for clarity. The only restriction on

Complementary template routing allows a wide range of possible joinery and inlay designs that are quick to make and reproduce, and dead accurate. The author uses his router method to make decorative drawer fronts and panels, marquetry and structural joints for furniture.

the joint line is that you cannot make curves so tight that the bearings of your piloted bits won't fit into them. In other words, a curved section can't be less in diameter than the outside diameter of the largest pilot bearing you'll use at any stage of the routing process.

Next, draw your joint line on the master-template stock. I use ½-in. "Medite" MDF, because it shapes easily, is dimensionally stable and holds screws well. But, any high-quality particleboard, other than underlayment grade, will do. Before cutting out the master, the joint line must be transferred 5/32 in. to the left to compensate for the offset created by the 5/16-in. bit and 5/8-in.-OD bearing combination used here to cut templates apart (see steps 1 and 2 in figure 1 on the next page). I do this by setting the legs of a compass 5/32 in. apart, and following the original joint line with the point, pivoting the compass around curves as necessary to keep the new line parallel. The left side of the particleboard will become the master template; therefore, saw on the new line with the blade on the right, or waste side, using a coping saw or bandsaw. Then, rasp, file and sand the work edge until it is smooth.

The master template can now be used to simultaneously cut the

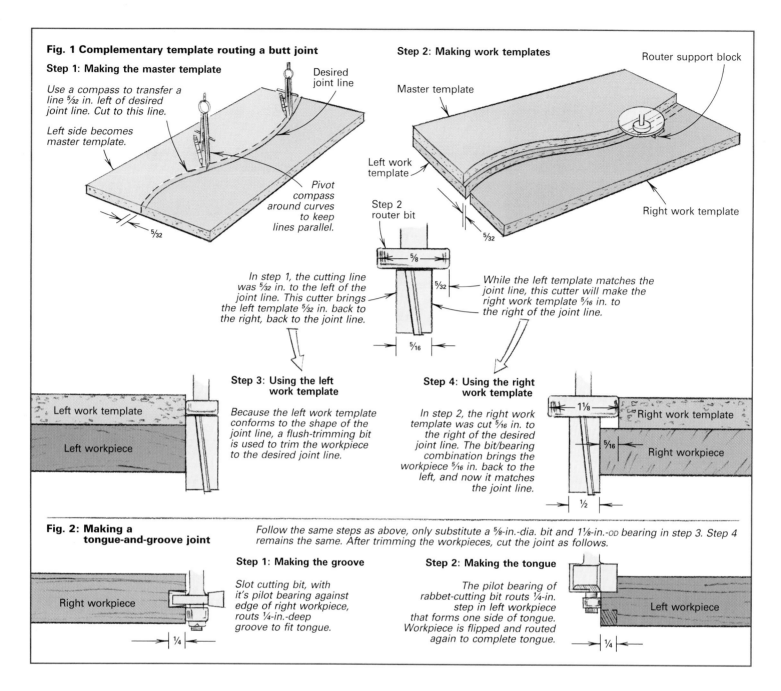

Fig. 1 Complementary template routing a butt joint

Step 1: Making the master template

Use a compass to transfer a line 5/32 in. left of desired joint line. Cut to this line.

Left side becomes master template.

Desired joint line

Pivot compass around curves to keep lines parallel.

5/32

Step 2: Making work templates

Router support block

Master template

Left work template

Right work template

5/32

Step 2 router bit

5/8

5/32

5/16

In step 1, the cutting line was 5/32 in. to the left of the joint line. This cutter brings the left template 5/32 in. back to the right, back to the joint line.

While the left template matches the joint line, this cutter will make the right work template 5/16 in. to the right of the joint line.

Step 3: Using the left work template

Left work template

Left workpiece

Because the left work template conforms to the shape of the joint line, a flush-trimming bit is used to trim the workpiece to the desired joint line.

Step 4: Using the right work template

In step 2, the right work template was cut 5/16 in. to the right of the desired joint line. The bit/bearing combination brings the workpiece 5/16 in. back to the left, and now it matches the joint line.

1 1/8

Right work template

5/16

Right workpiece

1/2

Fig. 2: Making a tongue-and-groove joint

Follow the same steps as above, only substitute a 5/8-in.-dia. bit and 1 1/8-in.-OD bearing in step 3. Step 4 remains the same. After trimming the workpieces, cut the joint as follows.

Step 1: Making the groove

Right workpiece

Slot cutting bit, with it's pilot bearing against edge of right workpiece, routs 1/4-in.-deep groove to fit tongue.

1/4

Step 2: Making the tongue

The pilot bearing of rabbet-cutting bit routs 1/4-in. step in left workpiece that forms one side of tongue. Workpiece is flipped and routed again to complete tongue.

Left workpiece

1/4

two work templates, as shown in the top photo on the facing page. Start with a large piece of particleboard. You want the two work templates to end up at least 5 in. or 6 in. wide, to leave room for clamping the templates to the workpieces later. I clamp or screw the master template on top of the particleboard, then clamp the assembly over a piece of scrap plywood. The scrap is needed to protect the workbench, because you'll be cutting clear through the particleboard to make the work templates.

The work templates are cut with a 5/16-in.-dia. straight bit in a 5/8-in.-OD pilot bearing. This bit/bearing combination results in a cut that's offset by 5/32 in., the same offset used in drawing up the master template, as previously discussed. To bear on the template, the pilot bearings must be above the cutter instead of below it, as is more usual on piloted router bits. Therefore, I use sealed ball bearings that have a 1/4-in.-ID (inside diameter) that will slide right over the 1/4-in. shank of the bit (see step 2 in figure 1). These bearings, as well as the others mentioned in the article, are available from Valley Chain and Gear Inc., 1320 Grand Ave., San Marcos, Calif. 92069; (619) 744-4200. I stack two bearings on the bit's shank to ensure solid contact with the template and to prevent any gouging of the particleboard edge. A drop of Locktite (available from auto-

supply stores) between the shank and the inner race of the bearings will keep them from riding up on the shank, if that becomes a problem. For the bit itself, use only carbide straight bits with a cutting length long enough to cut through the work-template stock. The bit's shank should be long enough to hold the bearings and still have at least 5/8 in. chucked in the router's collet.

With bit and bearing chucked in the router, I cut through the particleboard in one pass. Following the contour of the master, concentrate on keeping the router's base flat and the pilot bearing tight against the template's edge. To help keep the router from tipping, I screw a small, 1/2-in.-thick scrap (the same thickness as the master template) to my router base, to slide on the right work template as I cut. If the contours of the master are very curvaceous or convoluted, the router will want to pull away from the template as the cut changes directions. To prevent this, use the biggest router you have, to dampen the cutting forces. Try to keep full, even pressure at a right angle to the tangent of each curve you follow. Fortunately, even if the bearing loses contact and the cut deviates, the pair of work templates can still yield a tight joint, because the deviation is transferred to both templates equally and will be complementary in the final joint.

Drawing: Roland Wolf

Routing the workpiece—Once the work templates are cut, you're ready to use them to shape the joint on the workpieces. Once again, a combination of straight bits and ball-bearing pilots provides offsetting cuts. If you follow the bit/bearing combinations in the chart, you'll see that for a butt joint, you'll need a bit/bearing combination that yields a ⁵⁄₁₆-in. offset for the right half of the joint and a flush trim bit (one that yields zero offset) for the left half. Like the bit/bearing combinations for making the work templates, use a carbide straight bit. The bearings you'll need are listed in the chart by their outside diameter; the inside diameter should be chosen to fit the shank of the bit you use—¼ in., ⅜ in. or ½ in.—depending on what your router will handle. The flush-trimming bit can be any diameter, as long as the pilot bearing's outside diameter matches the bit's cutting circle. I prefer to use larger-diameter ⅜-in. or ½-in. shank bits, like the ones shown in the lower photo at right, because they are less susceptible to flexing and chatter.

To cut the butt joint, follow steps 3 and 4 in figure 1 on the facing page. Trace the outline of the left work template on the left half of the joint and bandsaw away the waste to within ¹⁄₁₆ in. of the line. Clamp the left template and workpiece to the bench and shape with the flush-trimming bit. The procedure is the same for the right half, except shift the joint line you trace from the right work template ⁵⁄₁₆ in. to the left. Use the ⁵⁄₁₆-in.-offset bit combination to take the final trim cut; always keep the router base flat and the pilot bearings against the template. If you've routed carefully, the right and left workpieces should fit together with less than .003 in. to .005 in. of variation along the joint line.

Tongue-and-groove joint—A butt joint is adequate if the two pieces are glued together with mostly long-grain to long-grain contact. But, if the parts join cross-grain, or if the joint needs to be reinforced, say for curved joints where the seat rails join the rear legs of a chair, I prefer some sort of interlocking joint. Fortunately, the same work templates created for a butt joint can also be used to make interlocking joints: The chart lists the bit/bearing combinations necessary for making two different-size rabbet or tongue-and-groove joints. These joints strengthen the mechanical connection between the workpieces and provide a better glue surface, even if the pieces join entirely cross-grain to one another. Further, an interlocking joint helps to register the two pieces, to keep them from sliding during glue-up; if the ends of the joined pieces are visible, they provide a nice bit of visual detail.

To make a tongue-and-groove joint, prepare the master and work templates exactly as described above. When you're ready to trim the workpieces, trim the joint surfaces on the workpieces just as shown in steps 3 and 4, but substitute the bit/bearing combinations from the chart that are designed for a tongue and groove or rabbet, either ¼ in. deep or ³⁄₁₆ in. deep (see figure 2 on the facing page).

After trimming the joint, I rout the tongues and grooves using a rabbeting bit for the tongues and a slot-cutting bit to plow the grooves. Make the groove in the right workpiece first, taking care to center the piloted bit on the thickness of the workpiece. For the tongue, choose a piloted rabbeting bit that cuts a shoulder the same width as the amount of overlap: ¼ in. or ³⁄₁₆ in. Set the depth of cut so that after passes are taken from both sides of the left workpiece, the resulting tongue will fit snugly into the groove. The advantage to this method is that by making passes from both sides of the stock, the tongue will automatically be centered. Make a test piece from a scrap of stock the same thickness as the workpiece to test the fit. If your stock is thin enough, you can get by using the slot cutter as a rabbeting bit to cut the tongue as well as the groove. The joint-making process is the same for making a rabbet joint, but only a single rabbet cutter is needed to rout

Using a master template to guide a router fitted with a ball-bearing piloted straight bit, a piece of particleboard is cut into left- and right-hand subtemplates. These templates are used to rout both halves of a joint so two pieces can be fitted together accurately.

The author fits most of the router bits used for his complementary routing process with a ball-bearing or two slipped down on the shank, to serve as a pilot. Each bit/bearing combination is chosen to give a prescribed amount of offset, for snug-fitting joints.

Bit/bearing combinations for trimming workpieces

Type of Joint	Left workpiece		Right workpiece	
	Bit dia.	Bearing OD	Bit dia.	Bearing OD
Butt joint	Flush trim bit (same dia. bit and bearing)		½ in. ¾ in.	1⅛ in. 1⅜ in.
Tongue and groove or rabbet ³⁄₁₆ in. deep	½ in. ¾ in. 1 in.	⅞ in. 1⅛ 1⅜ in.	½ in. ¾ in.	1⅛ in. 1⅜ in.
Tongue and groove or rabbet ¼-in. deep	⅝ in. ⅞ in.	1⅛ in. ⅜ in.	½ in. ¾ in.	1⅛ in. 1⅜ in.

complementary lips on both workpieces.

My complementary-template method isn't limited to the joints I've described: You can use other bit/bearing combinations to make more elaborate joints, like the glue-lock joint. You can do this by figuring out the bit-diameter/bearing-outside diameter combinations needed to give the proper amount of offset to make a joint with the bit you've chosen. The amount of offset is calculated by subtracting the cutting diameter of the bit from the outside diameter of the pilot bearing and dividing by two. □

Patrick Warner lives in Escondido, Calif. He teaches classes in router techniques and making jigs and fixtures.

Routing Rectangular Recesses

Circular templates make setup easy

by Ralph J. Harker

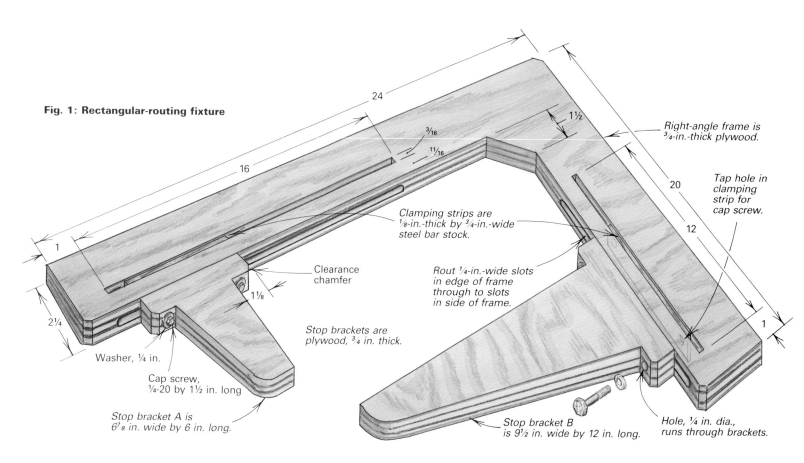

Fig. 1: Rectangular-routing fixture

24

16

3/16

11/16

1 1/2

Right-angle frame is 3/4-in.-thick plywood.

Tap hole in clamping strip for cap screw.

20

12

1

Clamping strips are 1/8-in.-thick by 3/4-in.-wide steel bar stock.

Clearance chamfer

Rout 1/4-in.-wide slots in edge of frame through to slots in side of frame.

1 1/8

Stop brackets are plywood, 3/4 in. thick.

2 1/4

Washer, 1/4 in.

Cap screw, 1/4-20 by 1 1/2 in. long

Stop bracket A is 6 7/8 in. wide by 6 in. long.

Stop bracket B is 9 1/2 in. wide by 12 in. long.

Hole, 1/4 in. dia., runs through brackets.

1

Routing a rectangular slot or a shallow recess is a common operation in furniture and cabinet work. Cutouts such as these are used for insetting mechanical components, like clockworks or locks, as well as for stopped dadoes or mortises to receive shelves or tenons. I've always found it difficult, time-consuming and inaccurate to rig up temporary router guides for this type of repetitive operation, and so I designed the plywood fixture shown above, which can be set up quickly to rout a series of identical mortises.

The fixture's right-angle frame carries two adjustable stop brackets that are perpendicular to each other and that can be locked to the frame to create a rectangular opening. Then the fixture is clamped to a workpiece and a router is moved around inside the rectangle. Since the router base is held captive within the frame and stop brackets, a rectangular cut is generated. A plunge router is ideal for use with this fixture, but a standard router can also be used.

To make it quick and easy to set the stop brackets for a particular mortise size, and to position the fixture on the work, I made two circular templates from 1/4-in.-thick plywood, bandsawn round and then trued up and sized on the lathe (see figure 2 at left on the facing page). The large template is used for setting the stop brackets and the small template is for positioning the fixture on the work. Template sizes are determined by the diameter of the router base and the bit you use. To calculate template size, measure the diameter of the router base and divide it in half to get its radius, which is the distance from the center of the bit to the edge of the base. From this radius, subtract half the diameter of the bit you will be using, and this gives you the diameter of the small template. The large template will be twice the diameter of the small one. I designed my fixture and templates for use with a router that has a standard 6-in.-dia. base fitted with a 1/4-in.-dia. bit, and so the dimensions in the drawings are based on these criteria. The fixture shown will allow you to rout recesses ranging from a 1/4-in.-dia. hole up to a rectangle measuring 2 3/4 in. by 9 1/2 in. Of course, the fixture's dimensions could be increased if larger mortises are required.

Construction—The frame and the two stop brackets are sawn from 3/4-in.-thick plywood, following the dimensions in figure 1. The frame's two inside faces and the stop brackets' bases and working faces must be square. The brackets are held to the frame

Photo: Sandor Nagyszalanczy; drawings: Aaron Azevedo

Fig. 2: Sizing template

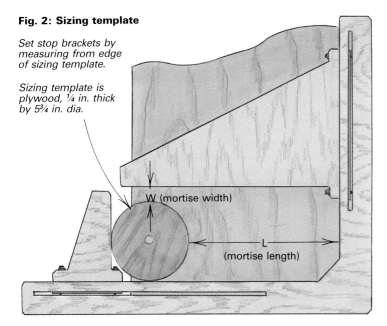

Set stop brackets by measuring from edge of sizing template.

Sizing template is plywood, ¼ in. thick by 5¾ in. dia.

W (mortise width)

L (mortise length)

Fig. 3: Positioning template

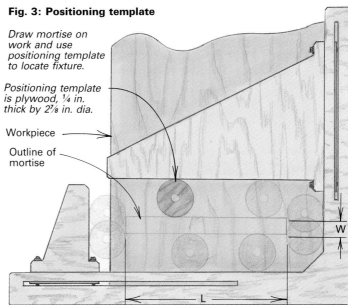

Draw mortise on work and use positioning template to locate fixture.

Positioning template is plywood, ¼ in. thick by 2⅞ in. dia.

Workpiece

Outline of mortise

W

L

with cap screws, which extend through slots in the edge of the frame and thread into holes tapped in the ⅛-in.-thick by ¾-in.-wide steel clamping strips. The ³⁄₁₆-in.-wide slots that house the clamping strips are cut on a table-mounted router. Then the frame is clamped in a bench vise and ¼-in.-wide slots are routed in the inside edges of the frame. These edge slots extend all the way through to the clamping strip slots and provide the track for adjusting the stop brackets. You'll need to chamfer the inside corner of each bracket, as shown, to provide clearance for the router base. Then, drill two ¼-in.-dia. holes in each bracket for the 1½-in.-long, ¼-20 cap screws that lock the brackets to the frame.

Each clamping strip is the same length as the base of the bracket it goes with: 6⅞ in. for the small bracket and 9½ in. for the large one. Drill two ¹³⁄₆₄-in.-dia. holes in each strip that align with the holes in the brackets, and then tap the holes in the metal to receive a cap screw. Finally, mount the brackets on the frame and make sure they slide freely along their entire stroke.

Setting and positioning the fixture—Remember, my fixture is designed for a 6-in.-dia. router base and a ¼-in.-dia. bit. For these two dimensions, the horizontal and vertical stop brackets must define a rectangle that is 5¾ in. larger in both directions than the actual size of the desired mortise (see figure 2 above, left). So place the 5¾-in.-dia. sizing template in the corner of the frame, and adjust each bracket to leave the actual size of the mortise between the bracket and the template's edge. Once the stop brackets are positioned and tightened, exact mortise size can be verified by clamping the fixture to a piece of scrap and routing a trial mortise.

To position the fixture, I draw the desired mortise on the workpiece and locate the fixture using the 2⅞-in.-dia. positioning template. When the template is rolled around inside the fixture's rectangular opening, its outer edge should follow the mortise outline exactly (see figure 3 above, right). When the fixture is precisely located, clamp it and the work securely to the benchtop. Spacer blocks are usually needed to support the fixture where it overhangs the workpiece (see the photo at right).

Routing the mortise—All you have to do now is plug in your router, place it within the fixture and move it clockwise inside the rectangle. For deep mortises, make shallow cuts and lower the bit in increments until you reach full depth. For wide mortises, rout the outside perimeter first and then remove the waste from the

center of the mortise. The router is captive in all directions and so the exact mortise size is reproducible on any number of workpieces.

Comments—Although the corners of the mortises have ⅛-in. radii, they can be squared up with a chisel, or if the mortise will receive a tenon, you can just round over the tenon's edges. When cutting multiple parts, you can simplify positioning the fixture on the workpieces by tacking slats on the back of the fixture's frame that will act as stops to give you a repeatable edge distance. In addition to mortising, the fixture can also be used for decorative veining in rectangular patterns. Or if you want to cut angles or curves, you can attach wedges or curved templates to the fixture's internal surfaces. □

Ralph J. Harker retired in 1985 after nearly 40 years as professor of mechanical engineering at the University of Wisconsin, Madison. Because Mr. Harker passed away before completing this article, his friend, Frank Fronczak of Madison, helped with its final preparation.

The fixture shown above is for routing a series of rectangular mortises. Two adjustable stop brackets are set to allow the router base just enough movement within the rectangle to hog out the desired mortise. The larger of the two circular templates (bottom, left) makes it possible to quickly set the stop brackets; the smaller template is for positioning the fixture on the work.

Adjustable Dovetail Jig

Let your router do the hard part

by Douglas Schroeder

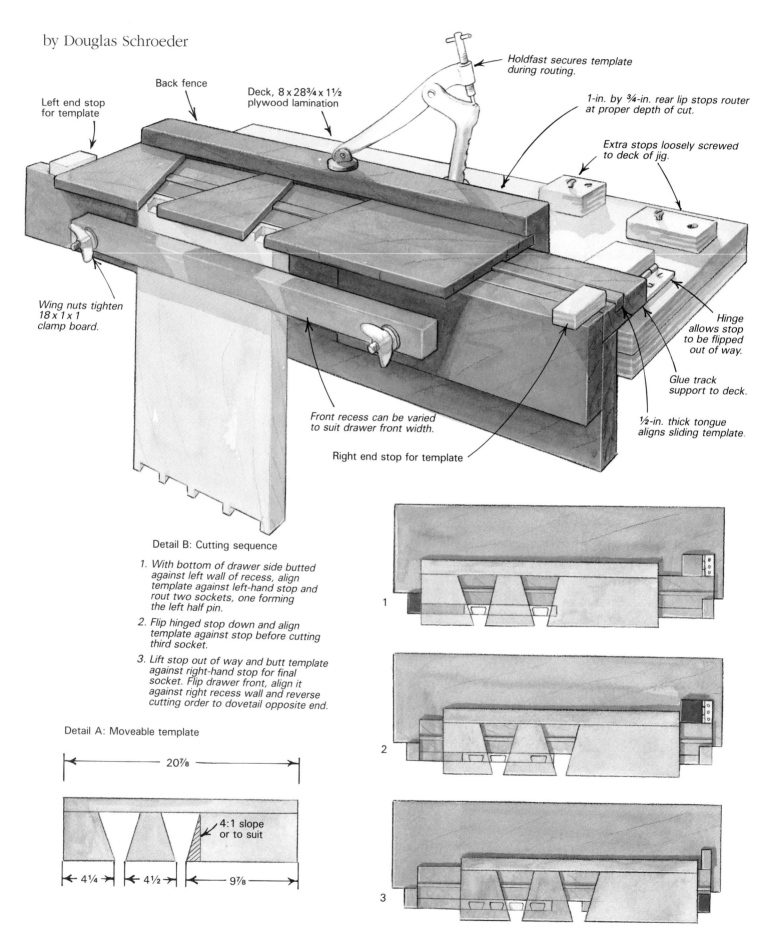

Left end stop for template

Back fence

Deck, 8 x 28¾ x 1½ plywood lamination

Holdfast secures template during routing.

1-in. by ¾-in. rear lip stops router at proper depth of cut.

Extra stops loosely screwed to deck of jig.

Wing nuts tighten 18 x 1 x 1 clamp board.

Hinge allows stop to be flipped out of way.

Glue track support to deck.

½-in. thick tongue aligns sliding template.

Front recess can be varied to suit drawer front width.

Right end stop for template

Detail B: Cutting sequence

1. With bottom of drawer side butted against left wall of recess, align template against left-hand stop and rout two sockets, one forming the left half pin.

2. Flip hinged stop down and align template against stop before cutting third socket.

3. Lift stop out of way and butt template against right-hand stop for final socket. Flip drawer front, align it against right recess wall and reverse cutting order to dovetail opposite end.

Detail A: Moveable template

20⅞

4:1 slope or to suit

4¼   4½   9⅞

From *Fine Woodworking* magazine (January 1988) 68:56-57

I recently was commissioned to build several large mahogany breakfronts and had to make 40 drawers in four different sizes. I wanted the look of hand-cut dovetails, but needed to produce them economically. The commercial dovetail jigs I'd examined wouldn't do the fine dovetails typical of the best 18th-century work, so I decided to make a jig that could rout both through and blind dovetails of different sizes and spacings. My jig is basically a platform equipped with a system of stops and a track accommodating a sliding template that can be adjusted to any size drawer front. The template guides the router as it cuts the sockets, leaving crisply formed pins. The tails are sawn on a bandsaw, then chopped out by hand in the conventional way.

Robert Mussey, furniture conservator at the Society for the Preservation of New England Antiquities, suggested the jig. It's based on one devised by Mario Genevesse, a master cabinetmaker in Natick, Mass.

As shown in the drawing, a rear lip stops the router at the proper distance from the face of the drawer front. For through dovetails, I put a piece of scrap behind the stock before routing. This enables me to rout all the way through the drawer front and partially through the scrap before the lip stops the router base.

I made my jig with mahogany and plywood, but any hardwood/plywood combination would work. The template guides are extra wide, because I wanted them to resist flexing when the router's template bushing was bearing against them. I worked out the size of the templates and the position of the stops by trial and error. I laid out the joint by hand, then sized the template and located the stops so that the router running against the template would cut the pins. Remember to account for the difference between the router bit and the template bushing—about 1/16 in. on my setup. The dimensions shown in the drawing are just guidelines; you'll have to adapt the jig to your own particular situation. It took me two days to work out the jig, but from then on, the drawers were a snap.

To build the jig, I dadoed the track support to accept the tongue, then glued and screwed the piece to a 1½-in.-thick laminated plywood deck. I cut a matching dado on the underside of a ½-in.-thick piece of stock, cut the correct slopes on the template fingers and glued them to the back fence, as shown. The stops shown in the drawing must be laid out carefully. The block on the left sets the position for the first and last half-pins. The drawer front's bottom edge should be clamped snugly against the left-hand side of the front recess. After routing the first two sockets, I slide the template down so it butts against the hinged block, then I cut the next socket. Finally, I flip the hinged block up and out of the way, and move the template against the right-hand block for the last socket.

Because the stops are fixed and the pins are unevenly spaced to accommodate the rabbet for the drawer bottom, the drawer front can't be flipped end-for-end to rout the opposite end. Instead, I align the jig against the right-hand side of the recess after the piece is flipped. The additional stops shown on the rear of the jig are added as the drawers decrease in size (about ¾ in. per drawer). My procedure is to cut all the joints on one end, then set up to do the opposite end. The routing procedure is the same, except this time I begin against the right-hand stop, move to the hinged stop and, finally, to the left-hand stop.

After routing the pins, I square the corners with a chisel, then scribe the tails directly from the pins (see top and middle photos). The tails are cut on a bandsaw fitted with a ¼-in. blade with no set, and the waste is chiseled out. A good way to remove the set is to push an oilstone against each side of the blade as it's running. □

Douglas Schroeder builds furniture in Hudson, Mass.

The router does the hard part by precisely locating the width and depth of the sockets, which can then be squared by jigging a chisel against the routed surfaces and slicing down to the corner.

The tails are scribed from the routed pins in the usual way.

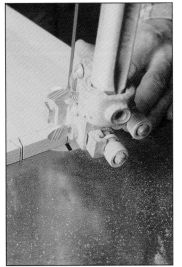

The tails are bandsawn freehand (left). A fine, smooth cut comes from using a blade whose set has been removed by running it against an oilstone. The waste is then chopped out (right).

Sliding Dovetails
Routed joint eases carcase assembly

by Mac Campbell

I have a physical limitation that handicaps me in some shop operations, particularly the assembly of large, complex carcases: I have only two hands. On carcases assembled with dowels or mortise-and-tenon joints, juggling clamps, cauls, glue and panels at the same time is a major problem. In the past, my solution was to assemble parts of the carcase separately, then put these together until the whole assembly was finally completed. This was unsatisfactory because it required large amounts of time and space, and made perfectly square assembly more difficult. Since I do a large amount of carcase work, this problem screamed for a solution, and eventually I found one: the sliding dovetail.

The sliding dovetail is a wonderful joint. Used throughout a carcase, it virtually guarantees that the piece will square itself. Slightly cupped or bowed panels will be pulled flat, and stay flat. The joint can be blind or left exposed; it allows one-piece-at-a-time assembly, requires no clamps, and can allow for cross-grain movement. Its only drawback is that because the joint's male pin must fit tightly into the tail, or female slot, it's devilish to cut accurately.

If the joint is cut with a 14° dovetail bit, which yields about a 1:4 ratio, cutting the male portion of the joint 0.010 in. too narrow allows a gap of 0.040 in., or just under $\frac{1}{16}$ in., between the two panels. Cutting it 0.010 in. too wide produces a joint that can't be assembled. Actually, it's worse than that. The joint can be partially assembled until it jams so tightly you can neither drive it home nor get it apart for another try. A joint that's too tight is a greater disaster than one too loose. The trick is to cut the joint accurately and quickly. There are machines that do this, but they're expensive. My system works and costs about a half-day to set up, plus a trip to the scrap pile for materials.

The female part of the joint, called the slot or socket, is fairly straightforward (**1**). Lay out centerlines for all joints, marking them clearly; also mark where the joints are to be stopped if they're not to be cut clear through. I use the hinged plywood fence shown and explained on the facing page. With the guide clamped in place, set the router to the desired depth. While I've cut a number of joints with $\frac{1}{4}$ in. penetration, I use $\frac{1}{8}$ in. as a standard. It's more than strong enough, and if two panels are to be joined to opposite sides of a $\frac{3}{4}$-in. central panel, it leaves more strength in the central piece. Another advantage is that if the joint's a bit too snug, $\frac{1}{8}$ in. of wood is easier to crush into place than $\frac{1}{4}$ in.

The trick to making a sliding dovetail joint work is cutting the male (dovetail pin) portion of the joint. Ideally, it would be cut by two dovetail bits opposite one another, cutting both sides of the pin at the same time. Since this is hard to set up, most methods I've seen cut the pin's two sides one at a time, and here the problems begin. The usual procedure is to cut one side, flip the workpiece and cut the other side. This depends on the piece being *absolutely* even in thickness across its width; any small deviation results in a large discrepancy in the joint. If the piece isn't perfectly flat, the situation gets worse, since on one pass it can rock, and on the other it can be lifted off the reference table by the bow.

The heart of my system lies in using an existing flat surface as a reference table and using the same side of the workpiece to reference *both* sides of the joint. I use the infeed table of a 15-in. jointer, but a tablesaw table or good bench would work as well. Photo **2** shows the general setup, with the router mounted on a pivoting subbase/fence. Photos **3** and **4** show the two sides of the pin being cut.

Assembling cabinets by yourself with this type of joinery is a relaxed process. I like to work on the floor so I can use my weight to slide panels into place. I usually start the joint together to see just how tight the fit really is. If it's too tight, I'll take it apart and take a discreet pass with a dovetail plane. If it's fairly tight, I'll partially assemble the joint and apply glue to the exposed parts of the joint in both panels. If the fit feels "just right," I'll apply glue just after the assembly is started, and if it's a little slack, I'll apply the glue to both halves of the joint, then wait for a few minutes before assembling to allow some swelling to take place. Usually, the panels slide smoothly into place, one after the other, and the swelling caused by the moisture in the glue locks the panels securely within a minute or two. If the joint involves cross-grain construction, apply glue to only one end of the joint just before it's completely assembled. Panels that seem loose can be clamped until the glue dries, but it's rarely necessary if care is taken in cutting the joint. It takes very little glue to lock the joint securely. If a joint binds and it's too late to disassemble it, it can be drawn into place using a pipe clamp with the faces rotated 90° around the pipe to engage each panel.

The sliding dovetail has become my standard joint for virtually all carcase construction in which panels meet in a T- or cross-configuration. It's quick, reliable, strong, and comfortable for an individual working by himself to use. The only drawback is that the joint requires considerable care and accuracy to cut, but that's really what cabinetmaking is all about. □

Mac Campbell runs Custom Woodworking in Harvey Station, New Brunswick, Canada. Photos by the author.

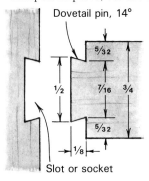

Dovetail pin, 14°

$\frac{5}{32}$

$\frac{1}{2}$ $\frac{7}{16}$ $\frac{3}{4}$

$\frac{5}{32}$

$\frac{1}{8}$

Slot or socket

1: I rout the slot or socket about ⅛ in. deep, using the shop-made fence shown in the photo above. The fence's hinged lip makes alignment easier: The hinged part is exactly half as wide as the router base, so that when the lip is flipped down, its edge marks the centerline of where the router bit will be. The first step is to draw the centerline of the slot on the work and align the flipped-down fence with it. After the fence is clamped in place, I flip the lip up out of the way for routing. The L-shaped extension on the end of the fence acts as a built-in stop when routing stopped dovetails.

2: Rout the male, or pin, part of the dovetail using a plywood subbase/fence attached at right angles to a reliably flat surface. I drilled and tapped holes in my jointer table to accept the jig, which adjusts by pivoting on one bolt (concealed by the router in the photo), and locking via the bolt and slot in the foreground. The hole for the dovetail bit should be just large enough for the bit, though it can be counterbored to allow clearance for the collet nut, if necessary. When mounting the jig, shim the subbase far enough away from the edge of the table so the bit can be lowered completely below the work surface (see photo 3).

3: All cuts are made with the same reference side of the board down. Set the router to cut one side of the joint and cut that side on all pieces. Try to feed the work with a uniform, comfortable speed and pressure; when you cut the second side of the joint, your goal will be to match that speed and pressure. I prefer making the cut with the bit climb-cutting (feeding with the bit's rotation), since this eliminates chipping. Otherwise, score the cutting line first with a cutting gauge to prevent tearout. Before changing the router setting, cut the joint on several pieces of scrap for testing the second cut.

4: When all the cuts of the first side of the joint have been made, re-set the router to cut the opposite side. Run the first of your scraps through, then test it in one of the female cuts made earlier, and adjust the router if necessary. (I have never had one fit on the first try, but I keep hoping.) Continue this adjustment process until you get the fit you want. Because of the built-in geometry of the joint, the slight swelling caused by the moisture in the glue can be enough to jam things up, so err on the side of looseness, but only slightly. Once you're satisfied with the fit, cut all the joints.

Router Joinery
Jigs expand the repertoire

by Bernie Maas

When I bought my first router in the mid-1960s, I thought that it might be useful for putting fancy edges on things. My attempts to do something more with it, like dado or rabbet, usually came to grief when the machine kicked out and gashed the piece. I kept at it though, and over the years, with the addition of a variety of sub-bases, jigs and templates, the limitless possibilities of the router became apparent to me. Today, I believe that the router is one of the more significant innovations in our craft in this century, particularly since the recent introduction of plunge routers.

The router is relatively safe, and it promises surety of performance without a lengthy apprenticeship—ideal qualities for the students in the shop that I run at a small Pennsylvania university. Shapers are expensive and they can be dangerous; I have neither the budget nor the inclination to buy one for our shop. The router can do much of what a shaper can do, and much that a shaper can't. The new generation of heavy-duty plunge routers can accept ½-in.-shank bits with the size and mass of some shaper cutters. Our 3-HP Hitachi TR12 plunge router, for example, comes with collets for ¼-in., ⅜-in. and ½-in. bits; it lists at about $300, although it can be found for half that price. Bits vary in price from a few dollars to over $100 apiece. Most of the jigs and fixtures I'll discuss here can also be used with much less expensive light-duty or medium-duty routers, and inexpensive cutters.

Perhaps the simplest router fixtures are auxiliary sub-bases. We commonly make two sub-bases for new routers, as shown at left and center in figure 1. We prefer to use ¼-in. Masonite or void-free plywood (such as Baltic birch), both of which are hard, slide easily, and wear well.

The first sub-base is similar to the router's original base, but we cut the center hole just large enough for the biggest bit we use to pass through. This reduces the chances of dipping or sniping when routing around corners or working small sections. Additional holes make it easier to see the cut in progress. The second base has a long, straight edge (12 in. or more) to guide the router against a fence for dadoing, rabbeting, or cutting grooves. The straight edge helps prevent loss of control when exiting a cut. The third sub-base shown in the drawing, which extends 6 in. either side of the router, is useful for spanning large templates. Make it as thick as possible while allowing the router's template guide to protrude.

An excellent partner for the straightedge sub-base is the shop-made T-square fence shown in figure 2. The blade is 30 in. to 36 in. long, and extends 6 in. to 8 in. beyond the head, to steady the router as it exits the cut. We make our fences from stable, defect-free hardwood scrap. Usually one clamp is enough to se-

cure the fence to the work. Clamp the fence on the side of the dado, groove or mortise that will be most visible. This limits wander or run-out to the "no show" side.

Trimming the ends of a wide panel square, smooth and true can be a stumbling block. A 40-in.-wide, 2-in.-thick tabletop can be a bear to wrestle through a tablesaw, a radial-arm saw doesn't have sufficient reach, and portable power saws leave rough surfaces at best. A router fitted with the straightedge sub-base will trim the ends dead square and glass smooth. We use a Freud 12-130 bit, a ½-in.-dia. straight, double-fluted carbide bit with 2½-in. working length, or a Freud 12-158, a similar ¾-in. bit with 2-in. working length. (Double-flute bits seem to cut cleaner than single-flute bits.) Both bits have ½-in. shanks.

Trim the panel to within ¼ in. of finished length, clamp a straightedge or T-square fence in place, and rout away. Blocks clamped to each edge of the panel, flush with the end and top surface, will prevent splintering at the ends of the cuts. End grain is very hard on edge tools, so make several very light, full-depth passes rather than one heavy one. Remember to cut against the bit's rotation, moving the router left to right as you face the end—moving the other way causes the bit to grab and tear.

Aligning boards for edge gluing is easily and accurately done with splines in routed grooves. Shaper-cut edge-gluing profiles aren't an option for us, and doweling jigs have proved inaccurate and error prone. Stopped grooves, such a nuisance on a tablesaw, are a snap with the router. We cut the grooves with a slotting cutter consisting of an arbor, ball-bearing pilot, and the cutter itself. No fence is needed because the pilot bears on the edge to guide the cutter. Cutters commonly have either two, three or four wings and come in a range of diameters and kerf sizes. I like four-wing cutters because they cut more smoothly and put less strain on the router. Set the cutter at about the middle of the edge; exact centering isn't important as long as you run the router on the same face of each board to be joined.

The only drawback to a slotting cutter is the vast amount of dust and chips it generates. The chips shoot out of the machine in a trajectory that is usually painfully in line with your forearm. To handle the dust and chips created by this and other large bits, we connect a Shop-Vac to the dust collector shown in figure 3. The collector is basically a cage-like device attached to the router in place of the normal sub-base. We make the top and bottom plates of Masonite or void-free hardwood plywood, and bandsaw the body from a block of any available lumber. The hole in the top plate (the sub-base), should be just as large as the cutter, and the clearance between the collector body and

From *Fine Woodworking* magazine (March 1986) 57:70-73

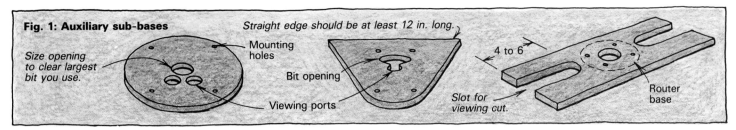

Fig. 1: Auxiliary sub-bases

Size opening to clear largest bit you use.

Mounting holes

Straight edge should be at least 12 in. long.

Bit opening

Viewing ports

4 to 6

Slot for viewing cut.

Router base

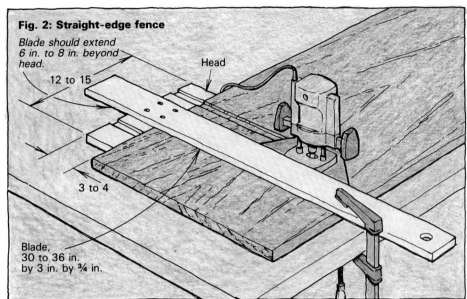

Fig. 2: Straight-edge fence

Blade should extend 6 in. to 8 in. beyond head.

12 to 15

Head

3 to 4

Blade, 30 to 36 in. by 3 in. by ¾ in.

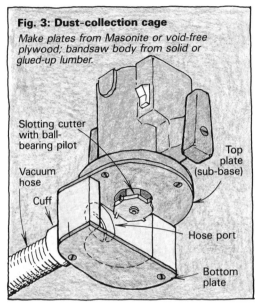

Fig. 3: Dust-collection cage

Make plates from Masonite or void-free plywood; bandsaw body from solid or glued-up lumber.

Slotting cutter with ball-bearing pilot

Vacuum hose

Cuff

Top plate (sub-base)

Hose port

Bottom plate

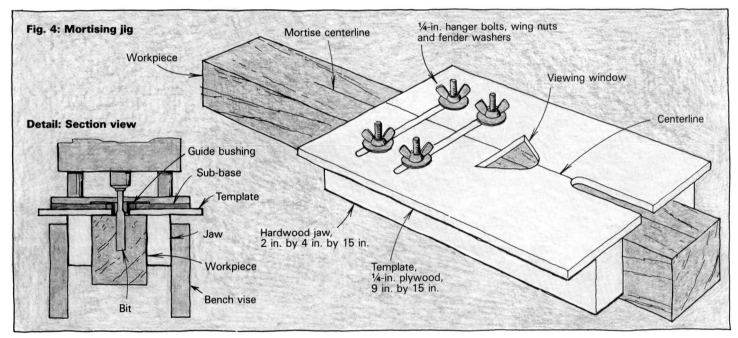

Fig. 4: Mortising jig

Workpiece

Mortise centerline

¼-in. hanger bolts, wing nuts and fender washers

Viewing window

Centerline

Detail: Section view

Guide bushing

Sub-base

Template

Jaw

Workpiece

Bench vise

Bit

Hardwood jaw, 2 in. by 4 in. by 15 in.

Template, ¼-in. plywood, 9 in. by 15 in.

the cutter should also be kept to a minimum. These close tolerances maximize available suction. We bored the hose port in the body with a multi-spur bit. Shop-Vac hose cuffs are usually 2¼ in. in diameter, and tapered; jamming the cuff into the hole should be sufficient to hold it without an additional fastener. Position the port so that its center is in line with the trajectory of most of the chips.

Mortise-and-tenon joints are strong, dependable, and basic to much woodworking. However, they require a flair for hand tools or a retine of expensive stationary power tools, both of which can be discouraging to novices. The plunge router presents a low-cost, quickly mastered alternative. It's possible to cut mortises and

tenons using just the factory-supplied machine-mounted router fence, but we developed a simple pair of jigs (figures 4 and 5) to eliminate the possibilities of wander or run-out that can occur when guiding the router with only the fence.

The mortising jig consists of two hardwood jaws, about 15 in. long, fastened by hanger bolts and wing nuts to a ¼-in.-thick template of void-free plywood. Oversized fender washers prevent damage to the template. Mill a slot down the center of the template, 5 in. or 6 in. long and just wide enough for a snug, sliding fit on your router's template guide bushing. A window in the template helps when aligning the template and mortise centerlines.

To use the jig, mount it on the workpiece, template resting on the top surface, then clamp the jaw/workpiece sandwich in a

Fig. 5: Tenoning jig

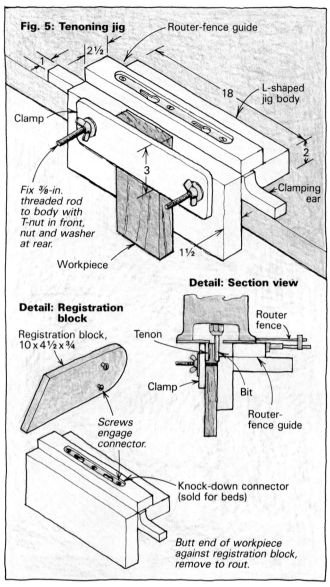

Router-fence guide

2½

1

Clamp

18

L-shaped jig body

Fix ⅜-in. threaded rod to body with T-nut in front, nut and washer at rear.

3

2

Clamping ear

Workpiece

1½

Detail: Registration block

Registration block, 10 x 4½ x ¾

Screws engage connector.

Knock-down connector (sold for beds)

Butt end of workpiece against registration block, remove to rout.

Detail: Section view

Tenon

Router fence

Clamp

Bit

Router-fence guide

Fig. 6: Jig for large tenons

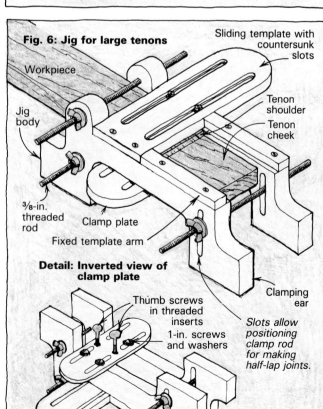

Sliding template with countersunk slots

Workpiece

Jig body

Tenon shoulder

Tenon cheek

⅜-in. threaded rod

Clamp plate

Fixed template arm

Clamping ear

Detail: Inverted view of clamp plate

Thumb screws in threaded inserts

1-in. screws and washers

Slots allow positioning clamp rod for making half-lap joints.

Fig. 7: Section view: Panel-raising jig

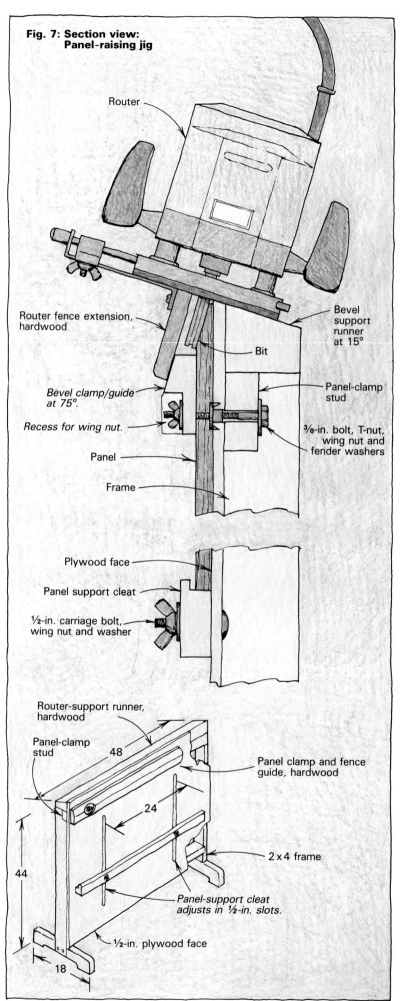

Router

Bevel support runner at 15°

Router fence extension, hardwood

Bit

Bevel clamp/guide at 75°.

Recess for wing nut.

Panel

Frame

Panel-clamp stud

⅜-in. bolt, T-nut, wing nut and fender washers

Plywood face

Panel support cleat

½-in. carriage bolt, wing nut and washer

Router-support runner, hardwood

Panel-clamp stud

48

Panel clamp and fence guide, hardwood

24

2 x 4 frame

Panel-support cleat adjusts in ½-in. slots.

44

½-in. plywood face

18

bench vise. Adjust the template to align the centerlines, then tighten the wing nuts. If you're cutting an open mortise on the end of a piece, as for a bridle joint, the template should extend an inch or so beyond the end so that the guide bushing is fully engaged before cutting starts. If you wish, clamp stop blocks for the mortise length. Cut the mortise in several passes. The same jig works for dovetail slots. Hog most of the waste with a straight bit, then rout the dovetail slot in one full-depth pass.

The tenoning jig (figure 5) is equally simple, and can be used with regular routers as well as plunge routers, though deep mortising is much easier with a plunge router. Built of 2-in. stock (any stable wood will do), it has an 18-in.-long L-shaped body that hooks over the edge of a workbench, where it is clamped by its two ears. Glued to the body's top surface is a precisely milled router-fence guide, about 1 in. thick by 2½ in. wide—make sure that it's thicker than the depth of your router fence. The guide is parallel to the front edge of the body and set back 1½ in. from it. The router's fence runs against the rear of the guide, making it impossible for the bit to wander or kick into the tenon. Two lengths of ⅜-in. threaded rod pass through the body to support the clamp that holds the workpiece. T-nuts at the front, and nuts and washers at the rear, lock the rod to the body. The top edge of the clamp should be level with, or slightly below, the upper face of the fence guide so it won't interfere with the router base. The detachable registration fixture positions the workpiece end at the correct height, although you could do this with a straightedge.

The tenon is cut vertically, the waste wood peeled away on the cheeks by the length of the bit, the shoulders cut square by the end of the bit. Adjusting the position of the fence varies the width of the shoulder and, therefore, the thickness of the tenon. Two setups are needed, one to cut each cheek. To register properly, the end of the workpiece must be square to its edges. Position the end of the workpiece with the fixture or straightedge, then tighten the wing nuts securely. Set the bit depth (or plunge depth stop) to the tenon's final length and adjust the router fence for the shoulder width. It's a good idea to cut a trial tenon in scrap to check the settings. Standing so the work is to your right, cut into the far edge of the workpiece slightly, pulling the router toward you. This prevents tear out when the cut is completed from the other direction. The bit will pull itself into the wood, so hold the router securely. Now, pushing the router, take several shallow passes to complete the cheek; for the last cut, push the fence firmly against the guide. Turn the piece around, re-register it, and cut the second cheek. You can trim the edges of the tenon in the same way, but for wide pieces it's just as easy to cut them on the tablesaw after routing the wide cheeks.

Using this jig, tenon length is restricted by the length of the router bit. In practice, we seldom cut them longer than 1¼ in. with this jig. For larger tenons, we use the jig shown in figure 6. The two halves of the jig slip over the workpiece, the sliding part of the template aligned with the shoulder line. The router rides on the template, the end of the bit milling the waste from the cheek. (Thumbscrews fitted in a plate under the jig push the workpiece tight to the sliding template.) For wide tenons, the extended router sub-base is helpful to span the jig. The guide bushing runs against the sliding template to cut the shoulder. (If your bit and guide bushing aren't the same diameter, be sure to allow for this when positioning the sliding template.) Repeat the process for the other cheek, and to remove the waste on the edges for the narrow cheeks, if you wish. By sliding the front bolt down in its slots, the jig can also be used to mill half-lap joints anywhere on the length of a board.

In frame-and-panel construction, beveling (also called "raising") the panel edges allows the panel to remain snug in the frame grooves as it expands and contracts with changing moisture content; raising also gives the panel a pleasing appearance. A century or so ago, panels were beveled with hand tools—saws and panel-raising planes—and a good deal of expertise. Today, the job can be done by machine, as well as by hand.

The shaper, tablesaw, jointer, and radial-arm saw all offer methods for panel raising, but they share two drawbacks. First, panels, often bulky and unwieldy, must be moved over a stationary cutter, presenting control problems that can result in sniping, blade burns, runout and kickback. Second, the panels must be dead flat or the beveled surfaces will be irregular.

Figure 7 shows the router panel-raising setup we developed in the school shop. The panel is fixed securely to the stand; any cup or bow is forced out by the stout clamp, which also guides the router fence. The router slides on the angled support runner that forms the top of the stand's frame. We use the Freud 12-130, ½-in. carbide bit to cut the bevel. Adjusting the router fence determines the depth of cut and, therefore, the final thickness of the tapered panel edge.

We used dressed 2x4s for the stand frame, hardwood elsewhere. The face of the stand is a 4-ft. square of plywood, glued and screwed to the frame—recess the screws to prevent marring the panels. Plunge-rout the ½-in. slots in the plywood face for the panel-support cleat. Oversized holes in the cleat will prevent the carriage bolts from binding. The support runner, angled 15° from the horizontal, can be mortised or screwed to the uprights. The 75° bevel on the clamp/guide combines with the angle of the top support runner to create a right angle—if you alter the angles, make sure they add up to 90°. The router fence extension should be at least 1 ft. long, and deep enough to provide good support and contact with the clamp/guide.

To use the jig, set the panel on the support cleat, adjusted to place the panel's top edge flush with the support runner, then tighten the clamp. Set the router fence and the bit depth, then hold the router base firmly on the runner, turn on the machine and slowly engage the panel. Make several passes, gradually easing the fence extension onto the clamp/guide. Make the final pass with the router held firmly against the guide. Set up for the next edge or end, and repeat. Because the unusually long bit is fully exposed, be extra careful to keep clear of it. The resulting panel should be uniformly raised, without burn marks, and with miters meeting precisely at the corners. Light rippling on the surfaces vanishes with normal sanding.

Much as I like routers, they do have drawbacks. They're terrific generators of noise and dust, so be sure to wear ear protection and a dust mask or respirator. When chucking a bit, especially a large one, slide it into the collet until it bottoms out, then back it off about ¹⁄₁₆ in. before tightening down. Bits seated against the bottom can vibrate loose, no matter how much torque you apply when tightening. Routers need very little maintenance—my 25-year-old Stanley still has its original brushes and bearings. Plunge mechanisms, though, need periodic cleaning and some type of dry lubrication, such as silicone spray. Dust in a switch can cause arcing at the contacts and failure of the switch. We've found that packing the switch cover housing in non-conductive Plasticine (children's modeling clay) seals out the dust. □

Bernie Maas teaches woodworking at Edinboro University in Edinboro, Penn.

Fig. 1: Typical drawer

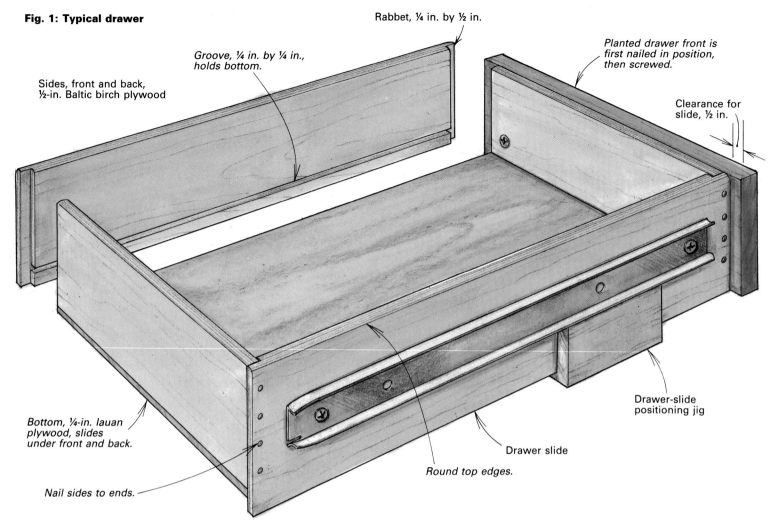

Rabbet, ¼ in. by ½ in.

Planted drawer front is first nailed in position, then screwed.

Groove, ¼ in. by ¼ in., holds bottom.

Sides, front and back, ½-in. Baltic birch plywood

Clearance for slide, ½ in.

Bottom, ¼-in. lauan plywood, slides under front and back.

Drawer-slide positioning jig

Nail sides to ends.

Drawer slide

Round top edges.

Production Drawermaking
Multi-router setup makes quick work of joinery

by Claude E. Graham III

Like many small-shop woodworkers, I've chosen to work in that vast middle ground of woodworking between the furniture studios producing one-of-a-kind pieces and the local shops churning out truckloads of doweled-together boxes with printed wood-grain exteriors. I prefer to stay close to my work and my fellow craftsmen rather than invest in computer-controlled routers or become a people pusher. I do my share of signed gallery pieces, but high-quality commercial furniture contracts make up more than half my business, and that's what pays most of the bills.

Since many of these contract casepieces contain several drawers, it seemed appropriate to devote some time, money and thought toward simplifying my drawermaking procedure. To make these jobs profitable, I needed an efficient system that

would work for everything from a pencil tray to a file drawer, yet still be simple enough to be managed by anyone in the shop, even that guy in the back who alternates his stare between the window and the clock. What I came up with was the simple, unvarying design for plywood drawers shown in figure 1 above—rabbet joints at the corners, rounded top edges and grooves to house plywood bottoms.

To handle the joinery, I set up a router table with three routers, as shown in the photo on the facing page. Shopmade fences and featherboards allow anyone to machine a drawer in about 30 seconds once the drawer parts are sawn out. The operator simply takes a stack of parts and works from router station to router station until all the rabbets, grooves and molded edges are cut. Although I just use the table for drawers, this multi-router system could be adapted to many other production situations.

The whole system, complete with stock routers and cutters, costs about $600. I've yet to find a commercial machine that can do the same work for under $4,000. If you don't produce great quantities of drawers, you could adapt the system to a one-router table with interchangeable fences. I find that leaving the router table permanently set up and ready to go takes the headache out of drawermaking runs. My router table is just a freestanding base made by rabbeting and screwing pieces of 1⅛-in.-thick particleboard together. The table itself is a 4-ft. by 2-ft. sheet of particleboard with a 1-sq.-ft. opening cut in the center. The 34-in.-high work surface is covered with plastic laminate, which makes it easy to slide workpieces past the cutters. I built a 2-in.-high box fence around the opening, as shown at right, so I could add a cover to contain dust and chips. A door installed in the base makes for easy cleanup.

Drawer design—Before describing the router operations in detail, I should explain how I designed the drawers. The budget for my typical project will not allow hand-cut dovetails even though I'm partial to them. Machine-cut dovetails, which I don't find objectionable at all, also chew too deeply into the profit margin. Dowels and knockdown fasteners are popular in Europe and in many American shops, but I don't care much for them. Butt joints are also not my cup of tea. The practical solution for me is a rabbeted joint. Besides being more than strong enough, the rabbeted joint is well suited to plywood, my material of choice for quality drawers in commercial work. Solid wood is fine, but cranking up the planer to make a drawer or two isn't very efficient, and then there is the question of warping and swelling.

Although many shops use standard 5-ply, ½-in. birch or other hardwood plywood, I've found that no amount of sanding will smooth the edges nicely. Most of my drawer sides are ½-in. Finland or Baltic birch plywoods, which have high-quality birch laminations and no voids. My only problem with imported plywoods is that they are often out of square, so I routinely square up the sheets before cutting out parts. Another quality product is Appleply, which can be obtained from some local lumber outlets and The Woodworkers' Store, 21801 Industrial Blvd., Rogers, Minn. 55374. This American-made plywood consists of nine plies of maple and alder that create a close-grain, easily finished edge. Bottoms are cut from ¼-in. lauan or similar plywood.

My next design decision involved drawer slides. If you like wood slides, I won't try to change your mind. Aesthetics aside, metal slides are simpler to install and easier to adjust, and they give years of trouble-free service. Oddly enough, they seem to work best when under full load. Generally, there are two categories of metal slides: Three-quarter-extension slides designed for chest and desk drawers and full-extension slides for file drawers or any drawer to which 100% access is required. In both cases, I prefer Accuride slides. (For the name of the nearest distributor, contact Standard Precision Inc., 12311 S. Shoemaker Ave., Santa Fe, Calif. 90670; 213-944-0921.)

Cutting lists—Once I had designed my standard drawer, I established a cutting-list system that helps me size all the parts. I first measure the drawer openings, then determine the drawer size that will allow a total of about ½-in. clearance in the drawer height, about ¼ in. above the drawer and ¼ in. below. Next, I make two headings on the cut sheet: one for sides and one for fronts and backs. The side measurements are simply the drawer height by the drawer length. For example, a drawer size of 5 in. high by 12 in. wide by 20 in. deep would need 5-in. by 20-in.

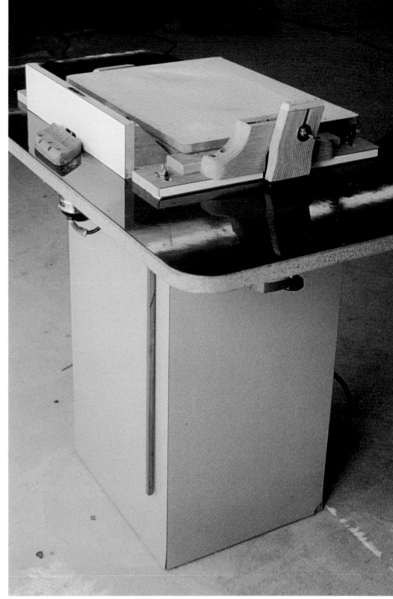

A freestanding table equipped with three routers is the key to the author's efficient and accurate drawermaking system. By moving drawer parts from station to station, a single worker can cut rabbet joints, groove the sides to house the drawer bottom and round all edges in a matter of seconds.

sides. Don't forget to account for the slides when determining part sizes. Slide lengths are typically on 2-in. even increments, so size your drawers accordingly. Most metal slides require ½-in. clearance per side or 1 in. total. The rabbet on the sides reduces the width of the drawer by ½ in.; therefore, you must make the fronts and backs only ½ in. less than the drawer width.

The drawer bottom fits into grooves on the sides, but slides under the front and back. To allow for the thickness of the bottom and the distance between the bottom of the groove and the bottom of the drawer side, the front and back pieces must be ⅝ in. less than the drawer height. For our example, therefore, the front and backs should be 4⅜ in. high by 11½ in. wide. Drawer bottoms are the width of the fronts (11½ in.) and the length of the sides (20 in.). The width measurement is critical. The bottoms are slid into place after the other components are assembled and nailed or screwed together at the front and back corners.

Routing procedures—The most efficient routing method is to perform one operation on all like parts before moving on to the

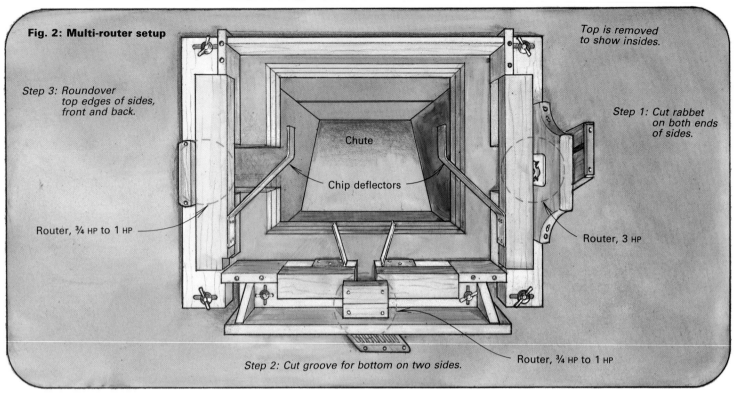

Fig. 2: Multi-router setup

Top is removed to show insides.

Step 3: Roundover top edges of sides, front and back.

Step 1: Cut rabbet on both ends of sides.

Chute

Chip deflectors

Router, ¾ HP to 1 HP

Router, 3 HP

Step 2: Cut groove for bottom on two sides.

Router, ¾ HP to 1 HP

Step 1: Routing rabbets

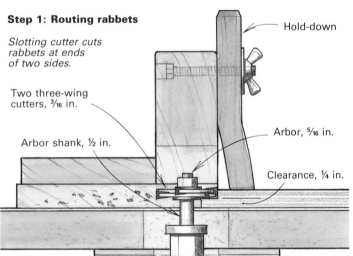

Slotting cutter cuts rabbets at ends of two sides.

Hold-down

Two three-wing cutters, ³⁄₁₆ in.

Arbor shank, ½ in.

Arbor, ⁵⁄₁₆ in.

Clearance, ¼ in.

A single pass under a three-wing carbide cutter rabbets the front and back ends of the side pieces. The cutter is set above the table to compensate for any variations in plywood thickness. A hold-down keeps the pieces flat on the table.

Step 2: Grooving sides

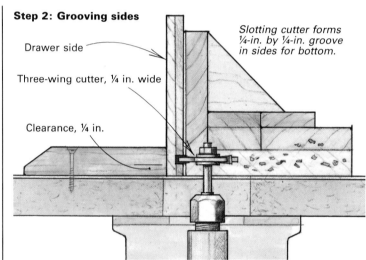

Slotting cutter forms ¼-in. by ¼-in. groove in sides for bottom.

Drawer side

Three-wing cutter, ¼ in. wide

Clearance, ¼ in.

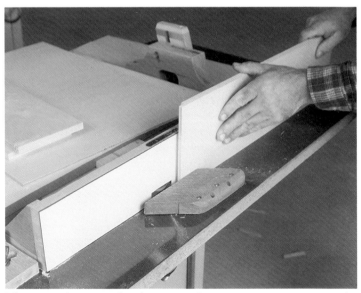

The second step in the drawermaking process is to groove the sides to accept plywood bottoms. Each side piece is run on edge past a ¼-in. slotting cutter. Because the bottom slides under the front and back, these pieces aren't grooved.

---

next. Step one is to cut the ¼-in. by ½-in. rabbet on the front and back ends of the side pieces. This operation uses a large cutter and removes a fair amount of stock from the edge of the plywood. I use a 3-HP router, which makes it possible to remove the rabbet with a single pass under two ³⁄₁₆-in. three-wing carbide-tipped cutters. These cutters, part #TF56110, available from Trend-lines, 375 Beacham St., Chelsea, Mass. 02150, are mounted together on a ⁵⁄₁₆-in. arbor, also available from Trend-lines, part #TF60100. To account for any variations in the plywood panel's thickness, I have permanently set the bit from the table surface so I'm sure I have ¼ in. of stock remaining against the table. The cutter is thick enough to eliminate any irregularities. The hold-down and cutter guard, shown in the bottom, left photo on the facing page, also increase the chance of an accurate cut and increase safety. Because the width of the pieces provides a good bearing surface on the fence and the opening for the cutter is so small, I carefully push the pieces past the cutter freehand. You could also dado the table for a miter gauge. One fine point: I always cut the stock so the crowned side of the plywood faces the inside of the drawer; when the bottom is inserted, the sides are pushed out straight.

Step two is to rout the ¼-in. by ¼-in. groove for the drawer bottom. This step is usually only performed on the drawer sides.

Step 3: Rounding over edges

Nosing cutter rounds over top edges of both sides, front and back.

Three-wing carbide-tip nosing cutter

Drawer side

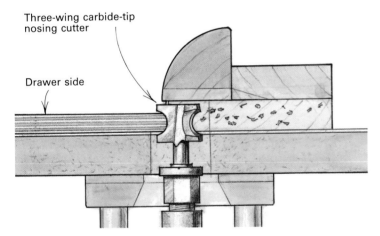

Graham rounds the edges of all the drawer parts with a single pass through the third router station, which is equipped with a carbide-tipped nosing cutter. The same operation could be done by making two passes by a roundover bit.

If you prefer to have the drawer bottom fully enclosed, then the fronts and backs should also be grooved, just be sure to adjust your cutting list if you do. The setup for this step is very similar to step one, and it uses the same arbor. But this time a ¼-in. three-wing carbide slotting cutter is used (Trend-lines, part #TF56112). This cutter can be powered by a ⅞-HP to 1-HP router. Again, I measure from the table surface to ensure proper placement of the groove and run the pieces on edge, bottom-side-down, past the cutter, as shown in the bottom, right photo on the facing page.

Step three entails nicely rounding the top edges of the sides, fronts and backs. This roundover effect also conceals small alignment blurbs during assembly. The bit here is a two-wing carbide-tipped nosing cutter (Trend-lines, part #TF82116), which rounds both edges at once, as shown in the photo below. You could also use a roundover bit and make two passes, but that seems inefficient to me. After all the parts are machined, the next step is to drill countersunk screw holes into the fronts so you can attach the show-wood drawer fronts later. Next, whip out the old orbital sander and smooth what will be the drawer interior with 100-grit paper. The exteriors are sanded after assembly and putting of the nail holes.

Drawer assembly—If you have an air nailer, assembly should take about 2.5 minutes to 3 minutes per drawer. If you don't have an air nailer, 3d finish nails work fine, just hammer them in the old-fashion way. If you are going to use this drawer system frequently, though, I think you'll find the method will pay for an air nailer in short order. Either way, my advice is to keep the glue to a minimum and turn the parts top-down on a flat surface while nailing. When the assembled drawers are dry and the nail holes puttied, finish-sand the exterior sides to taste. Finish as desired; I prefer lacquer because it is fast and sprayable.

Installing drawer slides—Put your clock-watching helper to work installing the slide rails on the drawers. Tell him to put a screw in a nonadjustable hole at the back and a screw in a vertically adjustable hole in the front. Make the quickie positioning jig shown in figure 1 to provide horizontal alignment. The next task is to install the case members. It may be necessary to cut some temporary supports to align the case part of the slide. If this is a factor, it's always better to start at the top of the case. In our shop, we put four to six screws in nonadjustable holes, depending on the anticipated load and how fast the clock is ticking. Cordless screwdrivers are ideal for this detail.

Next, you should put a bottom drawer in its new home and check for fit. Grab the appropriate drawer front and your air nailer. Align the front over the drawer and case opening. Reach inside the case, and with your air nailer, blast two or three nails through the drawer into the front. This will hold the front in place until all fronts are aligned, and it also allows a little fine-tuning, if needed. Continue this procedure, working up from the bottom. Quite often the top drawer opening is not accessible from the top for your air nailer. In this case, just pull out the drawer directly below and insert a shim or spacer to support the front directly above. Blast as needed. If you don't have an air nailer, you can screw your drawer fronts in place while they are held in the opening. When you are happy with the alignment, put a couple of screws in the front. The final adjustments for vertical positioning are made using the slide rail on the drawer. When you're pleased with the alignment, screw each rail securely in place. □

Claude E. Graham III operates Masterworks In Wood in Jacksonville, Fla.

Multiples on a router table

by Robin Cosman

My father was a woodworker in heavily forested New Brunswick, so I grew up around wood and tools. As far back as I can remember, I have worked with wood, whether it was making paddle-boats or carving handgrips for an air pistol. As a result, I've developed an affinity for small, well-crafted objects like the boxes I now produce.

I make these boxes in my spare time and earn a good profit selling them through local galleries. The boxes shown here sell for $65 retail, $32.50 wholesale. My boxes are very labor intensive, but I keep my overhead low because I don't need many power tools. Much of the work is done on a small, portable router table I built for cutting joints, grooving the sides and setting hinges on the boxes. Made in runs of 12, each box requires about two hours of labor. Building a dozen boxes at a time makes my part-time production profitable, without leaving me bored with the repetition.

Finger joints or miters decorated with the mock dovetail shown in figure 1 join the box corners. The lids pivot on a wooden hinge made from a dowel—a nice feature I learned about from Dale Nish at Brigham Young University. I've since learned this same hinge was used by 18th-century box makers in Scotland. (*Editor's note:* Despite their apparent ancient lineage, some wooden hinges may be protected by patents. Spider Johnson of Mason, Tex., has notified us that he has applied for such a patent.) The drawings and photos show the steps for making a box. One secret of efficient production work is to make consistently accurate parts. After I've surface-planed enough lumber for 12 boxes, I set up the tablesaw with a miter gauge and stop block to cut sides and ends precisely square. Before machining the sides and ends, I cut the box lids and bottoms, sand them smooth and oil them. For sanding, three orbital sanders with 150-, 220- and 320-grit paper are well worth the extra cost.

While the oil is drying on the tops, I set up my router table to cut the stopped grooves in the sides to house the box lid and bottom. There's less tearout if this step is done before the finger joints are cut. On boxes with sides that are 5/16 in. thick, a 3/16-in. bit makes an aesthetically pleasing finger. Although I prefer to cut my finger joints on the router table, they also can be cut on the table saw. After

With corner joints suited for quick construction on a router table, the author's small wooden boxes are a practical, profitable craft item.

Fig. 1: Joinery details

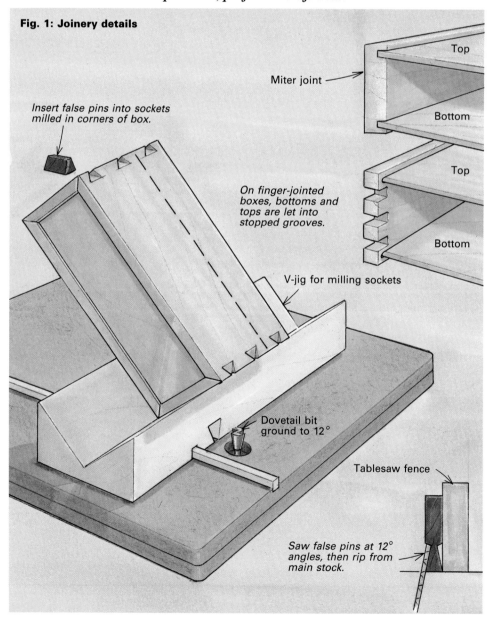

Insert false pins into sockets milled in corners of box.

Miter joint

Top

Bottom

On finger-jointed boxes, bottoms and tops are let into stopped grooves.

Top

Bottom

V-jig for milling sockets

Dovetail bit ground to 12°

Tablesaw fence

Saw false pins at 12° angles, then rip from main stock.

From *Fine Woodworking* magazine (May 1988) 70:49-50

The hinges are made from a dowel turned from the same species of wood used for the box body. A shopmade caliper assures consistent diameter. A semi-circular rabbet houses the hinge. It's cut on the router table with a core-box bit.

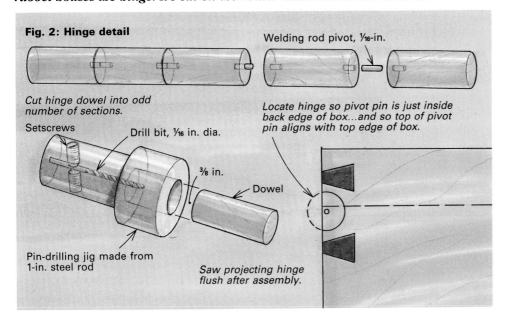

Fig. 2: Hinge detail

Welding rod pivot, ¹⁄₁₆-in.

Cut hinge dowel into odd number of sections.

Setscrews

Drill bit, ¹⁄₁₆ in. dia.

³⁄₈ in.

Dowel

Pin-drilling jig made from 1-in. steel rod

Locate hinge so pivot pin is just inside back edge of box...and so top of pivot pin aligns with top edge of box.

Saw projecting hinge flush after assembly.

the fingers are cut, the box is dry-assembled with the lid and bottom in place. If everything fits, I square up the box and apply Hot Stuff cyanoacrylate glue on the corners. The water-thin glue can be seeped into an already-assembled joint and then set with a shot of accelerator catalyst.

For the mock dovetails, I first miter the parts, then lay them end for end, outside face up. I run lengths of strapping tape along the parts, letting a few inches overhang the ends. After yellow glue is applied to the miters, I fold the pieces into a box, using the overhanging tape as a clamp. Once the glue is dry, I cut the sockets for the mock dovetails. Because commercially available bits don't produce a distinct enough dovetail, I ground a bit to about 12°.

After I have glued up all the boxes, I'm ready to slice off the lid on the tablesaw. I decide where the box should be cut apart and then, if the box is finger-jointed, center the cut in the middle

of a finger. Removing a ¹⁄₈-in. kerf down the middle of a ³⁄₁₆-in. finger leaves ¹⁄₃₂ in. on each half of the box. Working on a stationary belt sander, I use the remaining fingers as a guide— once they are sanded flush, the lid mates perfectly to the box.

The wooden hinge is next. As figure 2 shows, the hinge itself consists of a lathe-turned dowel made of the same wood species as the box. You could, however, use a standard hardware-store dowel. The dowel is sawn into an odd number of sections (odd numbers look better than even), which are let into a semi-circular rabbet routed into the back edge of both the box body and the lid with a core-box bit. The hinge pivots on ¹⁄₄-in. lengths of a ¹⁄₁₆-in.-dia. welding rod and, once assembled, the hinge sections are glued alternately to the lid and box body.

To turn the dowels safely and accurately, I use a mini drive center on my lathe, checking for consistent diameter

with a shopmade caliper consisting of a small scrap block with a groove milled in it by the same core-box bit that cuts the semi-circular rabbet. The dowels are initially turned 1 in. longer than the box, sawn into sections and then trimmed to final length. One of the biggest problems I've encountered is drilling perfectly centered holes in the dowels for the pivot pins. I solved the problem by having a machinist make the jig shown in figure 2. If you don't want to go to all this trouble to make just a couple of boxes, you could probably make the jig out of wood and then epoxy the ¹⁄₁₆-in.-dia. hinge-pin in place.

The semi-circular rabbets for the hinge are cut on the router table, beginning with the box body. The rabbet depth is critical; if it isn't correct, a sprung hinge might keep the box from closing or, worse, it will open too wide and jam. I cut the rabbet in the box body first. This rabbet must be positioned so the pivot points will be just inside the back edge of the box and tangent to the box's top edge. It's best to use a scrap piece to get the depth just right. To cut the lid rabbet, I lower the bit and move the fence forward, then using a scrap piece, I readjust the cutting depth and fence position until the lid fits with a tiny gap near the hinge end. This will prevent a sprung hinge.

The outermost hinge sections are glued to the box body and then alternate sections are glued to the lid. To avoid confusion, I pencil a "g" at points where the hinge is to be glued. A piece of cellophane tape stretched across the back of the box along the narrow edge of the rabbet prevents glue squeeze-out from seizing the lid. Apply a small bead of glue at the marked points—yellow glue or cyanoacrylate—and once everything is lined up, apply just enough clamp pressure to hold the box together. After the glue dries, I remove the projecting back of the hinge on the tablesaw, then sand everything flush, using the same sequential procedure as with the lids. A couple of coats of Minwax Antique Oil followed by two coats of Liberon Black Bison furniture wax leaves a satin-smooth finish. □

Robin Cosman is a student at Brigham Young University. He plans to open a furniture shop in New Brunswick upon graduation. Hot Stuff glue, mini-spur drive centers and Black Bison furniture wax are available from Craft Supplies U.S.A., 1287 E. 1120 S., Provo, Utah 84601; (801) 373-0917. Brass rod is available from Small Parts Inc., 6891 N.E. Third Ave., Miami, Fla. 33138; (305) 751 0856.

Decorative Routing on the Lathe
Special fixtures provide unlimited possibilities

by Daniel Agron

The addition of flutes (the concave designs on the interior and exterior of the bowl on the left) or reeds (the convex shapes on the exterior of the bowl on the right) enhances both the look and feel of turnings. Agron makes these and other decorative cuts with lathe-mounted router fixtures.

About 10 years ago, at age 55, I sold my business in Tel Aviv and my wife and I moved back to our hometown of Jerusalem. Our new house had a large basement for a shop, and I bought a small lathe and three turning chisels, and began fooling around. Pretty soon I was hooked on turning and my basement was filled with heavy, old woodworking machines, including a patternmaker's lathe equipped with a compound slide rest.

I read everything I could find about lathe work, but two books in particular really captured my interest. First and foremost was *The Principles and Practice of Ornamental or Complex Turning* by John Jacob Holtzapffel (1884, reprinted by Dover Publications Inc., 31 E. 2nd St., Mineola, N.Y. 11501; 1973), which describes the lathes that Holtzapffel designed specifically for decorating the surfaces of turnings with a large variety of intricate patterns. Another publication that I happened on was *Polychromatic Assembly for Woodturning* by Cyril and Emmett Brown (Linden Publishing Co., 3845 N. Blackstone, Fresno, Cal. 93726; 1982), which focused on constructing turning blanks from many tiny staves or wedges of various colored woods.

These influences inspired me to build two fixtures that mount on the lathe bed and hold a router so it can be moved in arcs and planes to make decorative cuts on turnings. An indexing ring, mounted outboard of the headstock, allows me to rotate the work-

piece in equal increments for routing radial flutes (concave) or reeds (convex) on the interiors or exteriors of bowls and platters (see the photo above and on p. 74). In addition to fluting preturned bowls, I use a router or drill for cutting recesses in workpieces to receive inlays of contrasting woods, thereby creating polychromatic, geometric designs (see the sidebar and the three bottom photos on p. 75).

I made the fixtures, which I call "compass" and "swing" (see figure 1 on the facing page and figure 2 on p. 74), by welding various steel parts together, but they could also be made from hardwood. Because I can vary the orientation of the router, the shape of the bit and the depth and angle of the cut, design variations are endless. I'll describe the basic setups and some of the ways that I've used the fixtures to decorate finished pieces, which will give you a taste of the possibilities.

The basic fixtures and attachments—My lathe is equipped with a compound slide rest like those found on metalworking lathes. A slide rest holds a cutting tool and moves it along the bed or across the bed by means of hand screws. A compound slide rest can also be rotated to allow fine adjustments at any angle to the work. Some of the setups that I use with my router fixtures require an auxiliary compound slide rest to facilitate setting up and fine-

From *Fine Woodworking* magazine (May 1991) 88:80-84

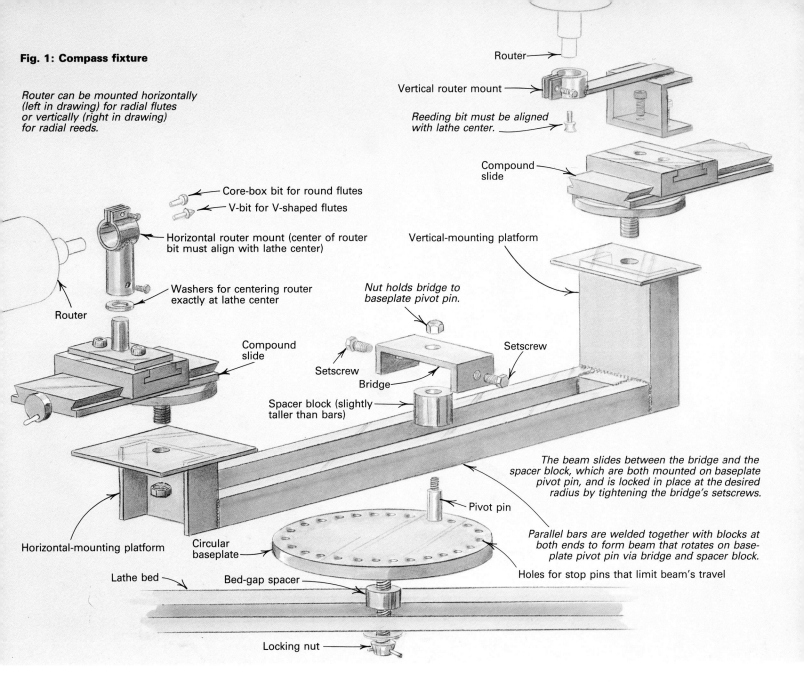

Fig. 1: Compass fixture

Router can be mounted horizontally (left in drawing) for radial flutes or vertically (right in drawing) for radial reeds.

Router

Vertical router mount

Reeding bit must be aligned with lathe center.

Compound slide

Core-box bit for round flutes

V-bit for V-shaped flutes

Horizontal router mount (center of router bit must align with lathe center)

Vertical-mounting platform

Washers for centering router exactly at lathe center

Router

Nut holds bridge to baseplate pivot pin.

Compound slide

Setscrew

Setscrew

Bridge

Spacer block (slightly taller than bars)

The beam slides between the bridge and the spacer block, which are both mounted on baseplate pivot pin, and is locked in place at the desired radius by tightening the bridge's setscrews.

Pivot pin

Parallel bars are welded together with blocks at both ends to form beam that rotates on baseplate pivot pin via bridge and spacer block.

Horizontal-mounting platform

Circular baseplate

Lathe bed

Bed-gap spacer

Holes for stop pins that limit beam's travel

Locking nut

tuning (see figures 1 and 2). You should be able to buy a slide rest from any company that sells machinist's lathes and you might even find one at a secondhand machinery store or flea market. Enco Manufacturing Co. (5000 W. Bloomingdale Ave., Chicago, Ill. 60639) has a compound mill and drill table, listed in its catalog for about $140, that could be adapted for use with my fixtures.

My lathe was not equipped with a built-in indexing system, and so I made an indexing ring and mounted it on the outboard end of the lathe's mandrel (see the top photo on p. 75). This allows me to rotate the workpiece in small increments and then lock it in place with a spring-loaded indexing pin. My ring has 72 evenly spaced holes on one face, 96 holes on the other face and 60 holes around the outer edge. Since I've been using it, however, I've found that 72 holes at 5° increments are adequate for most work. The indexing pin was designed so that fine vertical adjustments could be made, which are sometimes necessary when a workpiece is removed and then rechucked on the lathe.

I have two different clamping rings for mounting my Konnen router. The clamping ring, for mounting the router horizontally (shown at left in figure 1 above), is welded to a short length of round bar stock with its inside diameter turned to fit the slide rest's tool hold-down bolt. The clamping ring can then be rotated to set the router at the desired angle and locked in place by tight-

To cut exterior radial flutes, Agron mounts the router horizontally on the compass beam, which rotates on the baseplate's pivot pin via the bridge assembly (visible directly below the bowl).

Photos: Shuki Kook; drawings: Aaron Azevedo

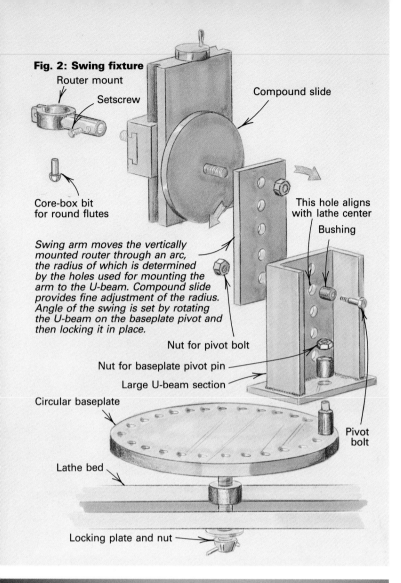

Fig. 2: Swing fixture

Router mount

Setscrew

Compound slide

Core-box bit for round flutes

Swing arm moves the vertically mounted router through an arc, the radius of which is determined by the holes used for mounting the arm to the U-beam. Compound slide provides fine adjustment of the radius. Angle of the swing is set by rotating the U-beam on the baseplate pivot and then locking it in place.

This hole aligns with lathe center

Bushing

Nut for pivot bolt

Nut for baseplate pivot pin

Large U-beam section

Circular baseplate

Pivot bolt

Lathe bed

Locking plate and nut

Flutes routed at an angle across the exterior surface of a bowl create a spiral effect, as shown above. The author routs these spiral flutes with his swing fixture, which holds the router vertically above the turning and allows it to be swung back and forth through various radii and angles. The swing mounts on the same baseplate as the compass fixture.

ening both the Allen setscrew tapped into the pipe and the nut that holds the bar stock to the slide rest. The other clamping ring is for mounting the router vertically on the compass fixture's beam for cutting radial reeds (shown at right in figure 1). You will have to adapt the mounting attachments to fit your router, but make sure the router will be firmly supported and exactly parallel or perpendicular to the bed.

The compass—I call the basic fixture for routing radial flutes and reeds the compass because it guides the router through various preset arcs. As you can see in figure 1, the compass is assembled from several component parts beginning with a circular metal baseplate. The baseplate has a ⅝-in. threaded rod tapped into the center of its underside. This means the plate can be secured any-place along the lathe bed by tightening a nut against a locking plate beneath the bed. A round guide block, center-drilled to slip over the threaded rod and sized to slide in the bed gap, centers the baseplate on the bed. A threaded pin, on which the compass beam pivots, is screwed near the rim on the top of the baseplate, and a ring of holes is drilled around the plate's outer edge for stop pins to limit the beam's travel.

The compass beam is made by welding steel blocks between the ends of two steel bars. A section of U-channel is then welded to each end of the beam to support the vertical and horizontal router mounting platforms. To mount the beam on the baseplate pivot, I milled a spacer block to slip between and stand just slightly higher than the parallel bars. I drilled a hole in the center of this block so it can be placed over the pivot and then I placed the beam on the baseplate with the parallel bars straddling the spacer block. A U-shaped bridge, which is also drilled to fit over the pivot, spans both bars and is secured with a nut on the pivot. Because the spacer stands slightly proud of the bars, the beam will still slide back and forth. Both ends of the bridge are drilled and tapped to receive setscrews to lock the beam after it is located at the desired radius. The beam should be considerably longer than the lathe's swing because when you rout the surface of shallow bowls or plates, the radius of the curvature will be larger than the radius of the workpiece.

For both horizontal and vertical mounting, a compound slide is mounted on the appropriate platform (see figure 1). When making the beam's platforms, keep in mind that the entire mounting assembly must be sized so the center of the router bit will align with the lathe's drive center. When the router is mounted vertically, this alignment can be fine-tuned by moving the bit in and out of the chuck. But no such easy adjustment is possible when the router is mounted horizontally, and so I made the platform a little low and then shimmed the router up to the lathe's center by inserting washers below the clamping ring's pipe (see figure 1). To decorate a bowl's exterior, the router must be mounted on the beam pointing toward the baseplate pivot; to decorate a bowl's interior, the router must point away from the pivot.

Routing flutes and reeds—Begin your work by preturning the bowl or platter. Then unplug the lathe and lock the workpiece in place by engaging the pin in one of the indexing ring holes. For cutting flutes, the router is mounted horizontally, level and at exact lathe center height, as shown in the photo on the previous page. If you want flutes to cover the entire surface of the bowl or platter, you only have to rough-turn the vessel close to final shape before setting up the fixture because the flutes will finish the job. However, if you want spaces between the flutes, you'll have to turn the bowl to the desired final shape before adding the flutes. You should also finish-sand the surface before fluting because sanding afterward will destroy the crisp edges of

(continued on p. 76)

Precise setups for inlaying turned forms

After playing around with the compass and swing fixtures described in the main article, I realized that the router mounted on a compound slide rest could be used to mill recesses for inlays in turning blanks. This method produces blanks with fewer glue-lines, and therefore less chance for errors, than conventional stave-lamination systems.

The vases shown here were constructed by stack-laminating preturned rings. I begin with blanks, which are discs of various thicknesses depending on their placement in the finished vessel, and I turn each blank to its proper diameter and shape. I inlay the edges of the blanks that will become the decorative bands and then I use a parting tool to separate the outer ring from the inner core of each blank. The core pieces from the larger blanks can be reused for the narrower parts of successive pieces. In some cases I use the router to cut mating rabbets in adjacent pieces before parting

off the rings. The rabbets ensure concentricity and make it easy to align the designs prior to gluing. The rabbets are made by slowly rotating the lathe by hand with the router locked in place perpendicular to the disc's face and fitted with a rabbeting bit. Always rotate the workpiece against the rotation of the cutter. After laminating the rings together, I mount the rough vessel on the lathe and carefully turn the exterior shape to refine the designs.

When cutting the recesses for the inlays, cuts should be made with the grain, that is from the larger to the smaller diameter of the blank. It's also advisable to arrange stops either by clamping blocks directly to the slides or by setting up adjustable rods, as shown in the left, top photo. The photos here of finished vases are accompanied by photos showing the setups I used for routing or drilling the slots for some of the inlays.   —D.A.

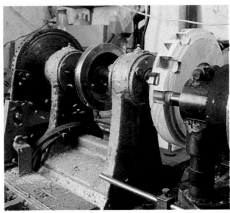

*A square wave pattern, such as that on the tall vase (**below**), is what you're left with if you alternate square slots in both edges of a blank and insert contrasting cubes in them. The setup is shown **above**. The router is mounted on the lathe's slide, fitted with a mortising bit, and moved into the blank with the slide rest's hand screw. When you reverse the blank to cut the second set of slots, you may have to adjust the indexing pin (at the far left in the photo **above**) slightly so these slots are exactly centered between the first slots. By leaving a little more than the thickness of the pattern at the base of the slots, you can true up both faces of the blank after the cubes are inlaid.*

*The feather pattern on the bottom of the vase in the photo **below** is made by routing large V-grooves in a preshaped blank with the router mounted horizontally on the lathe's compound slide, as shown in the photo **above**. Prism-shaped inserts are glued in the grooves and then turned flush with the blank's surface. To get outlined feathers, like those shown on the vase **below**, Agron inlaid dark-colored feathers, turned them flush, and then repeated the process with a shallower V-groove and light-colored inserts.*

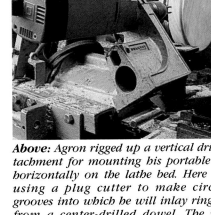

***Above:** Agron rigged up a vertical drill attachment for mounting his portable drill horizontally on the lathe bed. Here he is using a plug cutter to make circular grooves into which he will inlay rings cut from a center-drilled dowel. The rings should fit somewhat loosely in the groove to allow glue and trapped air to escape when they are inserted. Circles can be inlaid by using a Forstner drill bit instead of a plug cutter. The vessel shown **below** has a band inlaid with circles overlapping previously inlaid rings.*

Above: For cutting exterior radial reeds, the author mounts the router vertically on the beam's high platform. The beam rotates on the baseplate pivot pin and depth of cut is adjusted with the slide rest. Below: The author routs angled flutes using the swing fixture. The router is pivoted via the swing arm, which is bolted through a bushing to the vertical section of a large U-beam that is in turn bolted to the compass fixture's baseplate.

low sizing groove in the bowl's surface. You can then turn the bowl to match the radius of the sizing groove in either of two ways. First, if there is room on the bed to mount the lathe's tool rest, you can swing the router out of the way and hand-turn the bowl to this precise radius; or you can chuck a mortising bit in the compass-mounted router, set it for a shallow cut by adjusting the slide rest, and finish-turn the bowl's shape by swinging the compass through its arc while you rotate the workpiece by hand. Remember, if you will be leaving spaces between the flutes, you should finish-sand the surface at this time.

Next, you need to determine the amount of taper, the width (determined by size of bit and depth of cut) and the spacing of the flutes. This is done by trial. First, I create the taper by loosening the baseplate and rotating it so the router is pulled slightly away from the bottom of the workpiece. This results in a shallower and, therefore, narrower cut at the base of the piece. Next, I adjust depth of cut until it is as shallow as possible, but runs the full length of the final design. I clamp a bar across the slide as a stop to preserve this depth-of-cut setting. Then, to set the distance between cuts, I rotate the workpiece a number of holes along the indexing ring; this number must divide evenly into the total number of holes on the ring to ensure that the flutes will be evenly spaced around the bowl. I then make a second shallow cut, rotate the workpiece the same number of holes and make a third cut. Since the final width of cut and the spacing between cuts is determined by the size of the bit and the depth of penetration, I gradually increase the depth of all three cuts until the desired decoration is achieved. You may need to make minor adjustments in the taper as you proceed with the deeper cuts. Now you can clamp the depth stop at the final setting and rout all remaining flutes, rotating the bowl an equal number of indexing holes between them. To ensure a smooth finish cut, make at least two passes for each flute and make sure the last pass removes very little stock.

For cutting radial reeds, which are convex-shaped decorations, I follow the same system, except that the router is mounted vertically and I use a custom-made hollow-ground cutter, as shown in the top photo. You can align the bit with the lathe center by fine-tuning how far it is inserted into the chuck. The router attachment is again mounted on a slide rest for adjusting the depth of cut.

Using the swing to make spiral flutes—I designed the swing fixture (see figure 2 on p. 74 and the bottom photo here) for cutting flutes at an angle, which creates the spiral effect on the bowl in the photo on p. 74. The fixture consists of a 10-in. length of 8-in.-wide U-beam welded to a flat plate that is drilled to fit over the pivot on the compass' circular baseplate. The U-beam has a vertical row of arbitrarily spaced holes (one of which is aligned with the lathe's center) that will receive a pivoting bushing. The swing itself is a steel bar with holes bored along its length so it can be bolted to the U-beam and pivot on the bushing. The compound slide is bolted to the swing bar and the router is attached vertically to the slide. The desired radius of the swing is determined by selecting the appropriate holes in the U-beam and bar. The plane through which the router will swing, which determines the angle of the spiral, is determined by pivoting the U-beam on the circular baseplate before tightening it down. Fine adjustments of the radius and depth of cut are set with the compound slide. The procedures for rough-turning, presanding and determining the flute's taper and spacing are the same as for fluting with the compass fixture. □

Daniel Agron does decorative turning and occasionally teaches turning in Jerusalem, Israel.

the flutes. All cuts should be made from the larger to the smaller diameter of the workpiece whenever possible.

When cutting radial flutes, I first set the fixture's cutting radius, which is the distance between the pivots on the cutter and the compass beam. Then I set the center of compass rotation by sliding the baseplate along the bed and rotating it until the pivot is directly below the center of the desired radius of cut. Lock the baseplate to the bed and use the slide rest hand crank to finely adjust the desired radius and subsequently to control the depth of cut. To ensure that the compass fixture's radius is exactly the same as the bowl's preturned curvature, set the compass to a radius slightly smaller than the radius of curvature and then rout a shal-

Building an Art Nouveau Cabinet
Following the cold trail of the French masters

by Terrie Noll

My friend Page earned patron status when he referred me to a client who needed an Art Nouveau-style display case to house a collection of Gallé and other period glass. Armed with a portfolio of pictures gleaned from nearly two years of professional work and some borrowed books on the era, I approached the first meeting with my potential clients intending to assuage any anxieties about my skills and to ferret out their stylistic preferences.

After the portfolio, we started on the books, wending our way through the organic creepy-crawlies of the Nancy School and the sinuous Belgian lines that characterized turn-of-the-century Art Nouveau. From their comments, I could sense my clients' taste in art and get their ideas about the cabinet-to-be. As we turned a new page on the Parisian School's stylish grace, we found our aesthetic, done with finesse by Eugène Gaillard, a French master cabinetmaker whose work is prominent in the Art Nouveau School. Add a dash of interior lighting, a little carving here and there and voilà: the ingredients for a piece of fine furniture.

Back at the warehouse, putting magnifying glass to photo and eye to text yielded no clues about Art Nouveau construction. The single technical detail I unearthed—that pieces often were modeled in clay beforehand—only added to my confusion since you can't just glob on handfuls of wood to sculpt. The challenge was figuring out how to put material where I wanted it, take it away again and have a cabinet left over.

By scaling the agreed-upon dimensions—30 in. wide by "just a little taller" than my 6-ft. 4-in. client—I established my design territory. I immediately sectioned off the bottom third as too low for display, so it became a closed cupboard with paneled and relief-carved doors. The remaining space would be display area. With ballparked shelf spacing, I blocked in the carcase sides, flaring them all an inch forward and sideways. After adding an undulating profile, I had my basic cabinet.

There is no such thing as a square corner in Art Nouveau, so to my materials list I added a sheet of medium-density fiberboard for the curvy templates I'd need. Since the style didn't lend itself to visible joinery, and since I was more interested in representation than reproduction, I decided mortises with loose tenons throughout would be appropriate, affording me maneuverability while shaping. The cabinet elements could be glued up oversize, then

When Art Nouveau furniture was built in the shops of Paris around 1900, its sinuous lines were first modeled in clay, then sculpted by hand. Few clues about Art Nouveau construction have survived. For this Nouveau-style cabinet, Terrie Noll and Danielle Hanrahan followed template routing with hand carving.

Photo: Pablo Mason

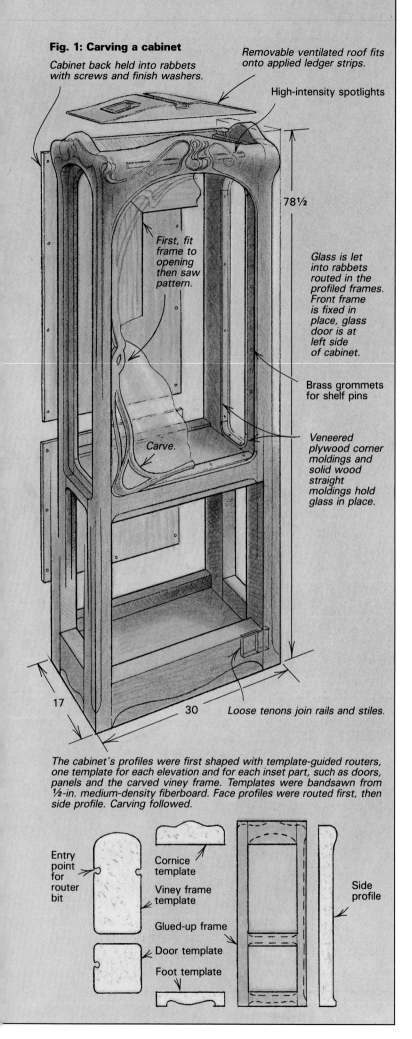

Fig. 1: Carving a cabinet

Cabinet back held into rabbets with screws and finish washers.

Removable ventilated roof fits onto applied ledger strips.

High-intensity spotlights

78½

First, fit frame to opening then saw pattern.

Glass is let into rabbets routed in the profiled frames. Front frame is fixed in place, glass door is at left side of cabinet.

Brass grommets for shelf pins

Carve.

Veneered plywood corner moldings and solid wood straight moldings hold glass in place.

17

30

Loose tenons join rails and stiles.

The cabinet's profiles were first shaped with template-guided routers, one template for each elevation and for each inset part, such as doors, panels and the carved viney frame. Templates were bandsawn from ½-in. medium-density fiberboard. Face profiles were routed first, then side profile. Carving followed.

Entry point for router bit

Cornice template

Viney frame template

Glued-up frame

Door template

Foot template

Side profile

sculpted down to the final profile. My three routers and a drawer full of flush-trim bits went on standby alert.

It dawned on me that if this cabinet were ever to be completed within a reasonable budget, and be Art Nouveau you could live with, it would have to be done *sotto voce*. After all, it was *for* display, not *the* display. This eliminated carving the side panels and relieved any notion of pasta-like diversions into foliage on the carcase sides. Unsure at this point how to embellish the cornice and foot, or what design element would travel down in the name of unity, I approached some troublesome details.

For starters, the frame of a front-opening door would infringe on the precious 24 in. of face glass; without widening the cabinet, it was structurally impossible to house a front door. But, by increasing the width of the carcase sides, I lost no critical glass and actually gained enough structure to dig a hole and bury a door there. Flush doors with Soss hinges fit both structure and design, and by making the carved reliefs double as door handles, I sidestepped the issue of finding period hardware.

Installing the glass was simple enough in the side door, but the big face glass could only go in diagonally through the top while the cabinet was face down. The glass was dropped into a rabbet, then held in place with a molding. With the glass set back fractions of an inch from the face of the 2-in.-thick wood, moldings to fill out the deep rabbets had to be very wide. For strength, the moldings transforming the curves into straightaways were of stacked ply, bandsawn to shape and veneered.

While synthesizing all these factors, a job at the San Diego Museum of Art led me to Danielle Hanrahan, the construction supervisor there. A discontented sculpture major, Danielle seemed karmically suited to moonlight on the display case. With this security blanket, I jumped into the abyss of living up to my famous last words: "Don't worry, I can build anything." I sent off a bid, then waited for a deposit to arrive. Magically, it did.

Using graph paper for layout, I realized I needed 12/4 lumber to accommodate the flared shapes, or else I'd have to glue up and tastelessly cut through a glue line. Considering the amount of carving and shaping to be done, and the species available in 3-in.-thick boards, I was fairly certain I'd choose the congenial workability of Honduras mahogany. Factoring in characteristics appropriate to the period—such as color, which had to be toward the light end so as not to lose the carving to massive darkness and subdued grain—mahogany won hands down.

While trying to sketch out tenon placement in several planes of cut-away material, I'm sure I suffered brain damage. I decided to follow the Krenovian approach: compose as you go and pray for divine guidance. By using loose tenons, I could cut all the parts to final length in basic chunks, then clamp the whole thing together into a full-size, three-dimensional worksheet. I could then see what would get cut away and what would not. With this decision, I felt safe to proceed, and began making full-size templates for every curve, outlining them in lumber crayon on my giant clamp-held box. Gaining the ability to look around corners and see what would become waste and where router bits would reach made deciding safe mortise placement a breeze.

A maelstrom of router shavings in the corner meant that Danielle was hard at work, wasting the ground on the lower doors' relief panels to a depth of ⅜ in. She then meditatively carved the now-raised design to final profile. Meanwhile—in the storm of my own router—the job of fashioning the carcase became, for me, a subtractive process of waste removal. Whoever invented Ocemco's ½-in. over-bearing flush-trim bit (Ocemco, 1251 51 Ave., Oakland, Calif. 94601) changed my life. Just slap

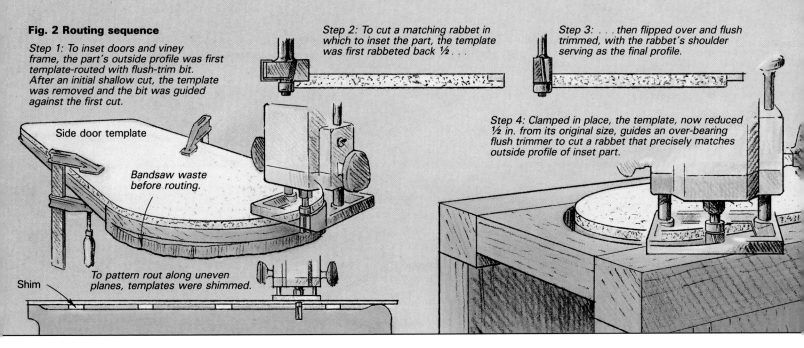

Fig. 2 Routing sequence

Step 1: To inset doors and viney frame, the part's outside profile was first template-routed with flush-trim bit. After an initial shallow cut, the template was removed and the bit was guided against the first cut.

Side door template

Bandsaw waste before routing.

Shim

To pattern rout along uneven planes, templates were shimmed.

Step 2: To cut a matching rabbet in which to inset the part, the template was first rabbeted back ½ . . .

Step 3: . . . then flipped over and flush trimmed, with the rabbet's shoulder serving as the final profile.

Step 4: Clamped in place, the template, now reduced ½ in. from its original size, guides an over-bearing flush trimmer to cut a rabbet that precisely matches outside profile of inset part.

on a template, cut the next bearing surface with the first pass, pull out the template and work your way down. With this bit and some longer ones of my own live-dangerously manufacture, I cut most of the way through, then finished up from the other side with a conventional flush-trim bit guided by the new profile and, occasionally, with hand tools, drum sanders, or a 4-in. right-angle body grinder.

Slightly more complex were the three double-duty templates for the outside curves of the two cupboard doors, the side door, and a press-fit and glued-in frame at the face opening, which was later inscribed with the viney design around the face glass. First, the templates were used to flush trim the initial outside shapes of the doors and the viney frame. Then, the templates themselves were modified—reduced in size by ½ in. around their perimeters—to serve as guides to rout the openings into which the doors and frame would fit. I used the process shown in steps 2 and 3 of figure 2 to modify the templates. The first cuts of all inside curves were made with a ½-in. bit guided against the now-reduced template, with the outer edge of the cutters doing the work. On the carcase sides, the stiles had been spaced at glue-up to the final dimension, so the bit just grazed the wood there. All of the real cutting was confined to the inside sweep of the rails, and this method made it easier to fit corresponding parts to openings.

A watchful eye on the sequence ensured that nothing got cut away before its time, thus destroying a vital reference edge. To simplify the process, the paneled doors' center rail was half-lapped in from behind after glue-up. Like the horizontal pieces at the waist, the rail was set 1 in. back from the front plane, and eventually all planes were faired smoothly together. As shown in figure 2, this meant that some templates had to be shimmed up, and the bit hung down, to create a shoulder to guide subsequent cuts without the template.

After all the openings in the face and sides plus the profiles of the top and bottom had been routed, I cut a rabbet to hold the side door in flush. Prior to the vertical profile being put in the carcase, a slotting cutter was used from the still-flat face to waste rabbets for the side panels, face glass and side glass. The viney frame was glued into place, leaving a flush surface on the inside for the face glass to butt against. This step completed, all vertical profiles were cut using the same template. With the cabinet on its side or back, and with some of my homemade monster over-

bearing flush trimmers, I could still only rout so deeply. Thus, the forward flare of the cornice, as well as the side flares, had to be faired in with a 4-in. grinder and some serious-grit sandpaper.

By the time the doors were carved and the cabinet shaped, we had completed enough work to boost morale by sanding the door panels together. Meticulous tool marks had to be swallowed as "distractive," so I watched what I once considered a liberal sanding budget disappear on those two panels, along with my dreams of Nouveau riches.

With the cabinet now fully profiled and the cornice still open to suggestion, Danielle sputtered on the runway before launching herself into Krenovian mode. I finished carving around the face glass, fit moldings and hardware, and built a removable ventilated roof. Once the mounting of the light track inside the cornice and concealment of wires and transformer were all provided for, I had nothing left to do but follow Danielle's work with 80-grit sandpaper in my hand and tape on all my fingers.

As we edged over 500 hours, I was working alone when sanding mercifully came to an end—I had plasticized into character the cabinet's few remaining crisp edges. With help from the shop downstairs, we moved the cabinet to my living room where we discovered that it had become a roller coaster ride for the eye, with tension-filled climbs, exquisite agony over the top, swoops into energy and climbs back up again. We sank into postpartum depression, but the idea of getting paid swept us into the finishing stage. We intended nothing more than a premature aging until the mahogany could go its own natural way. This was accomplished in a round-about manner: the analine-dye stain turned a panicky brick red and was brought back to gold by a wash of green-tinted sealer. A little brown Briwax toned it to an acceptable color, adding the shined-shoe patina I thought would fit the mood.

Into the windup, a smooth delivery and an honest pitch netted us some compensation for the hours we had surpassed the bid. The Gallè and Nancy glass glowed as never before under high-intensity spots. The cabinet emitted its own stately version of Art Nouveau liveliness. We glowed a little ourselves to know the Arts and Crafts movement was still alive and well in the 20th century, true to Walter Crane's aim of "turning our artists into craftsmen, and our craftsmen into artists." □

Terrie Noll builds one-of-a-kind furniture in San Francisco, Calif.

Building a File Cabinet
Router techniques for joinery and decoration

by Pat Warner

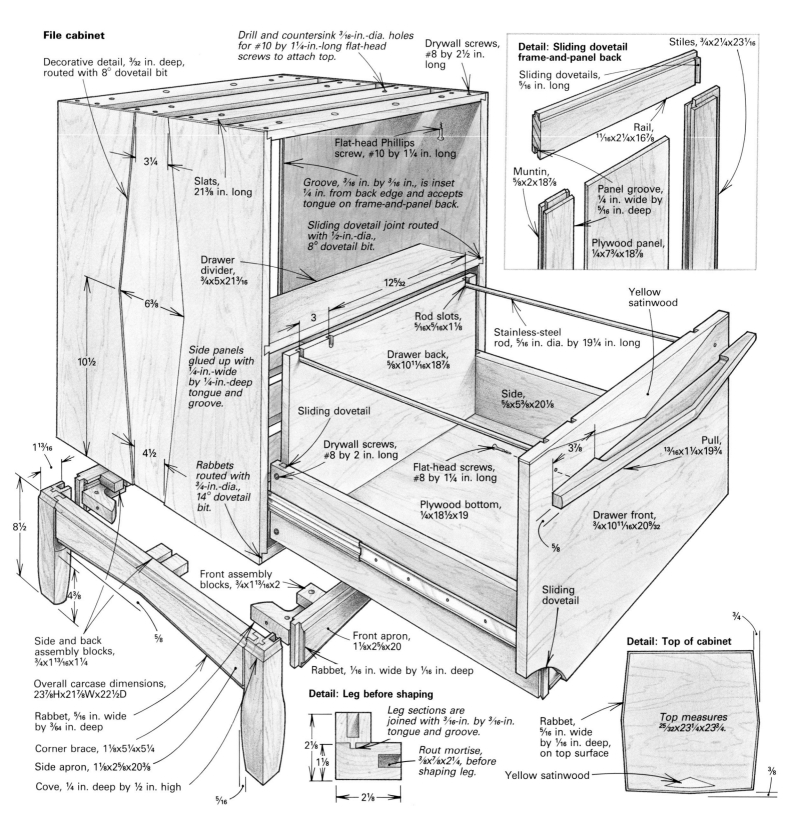

File cabinet

Decorative detail, ³⁄₃₂ in. deep, routed with 8° dovetail bit

Drill and countersink ³⁄₁₆-in.-dia. holes for #10 by 1¼-in.-long flat-head screws to attach top.

Drywall screws, #8 by 2½ in. long

3¼

Slats, 21⅜ in. long

Flat-head Phillips screw, #10 by 1¼ in. long

Groove, ³⁄₁₆ in. by ³⁄₁₆ in., is inset ¼ in. from back edge and accepts tongue on frame-and-panel back.

Sliding dovetail joint routed with ½-in.-dia., 8° dovetail bit.

6⅜

Drawer divider, ¾x5x21³⁄₁₆

12⁵⁄₃₂

10½

3

Rod slots, ⁵⁄₁₆x⁵⁄₁₆x1⅛

Detail: Sliding dovetail frame-and-panel back

Stiles, ¾x2¼x23¹⁄₁₆

Sliding dovetails, ⁵⁄₁₆ in. long

Rail, ¹¹⁄₁₆x2¼x16⅞

Muntin, ⅝x2x18⅞

Panel groove, ¼ in. wide by ⁵⁄₁₆ in. deep

Plywood panel, ¼x7¾x18⅞

Yellow satinwood

Side panels glued up with ¼-in.-wide by ¼-in.-deep tongue and groove.

Stainless-steel rod, ⁵⁄₁₆ in. dia. by 19¼ in. long

Drawer back, ⅝x10¹¹⁄₁₆x18⅞

Side, ⅝x5⅜x20⅛

1¹³⁄₁₆

4½

Sliding dovetail

Rabbets routed with ¾-in.-dia., 14° dovetail bit.

Drywall screws, #8 by 2 in. long

Flat-head screws, #8 by 1¼ in. long

Plywood bottom, ¼x18½x19

3⅞

Pull, ¹³⁄₁₆x1¼x19¾

8½

4³⁄₈

⅝

Front assembly blocks, ¾x1¹³⁄₁₆x2

Front apron, 1⅛x2⅝x20

Rabbet, ¹⁄₁₆ in. wide by ¹⁄₁₆ in. deep

Drawer front, ¾x10¹¹⁄₁₆x20⁹⁄₃₂

⅝

Sliding dovetail

Side and back assembly blocks, ¾x1¹³⁄₁₆x1¼

Overall carcase dimensions, 23⅞Hx21⅞Wx22½D

Rabbet, ⁵⁄₁₆ in. wide by ³⁄₆₄ in. deep

Corner brace, 1⅛x5¼x5¼

Side apron, 1⅛x2⅝x20⅜

Cove, ¼ in. deep by ½ in. high

Detail: Leg before shaping

2⅛

1⅛

2⅛

⁵⁄₁₆

Leg sections are joined with ³⁄₁₆-in. by ³⁄₁₆-in. tongue and groove.

Rout mortise, ³⁄₈x⅞x2¼, before shaping leg.

Detail: Top of cabinet

¾

Rabbet, ⁵⁄₁₆ in. wide by ¹⁄₁₆ in. deep, on top surface

Yellow satinwood

Top measures ²⁵⁄₃₂x23¼x23¾.

⅜

From *Fine Woodworking* magazine (March 1991) 87:44-47

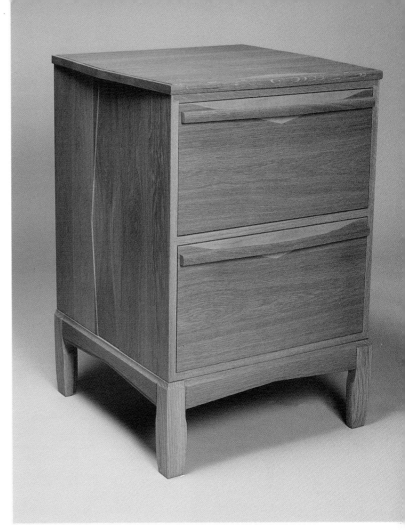

Most file cabinets look like department-store safes. My file cabinet started out as a chunky rectangular box, but I softened the lines and made it visually interesting by adding a separate base with shaped legs and by introducing a theme of triangles, which appear in many elements of the cabinet. The triangles first appear in the satinwood inlays in the drawer fronts and top, and the design is repeated in the shape of the top's edge, in the drawer pulls and in the shapes cut from the aprons on the base. Rabbets routed into the aprons and top and recessed opposing-triangle accents routed into the sides create shadow lines that reinforce these triangular designs. This is one of those rare projects that I wouldn't change if I were to build it again, but if you think it looks difficult, you could ignore most of the detail work, thereby simplifying construction, and still produce a good-looking, functional piece.

Building this file cabinet, shown in the top photo, is also a great learning project; it includes basic woodworking skills and is a tour de force of router techniques. The carcase is a simple white oak box that is joined with router-cut dovetailed rabbets, tongues and grooves, and sliding-dovetail joints. Designing the joints for the frame-and-panel back, shown in the bottom photo, was a challenge because each element is in a different plane. Although the back is unnecessarily complicated, it creates an extremely rigid carcase and makes the cabinet attractive enough to be used away from a wall. I decorated the drawers, which are joined with sliding dovetails, by routing a contrasting triangle of satinwood into each drawer front. Both drawer inlays and a satinwood triangle inlaid into the separate top were fitted by a process called complementary template routing: A router with a bushing or ball-bearing piloted bit is guided by a master template to simultaneously create complementary working templates. These templates then guide the router to create perfectly matching pieces that fit together snugly. (For more on this technique, see pp. 53-55.)

For maximum accuracy, I also used a template and a ball-bearing guided bit to shape many of the cabinet pieces, such as the overhanging sides and the front edge of the top and aprons. I usually assemble my own piloted bits by adding a bearing with an inside diameter matched to the shank of the router bit and an outside diameter suited to the job at hand. As a safety precaution, be sure that the cutting diameter of the bit is greater than the inside diameter of the bearing and that at least ¾ in. of the bit's shank is chucked in the router's collet. If the shank is long enough, I sometimes stack two bearings on the bit for greater depth of cut, to cover the shank on longer bits and to ensure solid contact with the template. A drop of Locktite (available from auto-supply stores) on the bearing's inner race will hold it in place. I bought my bearings from Valley Chain and Gear (1320 Grand, San Marcos, Cal. 92069) and the router bits from Paso Robles Carbide (731C Paso Robles St., Paso Robles, Cal. 93446) and MLCS Ltd. (Box 4053, Rydal, Pa. 19046).

Constructing the carcase—All carcase parts were milled to ¾ in. thick from 4/4 white oak and then cut to the dimensions in the drawing. The sides were glued up with tongue-and-groove joints to ensure flat, even pieces during clamping. I cut the tongues and grooves on a router table using a ¼-in. rabbeting bit for the tongues and a ³⁄₁₆-in.-thick three-wing slot cutter for the grooves. To center the slots and tongues, I made cuts in two passes, one from each face of the piece. I cut the tongues to be about 0.005 in. shy of the bottoms of the ¼-in.-deep grooves, to allow space for trapped glue and to prevent the tongues from bottoming out.

Rather than install a solid subtop and bottom, I used a series of slats joined to the sides with dovetailed rabbets that are glued and screwed. The slats eliminate normal carcase glue-up and simplify milling operations. Also, they can be cut from random widths of

Above: This white-oak file cabinet was made with a variety of router shaping and joinery. Its boxy appearance is softened by recurring triangular designs that appear in the inlaid drawer fronts and the top, in the shape of the aprons and overhanging top edges, and in the routed detail on the side panels.

Right: The author created this complicated frame-and-panel back, joined by sliding dovetails, as a personal design challenge. All the elements of the back are in different planes to create interesting shadow lines. A simple panel back can be substituted to ease construction.

lower-quality stock, and they let you install components one at a time, at a comfortable pace.

My slats are 4 in. to 6 in. wide, crosscut as shown in the drawing. The single-face dovetail that joins the slat to the side is half of a sliding dovetail cut with a ¾-in.-dia., 14° dovetail bit in a table-mounted router set to take a ½-in.-deep cut. I clamped the slat on end to a sliding fence attachment and adjusted the fence so the bit cut ¼ in. into the inside face of the slat (I was careful not to trap the workpiece between the fence and the router bit). I then drilled and countersunk two ¹¹⁄₆₄-in.-dia. holes in each end of the slat, for #8 by 2½-in.-long bugle-head drywall screws. The sharp twin-threaded screws are virtually unstrippable when screwed into ⁵⁄₃₂-in.-dia. pilot holes drilled into the sides. I lightly chamfered the edges of the slats and drilled $\frac{3}{16}$-in.-dia. holes in the subtop planks for the 12, #10 by $1\frac{1}{4}$-in.-long flat-head Phillips screws that secure the top. No allowance need be made for wood movement because the grain is oriented in the same direction for the top, subtop, bottom and sides.

I cut the mating dovetail rabbet in the sides with a hand-held router controlled by a template and a bearing-guided bit. I used the same dovetail bit as on the slats, but with a 1.125-OD bearing mounted on the bit's $\frac{1}{2}$-in.-dia. shaft. The template was positioned on the side panel and the depth of cut was adjusted so that the dovetailed slat end fit into the dovetailed rabbet in the side panel, as shown in the drawing. This setup is a trial-and-error process that should be practiced on scrap stock. Take light cuts and test the fit after each pass with one of the dovetailed slats until it is perfect. Then measure the fence setup on the practice piece and transfer it to the cabinet side. The offset-knob router subbase, shown in the top photo below, adds stability to this operation, particularly at the ends of the cut where only one-fourth of a regular router base would be on the template. (This subbase is available from Trendlines, 375 Beacham St., Chelsea, Mass. 02150.) I used a technique I call spring-clamping to secure some $\frac{3}{4}$-in.-thick material to the edge of the side panel to prevent tearout, as shown in the bottom photo below.

The frame-and-panel back is held in place by $\frac{3}{16}$-in.-sq. slots that I routed with a bearing-guided, $\frac{3}{16}$-in. two-wing groove cutter. I

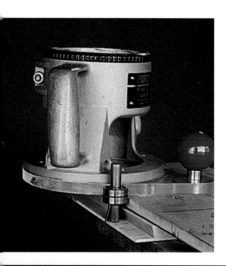

Left: The offset-knob router subbase, shown here with the router removed, increases surface area on the template for a more stable operation. The dovetail bit shows the correct setup for routing the dovetailed rabbet on the side panel.

Below: When routing the dovetail rabbets, a small piece of leather, clamped between the panel and scrap, levers the scrapwood tightly to the panel to help prevent tearout. This is a handy trick when a template interferes with clamping a scrap closer to the cut.

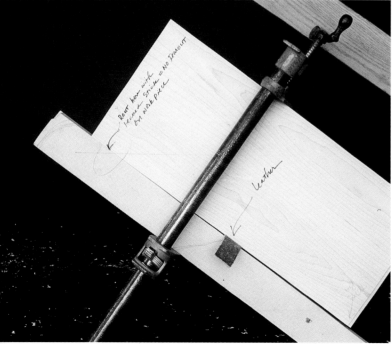

positioned the slots $\frac{1}{4}$ in. from the back edge of the carcase, on the inside edges of the sides and rear slats. Then I routed the optional opposing triangular detail in the cabinet sides, shown in the drawing on p. 80, with a bearing-guided, $\frac{1}{2}$-in.-dia. 8° dovetail bit in a hand-held router set for a $\frac{3}{32}$-in.-deep cut and guided by a template. Before beginning work on the back panel, I routed the sliding dovetails for the drawer divider. In a single pass, rout the 5-in.-long dovetail ways on the horizontal centerline of the side panels with a $\frac{1}{2}$-in.-dia., 8° dovetail bit mounted in a hand-held router controlled by a template and guide collar. Cut the dovetail pins with the same bit on the router table using the sliding fence attachment as previously described, only this time rout dovetails into both faces of the divider.

Backing up the cabinet—To finish the carcase, feel free to make the back any way you want. If the cabinet will be against the wall, a simple plywood panel may satisfy you. A more attractive solution would be ordinary frame-and-panel construction. Those with a more masochistic bent may decide to duplicate the sliding-dovetail frame-and-panel back that I developed, shown in the bottom photo on the previous page. To create interesting shadow lines, the rails, stiles, muntin and panels are all in different planes. This means the joinery must be offset to the rear of the panel. Although I show dimensions for the components of the back panel, you should dry-assemble your carcase and then cut these components to fit the opening in your particular carcase. After constructing the frame-and-panel back, as shown in the drawing, I routed a continuous $\frac{3}{16}$-in.-sq. tongue around its perimeter. The tongue is $\frac{3}{16}$ in. from the outside face of the stiles so that the entire back will be set into the carcase $\frac{1}{16}$ in., to produce yet another shadow line. All the parts, including the back edges of the carcase, were lightly chamfered.

I began assembling the carcase by temporarily clamping the two sides to one of the slats, forming a U-shaped assembly. Line up the top rear slat to the rear of both side panels and clamp it in place. Using the predrilled holes in the slat as a guide, bore the $\frac{5}{32}$-in.-dia. pilot holes into the sides for the #8 screws. Remove the clamps, and then glue and screw the slat in place. I used a 90° brace to clamp the slat in place before screwing, to ensure the carcase was square. After gluing and screwing all the slats on one end, turn the carcase over, sparingly glue up the upper half of the tongue on the outer edge of the back panel and the lower half of the slot in the carcase to avoid squeeze-out, slide the back into place, and begin assembling the opposite end starting with the rear slat. Finish up the carcase by gluing the drawer divider in place. Again, sparingly apply glue to the last half of the socket and the front half of the tenon. From start to finish, it took me about an hour to put the carcase together. But because of the step-by-step assembly, I didn't feel like I needed eight hands to control all the clamps, clamping pads and furniture components involved in carcase glue-up.

Building the base—Because of the weight of a full file cabinet, the base had to be rugged. I added stout corner braces to my mortised-and-tenoned base to resist the abuse of even the most ruthless mover. To beef up the base and allow it to protrude beyond the carcase ($\frac{5}{16}$ in. on the sides and front and $\frac{1}{16}$ in. in the back), I made the aprons, legs and corner braces from $1\frac{1}{8}$-in.-thick white oak, as shown in the drawing on p. 80. Although I could have mitered the leg sections together for a better grain match, I glued them together with a tongue-and-groove joint for easier assembly and a more precise fit, matching the pieces as well as I could. I glued up three 24-in.-long L-shaped units with $2\frac{1}{8}$-in.-wide outside faces from the $1\frac{1}{8}$-in.-thick stock. Cutting these units in half yielded six 12-in.-long legs. Although the legs will be a little long, the extra

Photos this page: Patrick Warner

length provides a safe handle for the machining operations you will perform before cutting the legs to their finished length of 8 1/2 in. I used one of the extra leg blanks to experiment with designs and the other for testing machine setups.

Before shaping the legs, rout an open, 3/8-in. centered mortise, 7/8 in. deep by 2 1/4 in. long, into each 1 1/8-in.-wide face on all the legs. To avoid vibration and deflection, I made multiple passes with a single-flute 3/8-in. bit chucked in a table-mounted router. Then, starting at the top of the leg, I routed 5/16 in. off the same face of the leg with a flush-trimming bit and a template to create the 4 1/8-in.-long section at the top of the leg. Now, using the same bit and a template with a 20-in. radius on its guide edge, shape the bottom of the leg on the edge you just shaped. I repeated that radius cut on both outside faces of the leg, first jigsawing the basic shape and then dressing up the face on my 4-in. edge sander. Finally, I hand-sanded a 1 3/4-in. radius onto the lower portion of the mortised face edge.

Dimension the aprons, according to the drawing, before routing the 3/8-in.-thick by 9/16-in.-long tenons with a bearing-guided rabbeting bit. Again, I ran a bearing-guided flush-trimming bit against a template to rout the triangular recess into the bottom edge of the front and side aprons. Next, rout the 5/16-in.-wide by 3/64-in.-deep rabbet on the face of each apron with a bearing-guided rabbeting bit. I also used a bearing-guided bit to rout a 1/16-in.-sq. rabbet at the tenon shoulder of each apron to provide another shadow line.

With a bearing-guided two-wing groove cutter, rout 3/16-in.-sq. slots on the inside face of each apron, to accept the tongued assembly blocks that fasten the base to the carcase (see the drawing on p. 80). Sand all members and glue up the frame. After assembly I routed a 1/4-in.-deep cove along the top edge of the front and side aprons, as well as the tops of the legs, with a bearing-guided 1/2-in.-radius cove bit, to blend the lines of the base into the carcase. I used very light climb cuts on the leg tops, moving the router from right to left to avoid end-grain tearout. But a safer technique is to stop the cut just shy of the leg edge and finish up the detail with sandpaper wrapped around a 1-in.-dia. dowel. Next, cut the corner braces and tongued assembly blocks, as shown in the drawing, and attach the front assembly blocks in place with #12 screws. To allow for wood movement, use pairs of blocks, spaced a screw width apart, on the sides and back. Locate the corner blocks so their holes or slots line up with the access holes in the corner braces. Then turn the carcase upside down, position the base upside down on the carcase and transfer the location of the holes in the assembly blocks to the bottom slats. Drill 5/32-in.-dia. pilot holes in the slats and fasten the base to the carcase with #12 by 1 1/4-in.-long round-head sheet-metal screws. Note that the carcase is fixed in front so that all movement will occur at the back, where the screws slide in the slots formed by the paired blocks.

Making the drawers—The drawers consist of a full-height front and back joined by sliding dovetails to half-height sides, which help reduce the weight of the drawers and conserve wood. The bottom slides into grooves on all four edges. To withstand heavy loads, I chose 18-in. Accuride #C3800 drawer slides with a load rating of 75 lbs., which I bought from Cabinet Hardware Manufacturing Co., 14560 S. Marquardt Ave., Santa Fe Springs, Cal. 90670. The slides require 1/2-in. clearance between each drawer side and the carcase, and so flanged, flush-inset drawer fronts work well. One caution: when measuring for the drawer compartments, allow 1/2-in. clearance for the hardware based on the inside dimensions of the carcase and not the drawer fronts; otherwise, the hardware won't fit properly.

Cut all drawer parts to size and then rout the sliding dovetails using the same 3/8-in.-dia., 8° dovetail bit set to take a 3/8-in.-deep pass for all joints. Again, although the drawing shows my drawer component dimensions, be sure to make adjustments as necessary to fit your actual carcase. I left 3/64-in. clearance on the sides of my drawers and a little bit more, about 1/16-in. clearance, on the top and bottom to prevent the drawers from sticking when their fronts expand. Also, leave at least 1/2-in. clearance between the drawer backs and the carcase back, because a carcase of this size can move as much as 1/4 in. with changing humidity levels.

Using the previously described technique of complementary routing to make templates, inlay the full-thickness yellow-satinwood triangles into the drawer fronts. Now rout the 5/16x5/16x1 1/8 rod support slots into each drawer front and back, as shown in the drawing on p. 80. The three slots are spaced 15 5/32 in. and 12 5/32 in. apart so the rods can support either legal- or letter-sized suspended file folder. The location of the slots is critical for smooth movement of the file folders, and so I suggest setting up the cuts first on a piece of scrap. To hang the file folders, I bought some 5/16-in.-dia. stainless rod at the junk yard, cut it to length, and dressed it by chucking it in the drill press set at its slowest speed and buffing it with 320-grit silicone-carbide paper and 0 steel wool. Finally, rout the groove for the 1/4-in.-thick plywood bottom; be aware that the groove is 3/16 in. deep on the sides and back, but 3/8 in. deep in front.

To assemble the drawers, first apply glue to the front sockets and to the pins on the front of the sides and then slide these pieces together. The plywood bottom slides into its grooves until it reaches the end of each drawer-front groove. The extra depth of this groove allows the bottom to slide past the front of the drawer back, which is then slid into position without glue. Pulling the bottom into the groove in the drawer back still leaves 3/16 in. of the bottom in the front groove so that the bottom is supported on all four sides. Now screw the sides to the back, as shown in the drawing. When finishing the piece, I removed the back and bottom, leaving these pieces and the inside of the carcase unfinished to minimize the outgasing of solvents within the cabinet.

The finger grips for the applied pulls are routed into oversize stock with a bearing-guided 1/4-in.-radius core-box bit and a template before the triangular-shaped pull is bandsawn. Sand the front edge to the correct radius, using a coved piece of scrap as a sanding block, and then cut the pull to length. Locate the centerline of the pull 1 1/8 in. below the top of the drawers and secure the pull with three #8 by 1 1/2-in.-long flat-head screws.

Topping off the cabinet—I made the separate slab top of 25/32-in.-thick white oak about 6 in. wider than the finished top is deep because I shaped and then ripped a strip from the back of the top and glued it to the front, to hide the edge of the satinwood inset. After gluing up the top, rout the satinwood triangle into its front edge using the same template and procedure as for the drawer fronts. Then using a template with a 60-in. radius, rout an arc across the back edge of the top. Rip a 2-in.-wide strip from the back and, using the same template, rout the complementary arc across the front edge of the top. Now glue and clamp the strip ripped from the back edge to the front edge. Finish shaping the top using a flush-trimming bit in a hand-held router guided by a template to cut the triangular edges on the sides and front (see the drawing). I routed a 5/16-in.-wide by 1/16-in.-deep detail around the edge of the top with a bearing-guided rabbeting bit. Sand the top's edge to a 7/8-in. radius with a piece of coved scrap and secure it to the carcase with 12, #10 by 1 1/4-in.-long flat-head screws. I finished the cabinet with three coats of Watco oil and wet-sanded the final coat. □

Patrick Warner teaches classes on router techniques and making jigs and fixtures. For more information, contact the author at 1427 Kenora St., Escondido, Cal. 92027.

Building a Shaker-Style Wardrobe

Beads and crown dress up a basic cabinet

by Tom Hagood

Fig. 1: Shaker-style wardrobe

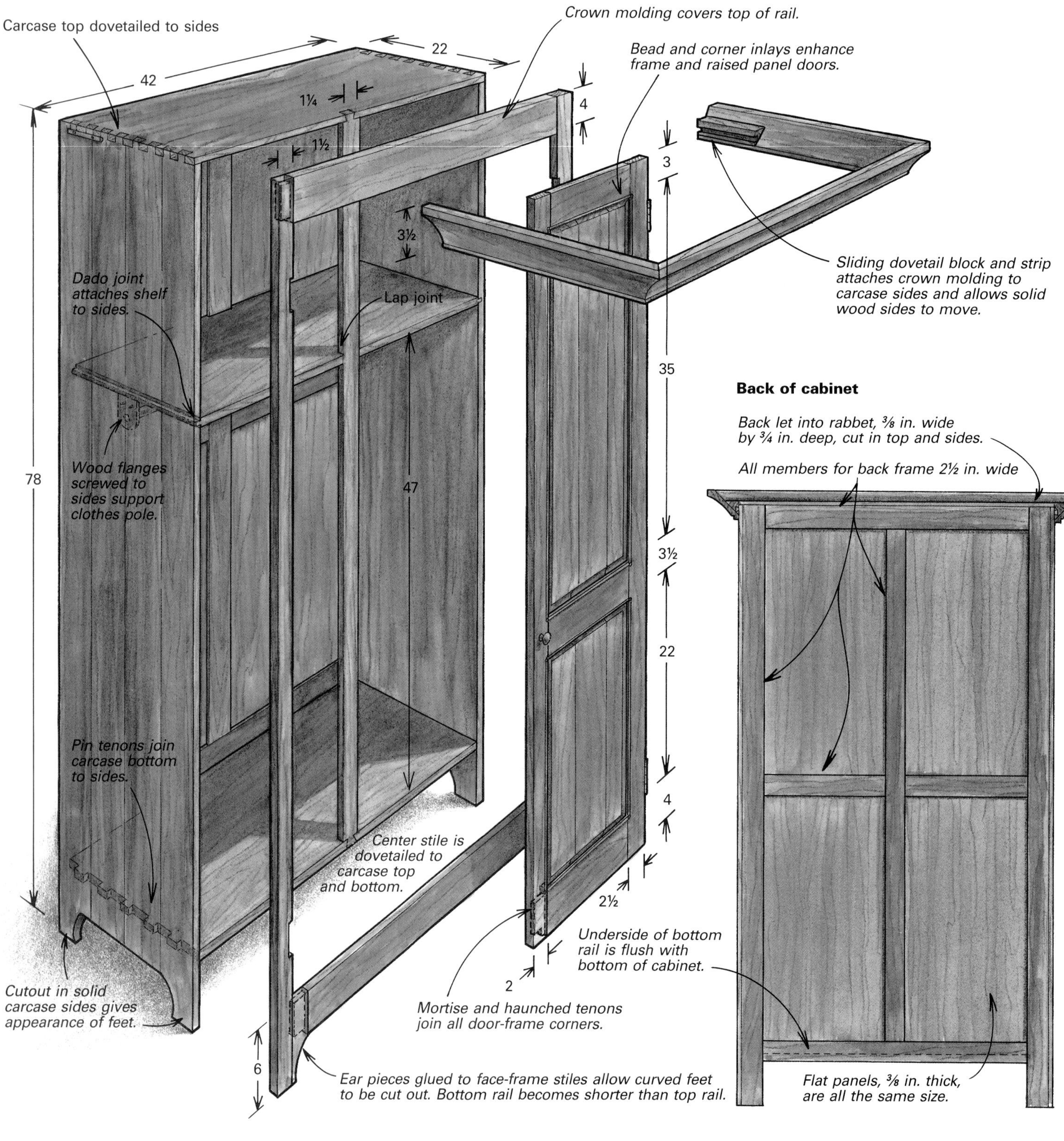

Carcase top dovetailed to sides

Crown molding covers top of rail.

Bead and corner inlays enhance frame and raised panel doors.

22

42

1¼

1½

4

3

3½

Lap joint

Dado joint attaches shelf to sides.

Wood flanges screwed to sides support clothes pole.

78

47

Sliding dovetail block and strip attaches crown molding to carcase sides and allows solid wood sides to move.

35

Back of cabinet

Back let into rabbet, ⅜ in. wide by ¾ in. deep, cut in top and sides.

All members for back frame 2½ in. wide

3½

22

4

Pin tenons join carcase bottom to sides.

Center stile is dovetailed to carcase top and bottom.

Underside of bottom rail is flush with bottom of cabinet.

2½

Cutout in solid carcase sides gives appearance of feet.

2

Mortise and haunched tenons join all door-frame corners.

6

Ear pieces glued to face-frame stiles allow curved feet to be cut out. Bottom rail becomes shorter than top rail.

Flat panels, ⅜ in. thick, are all the same size.

From *Fine Woodworking* magazine (January 1989) 74:58-61

I've never been especially fond of period furniture; therefore, the commission I received to build a traditionally styled wardrobe cabinet was quite a challenge. The client did not specify the style, but the piece had to fit into an Early American bedroom dominated by a huge antique mahogany bed—a family heirloom. Because all my previous work had been with contemporary designs, I had some reservations about accepting the commission; a contemporary wardrobe would clearly be out of place in this bedroom. Thus, I set out to find a period style that would be traditional yet allow for some creative interpretation so I could incorporate my own design details. In this article, I'll tell you how I developed my design, worked out the details and built the cherry wardrobe cabinet pictured at right.

Before I began designing the wardrobe, I searched through furniture reference books for a period piece to serve as a point of departure. In my search, I discovered a reference book called *Chests, Cupboards, Desks and Other Pieces* by William C. Ketchum, Jr. (published by Random House, Westminster, Md. 21157). Although primarily a book for furniture collectors, I find it a valuable resource for furniture designers: The book includes photographs and drawings of a dizzying number of styles, from English and French period pieces to Shaker designs to Wendell Castle stack-laminated work. The book even includes joinery details and dimensions for many of the pieces.

Ketchum's book contains a photo of a simple Shaker wardrobe that seemed to fit my needs. The piece is traditional looking yet plain enough to benefit from the addition of some of my decorative details. I was already somewhat familiar with Shaker furniture and crafts, having at one time manufactured Shaker-style steam-bent oval boxes, and I like the Shakers' straightforward, functional approach to furnituremaking. There are also modern interpretations of the style that I like, such as the work of furnituremaker Thomas Moser of Maine.

It was necessary to adapt the dimensions of the wardrobe to fit the client's room and accommodate the amount of clothing the cabinet would have to hold. To help visualize how the cabinet would relate to its surroundings, I made a perspective sketch of the room, including a view of the ceiling and other bedroom furnishings. I chose to make the wardrobe 78 in. tall and 42 in. wide to fit harmoniously with the client's large bed, and I made the wardrobe 22 in. deep to easily handle bulky winter clothes hung on a clothing pole inside.

Pleased with the proportions of the cabinet, I went back to the drafting table to work out the small details, such as the cutout base beading around the door frames, the profile of the crown molding and the joinery to hold the cabinet together. Because solid wood would be used throughout, I had to design the cabinet to allow for expansion and contraction. In addition to frame-and-panel doors, this meant making a frame-and-panel back and a sliding joint for attaching the crown molding to the top of the carcase. The top, bottom and sides of the carcase would consist of edge-glued boards joined with dovetails at the top and pin tenons at the bottom. A face frame would be glued to the front of the carcase, and the back frame would be fitted into a rabbet in the carcase sides. I also shaped door, base and crown molding details to give the cabinet individuality.

Carcase construction—I began by building the basic carcase. After edge-gluing several narrow 4/4 boards to make the sides, top and bottom, I cut the dovetails at the top of the case by hand, using a chisel, mallet and dovetail saw. You could also use a router and dovetail template. Next, I laid out and chopped the mortises at the bottom of the sides to accept the multiple tenons on the carcase bottom. These mortises were cut with a straight bit in a router

Photo: Tom Hagood

The design of the author's cherry wardrobe cabinet, above, is based on a traditional Shaker piece that he modified, adding his own details to the doors, base and crown molding.

By changing the position of the two movable rails that guide the router, the author works his way across the bottom of the carcase side, chopping mortises for pin tenons that will join the sides to the bottom of his wardrobe cabinet.

guided by a homemade jig, as shown in the smaller photo above. The jig is a square template made up of two rails and two adjustable fences. A plunge router is set into the square, the bit is plunged and the router is then moved around inside the fenced area (router base bearing against the fences and rails) until the mortise is completed. The two adjustable fences, pinned into place with removable dowels, are repositioned for each of the seven mortises across the width of the two carcase sides. The routed mortises have rounded corners that must be squared up with a chisel.

Next, I cut the multiple tenons on the ends of the carcase bottom. After marking these tenons by transferring lines from the mortises, I bandsawed away most of the waste, then pared the tenons for a tight fit into their mortises. As an alternative, you can use a router to rough-cut the shoulders, then pare them with a chisel. Either of these

The author makes raised panels for the wardrobe doors on the router table. In the first step, shown above, he reduces the thickness of each panel's edge by running the panel vertically by a straight bit. A fingerboard clamped to a spacer provides the pressure needed to stabilize the panel as it's fed. This fingerboard also prevents the climb-cutting bit from self-feeding the panel.

Hagood uses a homemade beading plane to detail the inner edges of the door frame. The mahogany plane has two nonsymmetrical bead-profile blades, one for cutting in each direction. A piece of quarter-round molding on the underside of the plane guides it along the frame's inner edge for a straight cut.

operations can be time-consuming, but I don't know a faster way to make pin tenons or an alternative joint that has the same integrity.

As with most wardrobes, mine has a high shelf for storing clothing above the hanging garments. The ¾-in.-thick shelf joins the inside of the carcase by sliding into a simple ⅜-in. by ⅜-in. dado plowed into the cabinet sides. The dado is the same depth as the rabbet cut along the back edges to accept the frame-and-panel back. I cut the dado with a ⅜-in. straight bit in a router, using a straight board clamped across the cabinet side as a fence. Because the 4/4 shelf must span the width of the 42-in. cabinet, I supported the middle of the shelf with a lap joint on the 1½-in.-wide center stile. Dovetails at the top and bottom of the stile connect to the front edges of the carcase top and bottom, as shown in the draw-

ing on p. 84. The shelf is notched so the edge of the shelf is flush with the front of the stile.

Originally, I'd planned to let the base of my wardrobe rest on the floor, with a decorative molding at the bottom edge. However, I saw another base treatment I liked in the Ketchum book and adapted this base to fit my wardrobe. With this new base, the carcase is cut out to make four feet, with gentle convex curves coming up from the floor along the insides of the feet—a pleasant visual effect. Drawing in scale, I experimented with various curves until I came up with one I liked. I scaled up this curve on graph paper to make a full-size plywood template, which I used to mark out the cabinet sides. After roughing out the curve with a sabersaw, I clamped the same template to the cabinet side and routed the final shapes with a piloted straight bit bearing against the template.

Creating the same curved feet on the front of the wardrobe involved modifying the cabinet's otherwise straightforward face frame. I used a typical face frame, assembled with mortise-and-tenon joints, on the front of the cabinet and a frame-and-panel back. But the stiles weren't wide enough for the same curve I had cut on the cabinet sides, so I glued 1½-in.-wide ears to the inside edges of the stiles, providing stock for the curved feet. I cut the bottom rail shorter than the top rail and tenoned it to the ear pieces instead of the stiles. If I'd made the bottom rail extra wide to accommodate the cutout, I would have created a wood-movement problem by joining a 6-in.-wide rail cross-grain to the face frame's stiles.

Gluing up a cabinet of this size was quite a task in my small shop. The cabinet's size stretched every clamp in the shop to its capacity. The carcase dovetails were tight enough that they didn't need clamping, but the pin tenons needed to be pulled into their mortises with pipe clamps. A 2x4 I had carefully bandsawn into a bow shape (convex surface toward the cabinet) was used as a caul to distribute clamping pressure across the sides. After the carcase was dry, I glued on the already assembled face frame.

Though plywood is a suitable and more-often-selected choice for the back of a large cabinet, I decided to stick to the more traditional solid-wood frame-and-panel back. This frame consists of three stiles and four rails mortised and tenoned together, dividing the back into four panels. The panels themselves are flat and only ⅜ in. thick, the same thickness as the grooves in the frame. The entire glued-up back recesses into the rabbet cut in the back of the carcase earlier.

Building frame-and-panel doors—After measuring the face-frame opening, I made a pair of door frames that fit snugly into the opening. The frames are joined with haunched mortise-and-tenon joints, and each member has a ⁵⁄₁₆-in.-wide groove, cut with a dado blade on the tablesaw, to hold the panel. The bottom door rails are wider than the top rails, to overcome visual foreshortening, which makes bottom rails look narrower than they are. I let the stiles run long to prevent splitting during mortising, then trimmed them to length after the doors were assembled.

I raised my panels with a router, homemade router table and two different bits. The first operation was to reduce the thickness at the panel's edge with a ½-in. straight bit. The panel's edges were routed with the panel on edge and held tight against the fence by a fingerboard clamped directly above the bit, as shown in the top photo on this page. To produce the cleanest cut possible, especially while shaping the panel's endgrain, I climb-cut the panels, feeding them into the bit counter in the same direction it was spinning. If you try this, make sure to take several shallow passes on each edge, to prevent dangerous self-feeding, which can occur when climb-cutting. The pressure of the fingerboard also prevents self-feeding, and it shields your fingers from exposure to the whirling bit.

After the panel edges were thicknessed, I cut a cove to finish the panel raising. I used a ½-in. core-box bit in the router, shaping the panels on the router table. I laid the stock flat on the table and shaped the cove in a few passes, raising the bit each time until its tip just contacted the flat in the panel edge cut from the previous operation. I then sanded the panels and glued up the door frames with the panels in place.

The next step is to detail each door with a cock bead around the inner edge of the frame. I originally scratched the bead with an old scraper blade filed to the correct profile, but I was unhappy with the fuzzing and tearout. I chose instead to make my own beading plane, shown in the bottom photo on the facing page. The plane is designed to cut into the corners from two directions for work on an already assembled frame. (You can plane the bead in the frame edges prior to assembly, but you need to stop the beads on the stiles where they meet the rails.) One of the plane's blades is a standard cutter from a Stanley #55 Multiplane set. The other cutter, a mirror image of the first, is made by modifying a straight plane blade. Both blades are held in place with removable wedges, making it easy to lower one cutter and retract the other, depending on the direction of the cut. A strip of molding on the underside of the plane body acts as a fence to keep the cutter parallel to the frame's edge as it cuts the bead.

Traditionally, the corners of a beaded frame were carved so the beads look mitered into one another. This is because the beading plane or scratch stock can't shape the bead all the way into a corner. Instead, I glued an end-grain dowel precisely into each corner, to serve as a return for the bead detail and to give the cabinet an original touch, as shown in the photo above, right. I made a drilling guide by boring a hole through a scrap and gluing a tiny triangle to the bottom to reference against the frame's inside corner. Clamped in place, the guide established the precise location of the hole and kept the bit straight as I bored each ¼-in. corner hole with a hand drill. A tape flap stuck to the bit told me when the hole was deep enough. The dowels for the corners were made from cherry scraps, using a plug cutter in the drill press. Each dowel was glued in with epoxy, then trimmed and sanded flush with the surface of the door frame.

Crown molding—For this highly visible detail, I chose the fanciest piece of cherry I had. To shape the crown's cove profile on the tablesaw, an improvised fence was diagonally clamped across the saw table and a length of stock long enough for the entire crown was passed over the blade, which is raised a little at a time. By varying the angle of the fence and depth of cut, you can produce many different cove shapes. I experimented until I had a profile that mimicked the curve of the feet. After coving, I angled the molding's edges as detailed in the drawing on p. 84.

The bead detail where the crown molding meets the cabinet is the same as the bead on the doors, adding visual detail and making any irregularity in the seam between the cabinet and molding less obvious. To hold the molding at the correct angle for beading, I first cut some small plywood triangles and hot-glued them to the bench in a straight line. I then hot-glued the noncoved side of the crown molding to the triangles so the molding's bottom edge was facing up and level. The narrow edge gives the beading plane little support, so it is a bit tricky to get a straight bead. To stabilize the plane, try laying one hand on the molding alongside the plane as you walk down the length of the molding taking the cut. It'll take several passes to get the full bead profile, but in the end, this great-looking detail makes it all worthwhile. After scraping the cove smooth with a curved scraper blade and sanding its show

The beaded inner edges of the door frame and inlaid corners, as well as the cove-and-bead crown molding, provide the author's wardrobe with a distinguished degree of visual interest.

surfaces smooth, I cut the length of crown molding into three pieces and joined the mitered corners with splines and epoxy glue.

Crown molding has been traditionally nailed or glued on old cabinets, but this method can create problems. The molding, attached crossgrain on the cabinet sides, loosens over time because of expansion and contraction of the cabinet's sides. To compensate for this movement, I attached the assembled crown to the cabinet's side with a sliding dovetail joint. This allows the cabinet sides to move while holding the molding securely to the cabinet.

The crown is fastened to the cabinet sides with two 3-in.-long male dovetail strips—one screwed to each cabinet side. These strips slide in female dovetails cut into angled blocks glued to the back of the molding. After the male strips were in place, an assistant held the molding while I screwed the front molding on from the inside of the cabinet. Then, I applied hide glue to the female dovetail blocks and slid them onto the dovetail strips from the back. I held the components in alignment until the glue set. This procedure is not as difficult as it sounds, especially if you're good at cutting sliding dovetails. In addition to alleviating wood-movement problems, this method avoids difficult clamping procedures and ensures that the molding is perfectly aligned. The whole crown is removable: This makes finishing the cabinet sides easier and lightens the heavy wardrobe, in case it needs to be moved.

After final sanding and finishing (I used Watco oil to bring out the cherry's color, but you can use any finish you like), I attached the knobs, mortised in the locks on the doors and hung the doors on the cabinet. Keeping with the Shaker style, I turned two small, plain cherry knobs. Each has a dowel turned on its back that is glued and wedged into a hole drilled through the door stile. I used standard 2½-in.-long butt hinges to hang the doors, three per door, and mortised them into the door frame and face frame for a clean fit with very little gap around the doors. Finally, I mounted a removable clothes pole inside the cabinet just below the shelf.

My client is pleased with the wardrobe, and so am I. The adaptations I made to the design seem to mediate well between the room's ornate furnishings and the cabinet's simple Shaker origins. While the extreme austerity of original Shaker designs is not always completely satisfying to me, I enjoyed reinterpreting the Shaker wardrobe design. But, I'll always acknowledge the Shakers' basic premise: "Keep it simple." □

Tom Hagood is a woodworker in Birmingham, Ala.

Building a Display Cabinet
Production-shop speed with small-shop tools

by Jeffrey Greef

I work in a custom architectural millwork shop, and when I wanted to make a wall-hung display cabinet, I decided to scale down our production methods to suit a small piece of casework. This seemed logical, because our methods for producing large quantities of millwork at the Davenport Mill are accurate and economical. Further, the operations we use for making full-size doors and windows—cutting mortise-and-tenon joinery and cope-and-stick work—are essentially the same for making the parts for a cabinet frame. But cutting small parts on a shaper normally used for thicker stock seemed much too risky for the parts and my fingers. Also, I didn't have the right shaper cutters to allow the cabinet frames to accept glass panels, nor were standard cabinet-door router-bit sets compatible with my design. Not wanting to compromise the joinery or the look of my cabinet, I developed some router techniques for cope-and-stick work and for other shaping on the

The author's handsome walnut display case is built with a combination of production joinery techniques adapted for a router and stock bits. Although the cabinet is designed to hold adjustable glass shelves, here it is shown without them, displaying two Sundanese rod puppets made in West Java by Aming.

cabinet. I used stock bits and employed plywood jigs and templates to set up repetitive operations that allow me to build several cabinets in a single production run, if I desire.

My display cabinet, shown below, left, consists of a carcase constructed from front and back frames with shaped stiles and curved top rails, joined together with mortises and tenons. These frames are plate-joined to the side frames. The side frames, as well as the cabinet's hinged door, are cope-and-stick cut and rabbeted to hold glass. The cabinet's arched top is steam-bent and laminated, and it fits into grooves dadoed in the top rails of the frame. The back is a panel covered with fabric. Pins in shelf holes support adjustable glass shelves inside the case.

Although most of the work for this piece requires only basic cabinetmaking skills, an understanding of sash-making is necessary. In a cope-and-stick sash frame, the inside edges of both the stiles and rails are molded; this is the "sticking." For the sticking to mate in the corners, the rail ends are shaped or "coped" to fit the sticking.

Building the case—The first job is to size and cut the parts from ¾-in.-stock for the front, back and side frames and the door. It's crucial that all your stock is accurately planed to exactly the same thickness; otherwise, you'll have problems later with the alignment and fit of both the joinery and the molding profiles of the cope and stick. Following the dimensions in figure 1 (facing page), rip all the straight frame members to width, adding ¼ in. extra to those that will receive sticking. The stiles for the front and back cabinet frames are ripped straight, and the curved pattern on the outside edges is cut later. Note that the stiles for the back frame are ¼ in. wider than the front ones, to provide extra width for the sticking. Next, cut all frame members to exact length, leaving an extra 1¾ in. on the rails for ⅞-in.-long tenons on the ends.

To avoid the weakness of cross-grain, each of the cabinet's three curved top rails (two for the cabinet frames, one for the door) are glued up from three separate pieces joined together, as shown in figure 2. This rail assembly may not look as good as one cut from a single, wide board, but it will be stronger and less subject to distortion from expansion/contraction. To keep the pieces from shifting out of alignment due to clamping pressure during glue-up, tack on a small scrap strip at the joint before clamping. Don't drive the nails in too far; otherwise, the holes will show in the finished rail. After tightening the clamps, check for flatness by laying a ruler on the stock perpendicular across each joint.

I template-rout the rails to ensure that the outside curve of the door will match the inside curve of the front rail. Two templates need to be made: one for the carcase rails and one for the door rail. I make the templates from ¼-in. Baltic birch, each the same

Drawings: Joel Katzowitz

Fig. 1: Display cabinet

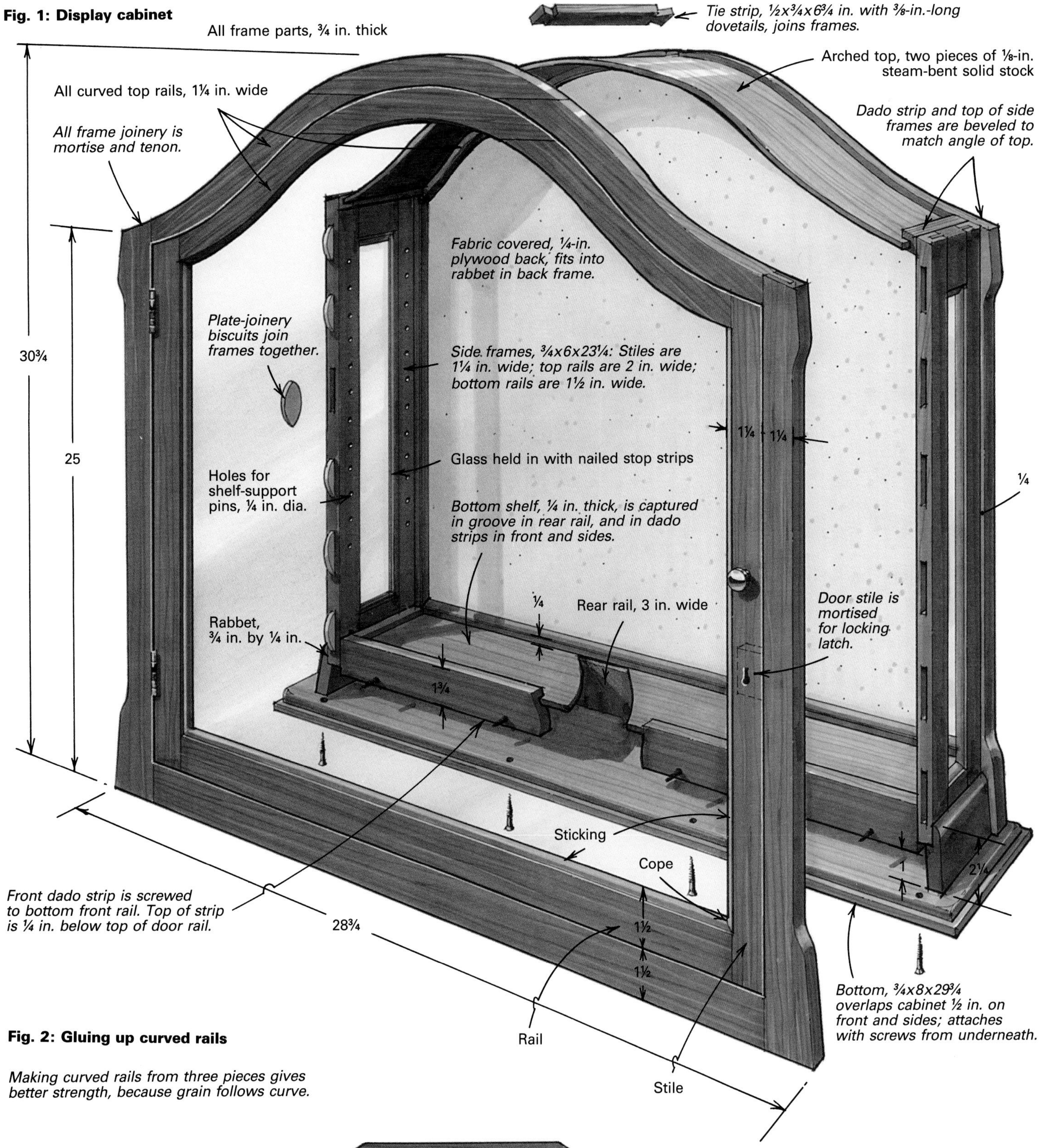
All frame parts, ¾ in. thick
Tie strip, ½x¾x6¾ in. with ⅜-in.-long dovetails, joins frames.
Arched top, two pieces of ⅛-in. steam-bent solid stock
All curved top rails, 1¼ in. wide
All frame joinery is mortise and tenon.
Dado strip and top of side frames are beveled to match angle of top.
Fabric covered, ¼-in. plywood back, fits into rabbet in back frame.
Plate-joinery biscuits join frames together.
30¾
Side frames, ¾x6x23¼: Stiles are 1¼ in. wide; top rails are 2 in. wide; bottom rails are 1½ in. wide.
1¼
1¼
25
Glass held in with nailed stop strips
Holes for shelf-support pins, ¼ in. dia.
¼
Bottom shelf, ¼ in. thick, is captured in groove in rear rail, and in dado strips in front and sides.
¼
Rear rail, 3 in. wide
Door stile is mortised for locking latch.
Rabbet, ¾ in. by ¼ in.
1¾
Sticking
Cope
1
2¼
Front dado strip is screwed to bottom front rail. Top of strip is ¼ in. below top of door rail.
28¾
1½
1½
Bottom, ¾x8x29¾ overlaps cabinet ½ in. on front and sides; attaches with screws from underneath.
Rail
Stile

Fig. 2: Gluing up curved rails

Making curved rails from three pieces gives better strength, because grain follows curve.

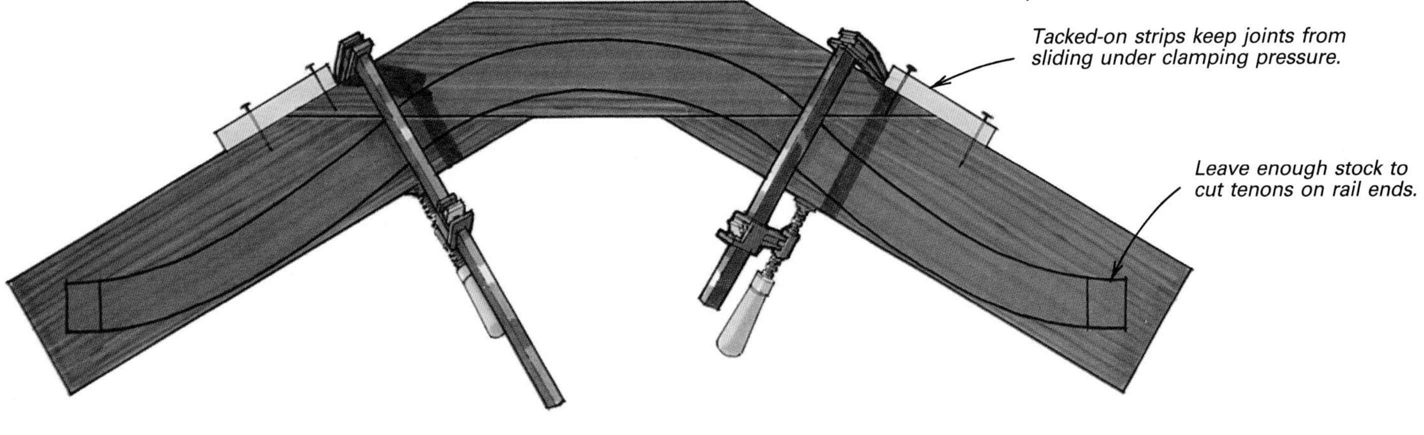
Tacked-on strips keep joints from sliding under clamping pressure.
Leave enough stock to cut tenons on rail ends.

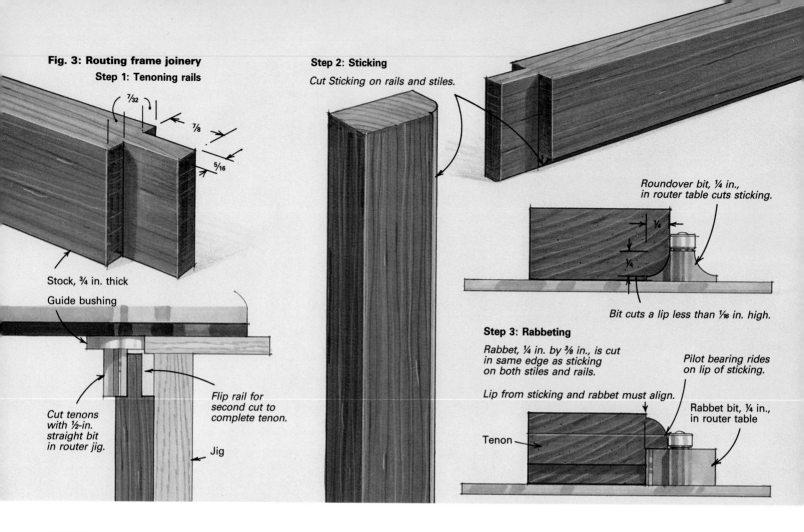

Fig. 3: Routing frame joinery

Step 1: Tenoning rails

7/32

7/8

5/16

Stock, ¾ in. thick

Guide bushing

Cut tenons with ½-in. straight bit in router jig.

Flip rail for second cut to complete tenon.

Jig

Step 2: Sticking

Cut Sticking on rails and stiles.

Roundover bit, ¼ in., in router table cuts sticking.

¼

¼

Bit cuts a lip less than 1/16 in. high.

Step 3: Rabbeting

Rabbet, ¼ in. by ⅜ in., is cut in same edge as sticking on both stiles and rails.

Lip from sticking and rabbet must align.

Pilot bearing rides on lip of sticking.

Tenon

Rabbet bit, ¼ in., in router table

Above: Using a flush trimmer in the router table, the author does the final shaping on a curved rail for the cabinet frame. The template, temporarily screwed to the back of the rail, guides the cut and has two dowel handles for convenience and safety. Below: The tenoning jig allows router-made tenons to be cut in two passes. The jig has two fences and clamping stations, to accommodate flipping the curved rails for routing the second half of each tenon.

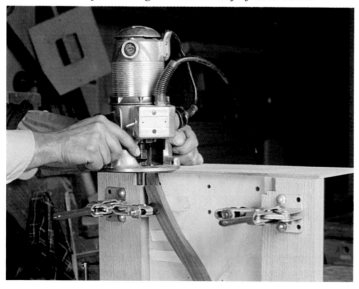

width as the final rail, with the curve carried past where the tenons will be cut on the ends. Mark a centerline on each template. To shape the 1¼-in. curved top rails, first bandsaw out the rough curves to lines scribed from the template, leaving about 1/16 in. on the edges for trimming and enough stock on the ends for the tenons. I screw two ¾-in.-thick, 6-in.-long dowels to the templates, to act as handles. Countersink the screw heads and temporarily screw the template to what will be the back side of the rail. Trim each piece to final shape by running the template against the pilot bearing of a flush trimmer in the router table, as shown in the top photo at left. The handles let you move the workpiece past the bit smoothly, and they keep your hands well away from the cutter. To avoid tearout as you trim parts of the curve against the grain, climb-cut these sections by feeding the work into the cutter in the direction of the cut, instead of against it as usual. Take the cut slowly, as a climb-cutting router can kick back the workpiece unexpectedly if it's fed too quickly into the cutter.

Before removing each rail from the jig, transfer the centerline mark from the template, to help you align the rail for trimming the ends. I do this by clamping each curved rail to a piece of plywood with three blocks glued to it. The ends are then cut on the radial saw, with the front edge of the plywood against the fence. By setting the cut according to the centerline on the jig, the two halves of the curved rail will be symmetrical, essential for a good fit between the door and the cabinet frame.

Frame joinery and shaping—Because I make most of the joints and shaped edges of the frame members with a carbide router bit guided by a pilot bearing, the order of operations is important, both to avoid tearout and to always give the pilot a surface to ride on. The order of operations, as shown in figure 3, above, is tenoning, sticking, rabbeting, mortising, coping and tenon trimming. You tenon before mortising, instead of the other way around, so that the pilot bearing

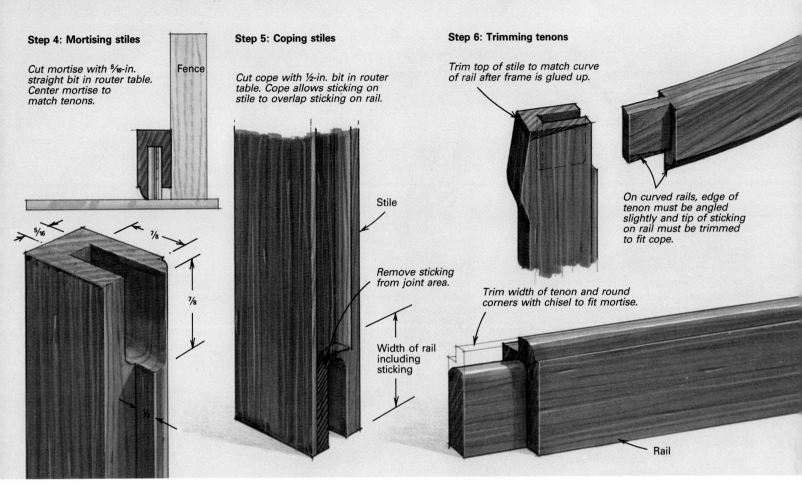

Step 4: Mortising stiles

Cut mortise with 5/16-in. straight bit in router table. Center mortise to match tenons.

Fence

5/16

7/8

7/8

1/4

Step 5: Coping stiles

Cut cope with 1/2-in. bit in router table. Cope allows sticking on stile to overlap sticking on rail.

Stile

Remove sticking from joint area.

Width of rail including sticking

Step 6: Trimming tenons

Trim top of stile to match curve of rail after frame is glued up.

On curved rails, edge of tenon must be angled slightly and tip of sticking on rail must be trimmed to fit cope.

Trim width of tenon and round corners with chisel to fit mortise.

Rail

of the rabbeting bit doesn't plunge into the mortise at the ends.

In step 1, the 7/8-in.-long tenons on the ends of both the straight and curved rails are cut using a jig that holds the pieces vertically, while a 1/2-in. straight bit in the router cuts both tenon shoulder and cheek in one pass. A template guide bushing on the router's base bears against the jig's fence and guides the cut. The rail is clamped to the jig, as shown in the lower photo on the facing page. Each tenon is cut on one side first, then flipped and cut on the other side. This automatically centers the tenons. The curved rails are aligned in the jig by resting both ends against the fence. After cutting half of the tenon on each end, the rail is flipped front to back and clamped on the jig's other side, where the tenon is completed.

Next, the sticking and rabbet are cut on the outside faces of the side and door frames and on the inside face of the back frame members, as shown in steps 2 and 3. Both operations are done on the router table, with a piloted 1/4-in. roundover bit for the stick and a 1/4-in. piloted rabbeting bit for the rabbet to hold the glass and back. Adjust the roundover bit's height for the sticking cut so the bit forms a lip that's less than 1/16 in. high. It's very important that the radius-cutting portion of the roundover bit be exactly 1/4 in. high (viewing the bit's profile). This is so the bit will not remove stock where the pilot of the rabbet cutter must bear. Also, when setting up the 1/4-in. by 1/4-in. rabbet cut, make sure the lip on the sticking and the rabbet align with each other (see step 3). These considerations are important if the tenon shoulders on the rails are to mate squarely with the stiles when the frame is assembled later.

It's best to cut the sticking and the rabbet in several passes, rather than in a single heavy cut. During the last light pass, make certain the work is flat on the table as it passes by the bit, as any variance will change the height of the cut. Take some care when doing the rabbeting, as the pilot bearing rides on the relatively delicate edge of the sticking cut in the previous step.

The mortises are cut in the stiles in step 4, with a straight bit,

A 1/2-in. straight bit in the router table cuts the cope in the ends of the stiles and removes the sticking where the rail and stile will mate. Here the stop block is set for cutting one end of each stile; the other ends are cut with the block left of the bit.

also on the router table. The mortise is open on the end of the stile so the stile can be slid along the fence and fed into the bit. I use a 5/16-in. bit to match the tenon's thickness and raise it 1 1/8 in. above the router table, the depth of the mortise plus the width of the sticking. The bit chatters nastily if you try to chop the mortise in one pass, so I cut it in stages, taking only 3/16 in. of depth in a single pass until I reach the full depth of cut.

The next step is coping the ends of the sticking on the stiles so that the quarter-round sticking will mate at the corners of the frames. I use a 1/2-in.-dia. straight bit, because its radius matches the 1/4-in. radius of the sticking. With the bit elevated 1/4 in. (the width of the sticking) in the router table, the fence and end stop are set so that the bit will remove the sticking and create the cope precisely where the rail will mate with the stile (see step 5 and the photo above). With the rabbeted side against the fence, cope one end of each stile, then move the stop to the other side of the bit to do the other ends. There may be some tearout problems when

A bending form, screwed together from scraps of ½-in. plywood, lends shape to the two ⅛-in.-thick walnut pieces that will form the cabinet's arched top. The radii of the jig are slightly tighter than the final shape of the top, to allow for springback when the steam-bent pieces cool.

making the right-hand cuts, because the bit cuts against the direction of the grain. If tearout occurs, gently lower the stile into the cutter from above, keeping the stile firmly against the fence.

Before final fitting the frame joints, the rail tenons must be trimmed in width and rounded to match the mortises. On the straight rails, I cut the excess tenon off with a scroll saw, then use a chisel to pare it flush with the tenon shoulder. I also use the chisel to round the tenons' corners so they'll approximately match the rounded mortises (precision isn't crucial here, as that part of the joint is hidden). On the curved top rails, one corner of tenon must be trimmed at an angle to fit the mortise and a small corner of the sticking must be chiseled down where it meets the cope. This final bit of trimming, again, isn't crucial, because the cope will cover it.

Arched top—The cabinet's ¼-in.-thick arched top consists of two separate ⅛-in.-thick steam-bent laminations. Bending it from two thinner slices instead of from one thick piece makes it easier to control springback after bending. The steamed pieces are clamped to the bending form, as shown in the photo above, right out of the steambox, and then left to cool. I don't glue them together, as they're easier to fit into the dado as more-flexible, separate layers.

The top rides in a groove dadoed into the curved top rails with a ¼-in. straight bit. A plywood template guides the router-base guide bushing to keep the bit centered and a uniform distance from the edge all the way along the curve. Cut the dado with the rail and template assembly clamped to the bench; make sure to align the rail's centerline to the template and dado only the inside surface. The ends of the top fit into two ½x¾x6-in. dado strips, made slightly diamond shape to match the angle of the top. Plow ¼-in.-deep, ¼-in.-wide dadoes in the strips and glue them to the side frames where the ends of the top will slide in.

I add a small dovetailed tie strip to keep the curved rails that support the floating top together in the center. I make the female dovetails on the rails with a ⅜-in. dovetail bit in a router guided by a scrap-strip fence I clamp to the rail. Set the fence to guide the router's base perpendicular to the center of the rail. The male dovetails on the ends of the tie strip are cut with the dovetail bit in the router table: Hold the piece vertically, with its edge against the fence, and run it past the bit for half the tail. Then, flip the piece and run the other edge against the fence to complete the tail. Bit height determines the length of the dovetail, and bit-to-fence distance will determine the final width of the tail.

A few more machining operations need to be done before the cabinet is assembled: Plate joints must be cut to attach the frames together to form the carcase. Lay the stiles flat on the workbench, and with a square, draw lines across to locate the biscuits in the same place on each stile. Transfer these marks on the edges of the side-frame stiles, and cut all the slots for #20 biscuits. For the cabinet's adjustable glass shelves, ¼-in. holes must be drilled in the frame stiles for pin-style shelf supports. Lay out these holes the same on all stiles so the shelves will be level. To hold the cabinet's bottom shelf at the rear, cut a dado in the 3-in.-wide bottom rail on the back frame. On the sides and front, the shelf is held in dadoed strips, like the ends of the arched top. Because the back bottom rail is wider than the front bottom rail, the strips bring the height of the bottom shelf up to where it's just ¼ in. below the door's bottom rail. This is to keep whatever is displayed in the cabinet in clear sight with the door closed. Two 2¼-in.-wide base moldings on the sides of the cabinet mate with the bottoms of the side frames, raising them to the same level as the bottom of the door frame. As shown in figure 1 on p. 89, the moldings angle slightly, to match the angle on the lower front and back frames. Make the molding's rabbet match this angle and round over the top edge. Mortise the door for inlaying the locking latch, unless you plan to use a bullet catch or other type of latch. Cut out a ¾-in.-thick piece for the cabinet bottom and rout its edges with a ¼-in. roundover bit, to match the sticking. Finally, sand all the parts to at least 280 grit.

Assembly and finishing—The first stage of assembly is to glue up the individual frames. To prevent distortion of the curved rails, run an extra clamp from the middle of the arch to the opposite rail and don't apply any more clamping pressure than necessary. Check for square and frame flatness, and allow the frames to sit overnight. After the clamps are off, flush-trim the stiles to conform with the curve of the top rails, and check the fit of the door into its frame. If it doesn't go into the opening, or if the fit is uneven, adjust with a handplane or spokeshave.

Before gluing the frames together to form the carcase, bandsaw the outside edges of the front and back stiles, and clean up the edges by flush-trimming them with the router, following a template temporarily screwed to the inside surface of the frame. Glue and nail the dado strips and base moldings on the side frames, and screw the front dado strip to the back of the front frame. As you glue the carcase up, slide the bottom shelf into its groove, and make sure the stiles align at the bottom evenly.

After cleaning up the glue drips and doing any touch-up sanding, screw on the bottom of the cabinet and plug the holes; now you're ready to apply the finish. For the back of the cabinet, I nail on a piece of ¼-in. plywood covered with fabric. Take care to drive the nails at an angle, to avoid nailing through the sticking. If you prefer a mirrored back, hold it in place with thin stop strips screwed into the back of the frame. To hold in the glass on the door and side frames, I use small stop strips that are held in with brads. I made the curved stop for the door by bandsawing a strip from an extra rail I template-routed earlier. To mount the cabinet to the wall, I screw two 3-in. "L" brackets (vertical leg of the L pointing up) to studs in the wall, to support the cabinet at the bottom. The top is secured by a hook bent from a piece of ¾-in. flat iron, attached to the wall with drywall butterflies. The hook will hold a flat-iron strip screwed to the top rail on the back of the cabinet. To attach, slide the cabinet down so the top strip engages the hook, and screw the brackets in the bottom. All that's left is to fill the cabinet with whatever treasures are to be displayed. □

Jeff Greef is a woodworker at the Davenport Mill in Davenport, Calif.

Newport-Style Tall Clock
Tackling the tricky details

by Robert Effinger

When I moved to Maine in 1970, I left behind a career as a tool-and-die maker. Working with wood instead of metal, I managed to eke out a living selling my turned bowls and wooden novelties to tourists who drove through town in the summer. One day a local gentleman stopped in to ask me if I could make a tall clock. I'd never attempted anything that ambitious before but I took the job. Since then, I've turned out quite a few. Along the way I've developed some methods that make short work of the details; I'll explain several of these in this article.

The clock shown is based on an 18th-century mahogany tall clock attributed to Newport, R.I., cabinetmaker John Goddard (1745-85). I scaled up the plan from a measured drawing in Wallace Nutting's book, *Furniture Treasury: Vol. III* (1933, MacMillan Publishing Co.).

I'm not a period purist so my clock isn't built exactly like the Goddard original. I'll improve on the old construction methods if I can. For example, unlike many old clocks, mine are built to allow for seasonal wood movement in places where the old clocks might have nails, glue blocks and, more often than not, cracks. The most radical change I've made is in the supports for the seat board—the horizontal board that supports the clockworks. On old clocks, the waist sides extended up into the hood and the seat board was nailed across them. My adjustable seatboard assembly slides up or down until the movement's at the correct height, then screws tight against the waist sides.

The ¼-in. plywood bottom of my clock is another break from tradition. Old clocks had a thick bottom that was often dovetailed to the base sides. This construction works fine until a weight cable breaks and the cast-iron weight wrecks the bottom, feet and sides of the clock. A falling weight will smash through my thin plywood bottom, without damaging the rest of the clock.

Buy the movement and make the dial before you start cutting anything. The depth of the movement determines the depth of the case and the dial must be made to fit the hood or vice versa. It's easier to make your own dial than it is to redesign the Goddard hood around a store-bought dial. Some of the fancy old engraved dials were made from brass, but I cut mine from 16-gauge sheet steel and sent it out to be hand painted. The sources of supply on p. 96 lists a few of the many companies that sell movements. The movement I used in this particular clock is a cable-wound, nine nested-bell movement (No. 213) from the Concord Clock Co., 96 Main St., Plaistow, N.H. 03865.

Think of the clock case as three separate sections: the base,

Built with the aid of 20th-century technology, Effinger's stately mahogany tall clock captures the graceful proportions and crisp carving of the 18th-century Rhode Island original. The dial face was hand painted by Judith W. Akey.

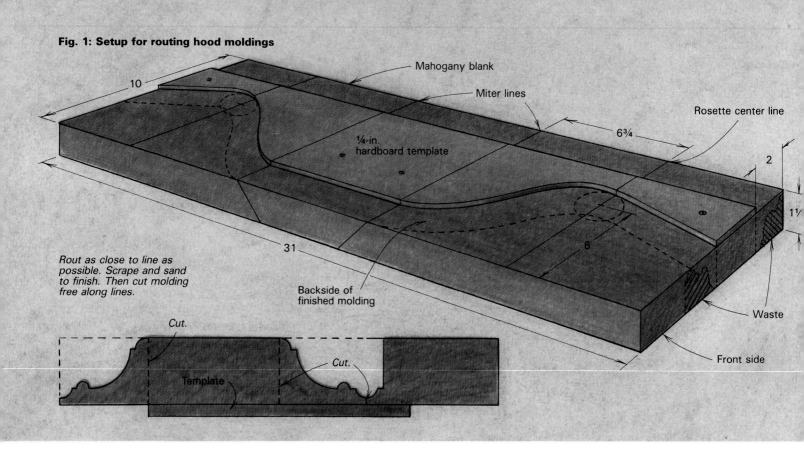

Fig. 1: Setup for routing hood moldings

Mahogany blank

Miter lines

Rosette center line

10

¼-in. hardboard template

6¾

Rosette center line

2

31

6

1½

Rout as close to line as possible. Scrape and sand to finish. Then cut molding free along lines.

Backside of finished molding

Waste

Cut.

Cut.

Template

Front side

waist and hood. Figure 3 (p. 97) and figure 4 (on pp. 98-99) shown how these sections are built and how they fit together. The waist sides screw to the base while the hood just rests on the waist. The hood slides off the front to allow access to the works. The ¾-in. pine back ties all three parts together, as shown in figure 4. In general, the waist must be about ¾ in. wider inside than the swing of the pendulum. Most old clock waists measure 13⅞ in. across the outside and 7 in. to 8 in. from front to back. I increased the depth of my clock case because modern musical movements are larger than the old ones.

I made the special one-piece hinges for the hood door from ⅛-in.-thick sheet brass. These hinges screw to the top and bottom of the door and pivot on ⅜-in. #2 woodscrews in the scroll board and hood molding. The waist door also requires special hinges with an offset to match the ¼-in.-thick lip on the hinge stile as shown in the detail, figure 4. Ball and Ball is the only company I've found that makes these hinges.

The curved goose-neck, or swan-neck moldings at the top of the hood are often the most intimidating part of a tall clock case. In the old days they were shaped by carving and scraping, but I prefer to make them with a pin router. My method of pattern routing cuts both of the curved moldings and both of the return moldings that run along either side of the hood at the same time, from the same piece of mahogany.

To make the moldings, I've converted my drill press into a pin router. My setup guarantees that the moldings will match up perfectly at the corner miters.

Start with a mahogany blank 1½ in. thick, 10 in. wide and 31 in. long. Make a template by drawing the molding curves on a 6-in.-wide piece of ¼-in. hardboard, as shown in figure 1 and bandsawing to shape. On this template, mark off the miter lines and the center lines for the rosettes.

Place the template on the bottom of the mahogany blank and transfer the miter lines and rosette center lines to the blank.

With a square, extend these lines across the width of the blank, extend the line of the curve over the end of the blank. Fasten the template to the mahogany with small screws making sure that the template marks line up with the lines drawn on the blank. Draw the molding profile on the ends of the blank as shown in the drawing. You'll set your router bit against this profile.

One-quarter-in.-thick wooden discs in increments of 1/16-in. in diameter fit over a pin in the auxiliary drill-press table directly underneath the bit. With the template side of the blank down on the table, I select a disc that positions the bit where I want it against the profile on the blank end, adjust the bit to the right height, then guide the template against the disc to make the cut, as shown in the photo on p. 95. One pass hogs the straight return moldings, and other pass at the same setting cuts the curves. Next I switch to a smaller disc to move the stock closer to the bit or a larger disc to move the stock away. The idea is to rout as close as possible to the molding profile you've drawn on the end of the blank. I do as much hogging as I can with a ⅝-in. straight bit then I switch to smaller straight bits followed by whatever curved bit gets closest to the line. After routing, I scrape and sand out any imperfections in the molding.

After routing, trace around the template on the back side of the blank. This line will become the cutting line for the top edge of the molding. Remove the template, set the tablesaw blade to 45° and cut the blank along the miter lines.

To mark for the rosette, score about ⅛ in. deep with a 2½-in.-diameter hole saw on the back of the blank. This gives you a definite line to follow later on the bandsaw. Rip the return molding off the blank along the straight template line. Now, with the back side up, bandsaw along the curved template line that marks the top edge of each goose-neck molding, including the radius marked by the hole saw. Flip the molding over. The cutting line for the bottom edge of the molding lies at the lowest point of the radius, as shown in figure 1. If you run a pencil along the bottom of this groove, it's easier to follow with the bandsaw.

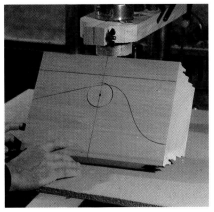

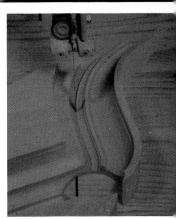

With his drill press converted to a pin router, Effinger routs out the pediment moldings. The template rides against a wooden disc over a pin under the work. Bit height is adjusted against the molding profile drawn on the end of the blank (above). After a pass along the straight molding, the goose-neck molding gets a pass at the same setting (top right). After sawing the miter, the rosette location is scored with a hole saw (right), then the goose-neck is bandsawn from the blank. After sawing the top edge and the rosette, the blank is flipped over and the lower molding edge is bandsawn free (far right).

The moldings are now ready to glue to the scroll board.

The smaller scroll-board arch moldings can be made using the same technique, but I find it easier to mount a router on a cobbled-up pivot to cut the semi-circular part and guide the hand-held router against a straight edge to cut the straight sections. You could also turn the semicircular molding on the lathe.

The quarter columns on the waist of old clocks were just that, ¼ of a circle. To my eye, these look sort of flat. I thought that the effect would be more dramatic if the columns were just slightly more than ¼ of a circle. Here's the method I developed to turn a "quarter" column that's really a 120° section of a circle.

Make a fixture from two pieces of ¾-in. scrap stock as long as the column. Rip one piece 2 in. wide and one 1¼ in. wide and butt glue them to make an L-shaped fixture, as shown in figure 2. Cut a 1¼-in.-square piece of mahogany for the column. Screw this square blank into the L-shaped piece as shown. Make sure that your screws are recessed enough that you don't turn into them later. Lay out the center on each end, remove the corners on the tablesaw, if you prefer, and turn the column and the jig to shape. A new L-shaped jig must be made for each quarter column.

If your lathe has an indexing head, you can rig up a router box and cut the flutes right on the lathe with a small veining bit in a router, but I have a different method. I have an old indexing jig that holds the column between centers and allows me to slide it across the drill-press table against a cutter chucked up in the drill press. My cutter is a ⁵⁄₃₂-in. Woodruff key seat cutter that I've ground to a radius as shown (available unground from Manhattan Supply Co., In., 151 Sunnyside Blvd., Plainview, N.Y. 11803). A bronze sleeve over the shaft acts as a bush and limits the depth of cut.

There are lots of ways to make ogee bracket feet but I think that my method is the easiest. I cut and glue up the joints while the stock is still square. By clamping the glued-up foot to a small

Fig. 2: Turning "quarter" columns

1¼-in.-sq. mahogany

¾ x 2 x column length scrap

¾ x 1¼

120°

Butt join scrap pieces and screw mahogany to scrap. Turn to shape.

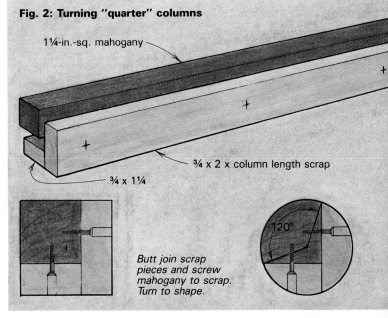

Author cuts column flutes with a Woodruff key seat cutter ground to a radius and chucked up in the drill press. Indexing jig rests on drill-press table and slides by cutter. Sleeve on cutter limits depth of cut.

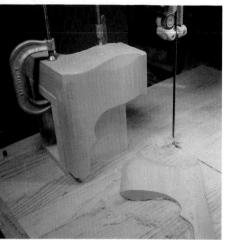

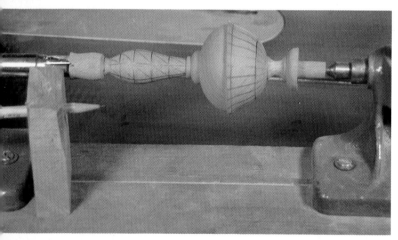

Ogee bracket feet are glued up while square then cut to shape on the bandsaw. Supporting the foot over a wooden box allows the ogee profile to be cut on the bandsaw (left). Finial is lathe turned, then flutes are marked out in indexing jig and carved by hand. To lay out the flame, divide flame into six longitudinal sections and five latitudinal sections to form a grid (below). Connect points on the diagonal to form spiral lines. Pencil holder shown marks out axis lines.

wooden box for support, as shown in the photo at left, I cut the ogee curve on the bandsaw.

The front feet are joined with a splined miter. I cut the spline slot on the tablesaw with the blade at 45°. The back feet are joined with half-blind dovetails. The rear section of the back feet is made from thinner stock and left flat to allow the clock to sit closer to a wall.

The flame finials that crown the hood are turned from 3-in.-square blocks about 8½ in. long. Turn the finial in the middle of the stock leaving about 1 in. of waste on each end, as shown in the photo. For now, just turn the flame section to shape—carving comes later. On the bottom of the urn, mark off 24 divisions for reeding and stop fluting. If your lathe has an indexing head, you can mark and carve the finial between centers. I carve the reeds with a V-tool working from larger diameter to smaller diameter. Tipping the tool to the left and right, I take off the sharp edges to round over the reed. About ⅛ in. down from the top of the reeding I mark a line around the circumference and another line about ¾ in. from the first. This designates the lengths of the shallow flutes within the reeds. I carve these with a small gouge.

On old clocks, the flames on the outside finials spiral in opposite directions. To lay out the flame spiral, I draw lines parallel to the finial axis that divide the circumference of the cylinder into six equal sections. Then I draw lines around the circumference, spaced ½ in. apart, to form a grid. I connect the intersections with diagonal lines to form the spirals. Carve between the spiral lines with a small gouge. After the flame has been carved, cut the waste off and finish to a point. I sand the completed finial with a 220-grit flap sander chucked up in the drill press.

One other detail worth specific mention is the shell carving on the waist door. Some of the old ones were glued onto the door panel after carving. I like to make the door panel and shell from one board as thick as the combined thickness of the shell and panel. I set the thickness planer to remove ⅛ in. and I stop the planer before the shell area goes through. The finished shell is about ⅛ in. higher than the panel and overhangs each edge by ⅛ in. I set the jointer for a ⅛-in. cut and joint the panel edge stopping when I get to the shell area. □

Robert Effinger makes period furniture in Fryeburg, Me.

Sources of supply

These firms sell tall-clock movements, clock supplies and hardware, except as noted.
Selva-Borel, 347 13th St., P.O. Box 796, Oakland, Calif. 94604.
Mason & Sullivan Co., 586 Higgins Crowel Rd., West Yarmouth, Mass. 02673.
Turncraft Clock Imports Co., 7912 Olson Highway 55, Golden Valley, Minn. 55427.
Klockit, P.O. Box 629, Highway H, North, Lake Geneva, Wisc. 53147.
Craft Products Co., 2200 Dean St., St. Charles, Ill. 60174.
Ball and Ball, 463 West Lincoln Hwy., Exton, Pa. 19341 (authentic reproductions of hood-door hinges, offset waist-door hinges and clock hardware).
Judith W. Akey, 173 Harbourton Rd., Pennington, N.J. 08534 (hand paints clock dials).
The Dial House, Rt. 7, Box 532, Dallas, Ga. 30132 (custom dials and hand painting).

Fig. 3: Hood construction

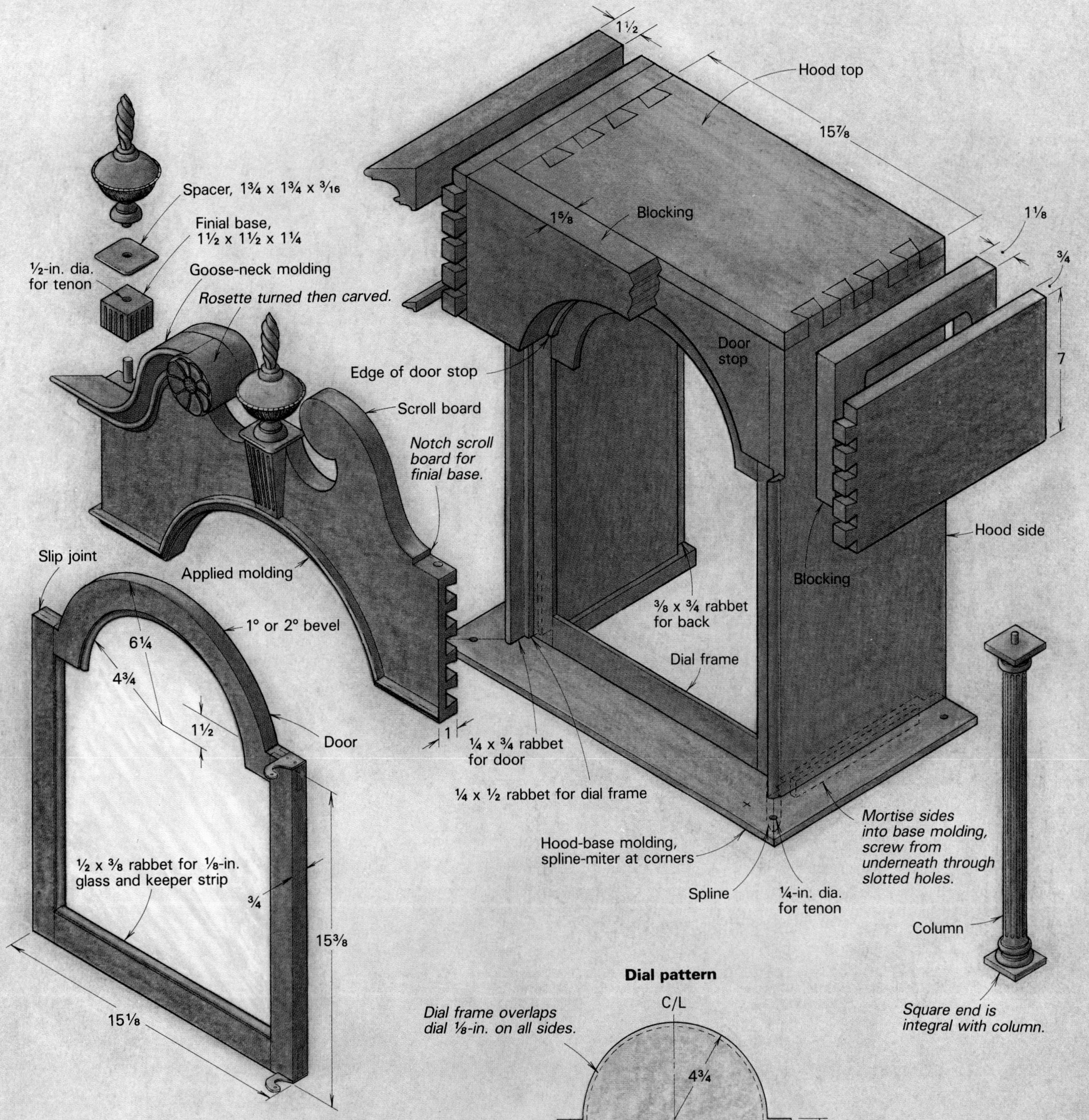

1½
Hood top
15⅞
Spacer, 1¾ x 1¾ x 3/16
Finial base, 1½ x 1½ x 1¼
½-in. dia. for tenon
Goose-neck molding
Rosette turned then carved.
1⅝
Blocking
1⅛
¾
7
Door stop
Edge of door stop
Scroll board
Notch scroll board for finial base.
Hood side
Slip joint
Applied molding
Blocking
⅜ x ¾ rabbet for back
1° or 2° bevel
6¼
4¾
Dial frame
1½
Door
1
¼ x ¾ rabbet for door
¼ x ½ rabbet for dial frame
Hood-base molding, spline-miter at corners
Mortise sides into base molding, screw from underneath through slotted holes.
½ x ⅜ rabbet for ⅛-in. glass and keeper strip
¾
Spline
¼-in. dia. for tenon
15⅜
Column
15⅛
Square end is integral with column.

Dial pattern

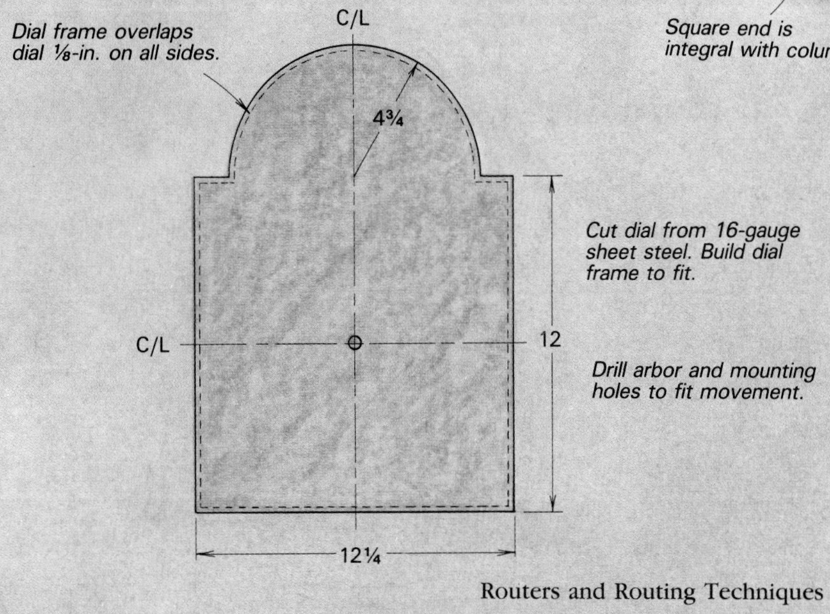

Dial frame overlaps dial ⅛-in. on all sides.
C/L
4¾
C/L
12
12¼
Cut dial from 16-gauge sheet steel. Build dial frame to fit.
Drill arbor and mounting holes to fit movement.

Hood-door hinge

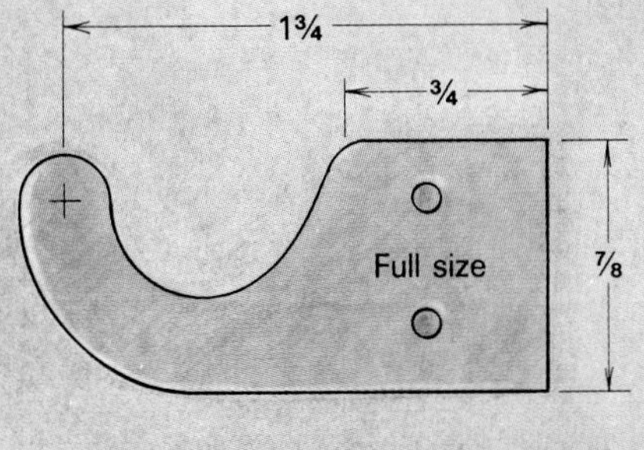

1¾
¾
Full size
⅞

Fig. 4: Newport-style tall clock

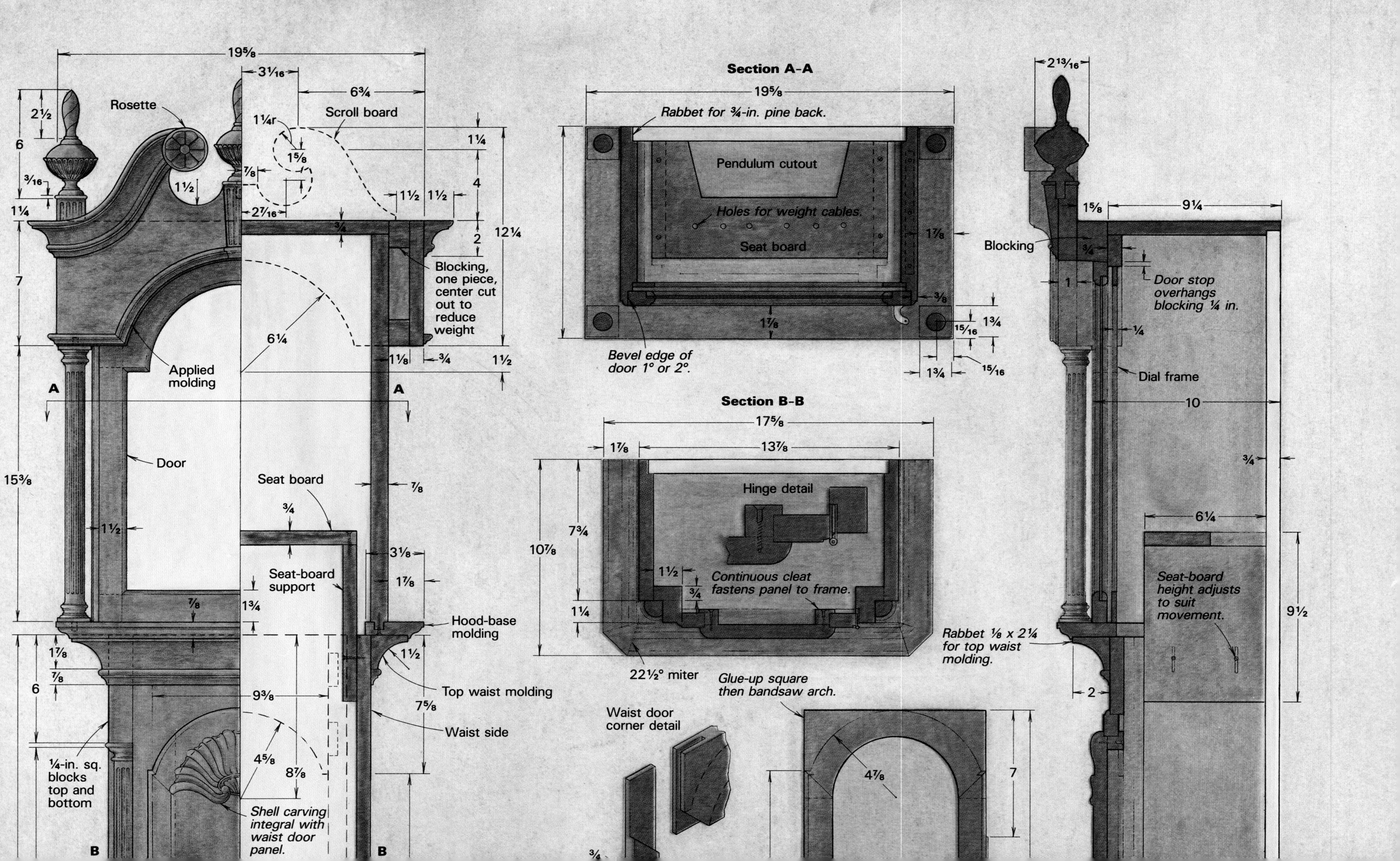

Section A-A

Rabbet for ¾-in. pine back.

Pendulum cutout

Holes for weight cables.

Seat board

Bevel edge of door 1° or 2°.

19⅝

1⅞

1¾

15/16

15/16

1¾

⅜

1⅞

Section B-B

Hinge detail

Continuous cleat fastens panel to frame.

22½° miter

17⅝

13⅞

1⅞

1½

¾

7¾

1¼

10⅞

Waist door corner detail

Glue-up square then bandsaw arch.

7

4⅞

Rabbet ⅛ x 2¼ for top waist molding.

⅜

Door stop overhangs blocking ¼ in.

Dial frame

Seat-board height adjusts to suit movement.

9¼

9½

¾

10

6¼

9¼

2¹³⁄₁₆

1⅝

¾

¼

1

Blocking

2

Rosette

Scroll board

Blocking, one piece, center cut out to reduce weight

Applied molding

Door

Seat board

Seat-board support

Shell carving integral with waist door panel.

Hood-base molding

Top waist molding

Waist side

¼-in. sq. blocks top and bottom

19⅝

3¹⁄₁₆

6¾

1¼

1⅝

⅞

2⁷⁄₁₆

1¼

1½

1½

12¼

4

2

1½

¾

1⅛

¾

6¼

1½

¾

7⅞

3⅛

1⅞

1½

7⅝

9⅜

1¾

⅞

4⅝

8⅞

1½

6

⅞

1⅞

⅞

7

15⅜

A

A

B

B

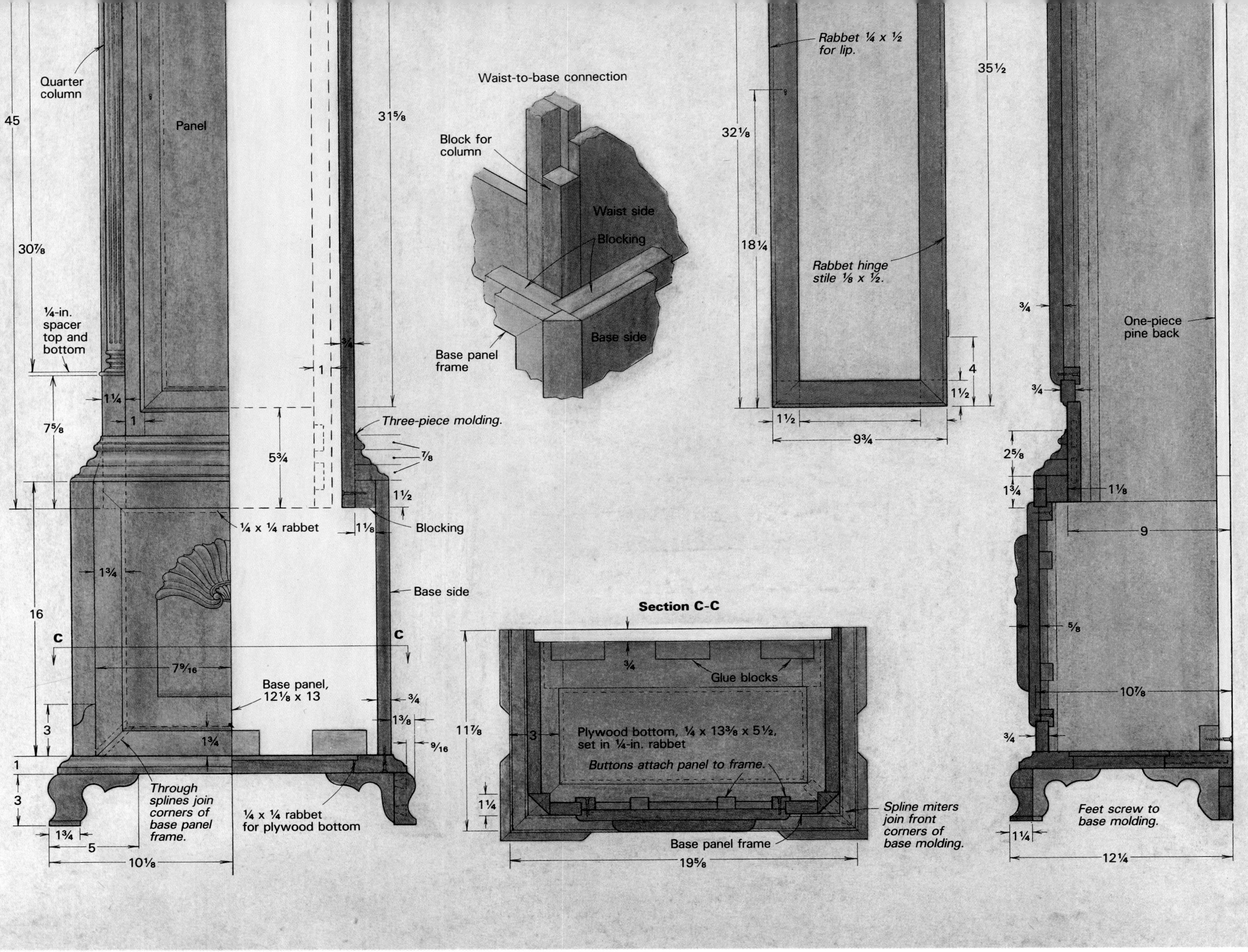

Quarter column
Panel
45
30⅞
¼-in. spacer top and bottom
1¼
1
7⅝
16
3
1
3
1¾
5
10⅛
1¾
7⁹⁄₁₆
¼ x ¼ rabbet
5¾
1
¾
31⅝
Three-piece molding.
⅞
1½
1⅛
Blocking
Base side
C
C
Base panel, 12⅛ x 13
1¾
¾
1⅜
⁹⁄₁₆
Through splines join corners of base panel frame.
¼ x ¼ rabbet for plywood bottom
Waist-to-base connection
Block for column
Waist side
Blocking
Base side
Base panel frame
Rabbet ¼ x ½ for lip.
32⅛
18¼
Rabbet hinge stile ⅛ x ½.
4
1½
1½
9¾
35½
Section C-C
¾
Glue blocks
11⅞
3
Plywood bottom, ¼ x 13⅜ x 5½, set in ¼-in. rabbet
Buttons attach panel to frame.
1¼
Base panel frame
19⅝
Spline miters join front corners of base molding.
¾
¾
2⅝
1¾
1⅛
One-piece pine back
9
⅝
10⅞
¾
Feet screw to base molding.
1¼
12¼

Tubular Table

A router makes the legs round

by Patrick Warner

I've always liked the light and airy configurations of steel tubing in contemporary stools, tables and chairs, but I prefer the look and feel of wood. Using simple joinery and a router, I combined the best of both worlds and came up with the end table shown here.

The construction is straightforward. The end frames are assembled, doweled, then routed round. I used rectangular stock so that after routing, the vertical pieces would appear to bend into the horizontal ones. If you're not interested in this illusion, you can start with square-section stock, and eliminate the rabbeting step (**4**) shown in the drawing. I aligned the end-frame pieces with a routed glue joint for gluing up (**1**), then bored and drove in the dowels after the glue had set (**2**). A simple dowel joint would work just as well; the glue joint alone won't. (I also used the routed glue joint in the top because I like the way it looks. By gluing strips of dark wood on the edges before milling, I made the decorative joint you see in the photo.)

The corner joints are vulnerable to racking stresses in light end frames like these, so I added stretchers to strengthen them. The stretchers can be located almost anywhere along the legs, but bore the relief holes and mortises for the stretchers before rounding the end frames (**3**). Holes for the screws that attach the end frames to the top should be counterbored and oversized to allow the top to expand and contract with humidity changes. Bore these holes before rounding, too. I made the top overhang the base so the screws would be well clear of the rounded edges.

After gluing, doweling and mortising the end frames, plane their faces flush. Then rout the inside surfaces as shown in the drawing (**4**). The piloted rabbet cutter establishes the curve that makes the frame appear to bend around the corners. The straight cutter follows, bearing on the rabbet to clear the rest of the waste.

Curve the outside of each corner by a similar method, but pilot the first cut against a template (**5**). The cutter I use is a TA 170 overhead flush-bearing carbide trimmer, which is sold for $13.50 by OCEMCO, 1232 51st Ave., Oakland, Calif. 94601. The template shown (which can be made of Masonite or plywood) produces an outside curve concentric with the inside one, but you can use whatever curve appeals to you. After the corners have been routed, each frame will be square in section. Figures **6** and **7** show how to round the frames with a flush-piloted, $\frac{5}{8}$-in. radius rounding-over bit. When routing the straight sections, be careful around the screw holes and mortises—if the bearing slips into the holes, the piece will be ruined.

Round the stretchers from 1-in. square stock with a flush-piloted, $\frac{1}{2}$-in. radius rounding-over bit. Cut the stock at least 5 in. longer than needed to give you an end to hold or clamp while routing. I routed the tenons using a rabbet bit with an end-mounted pilot (**8**).

I like a Watco Natural oil finish, wet-sanded during oiling with 400- to 600-grit wet-or-dry sandpaper. I follow this up with a light coat of wax four or five days later when the oil has stopped bleeding. □

Patrick Warner is a designer/furniture-maker in Escondido, Calif.

The tubular legs of this white oak table were routed round after assembly.

Photo: Ernie Cowan and Scott Campbell

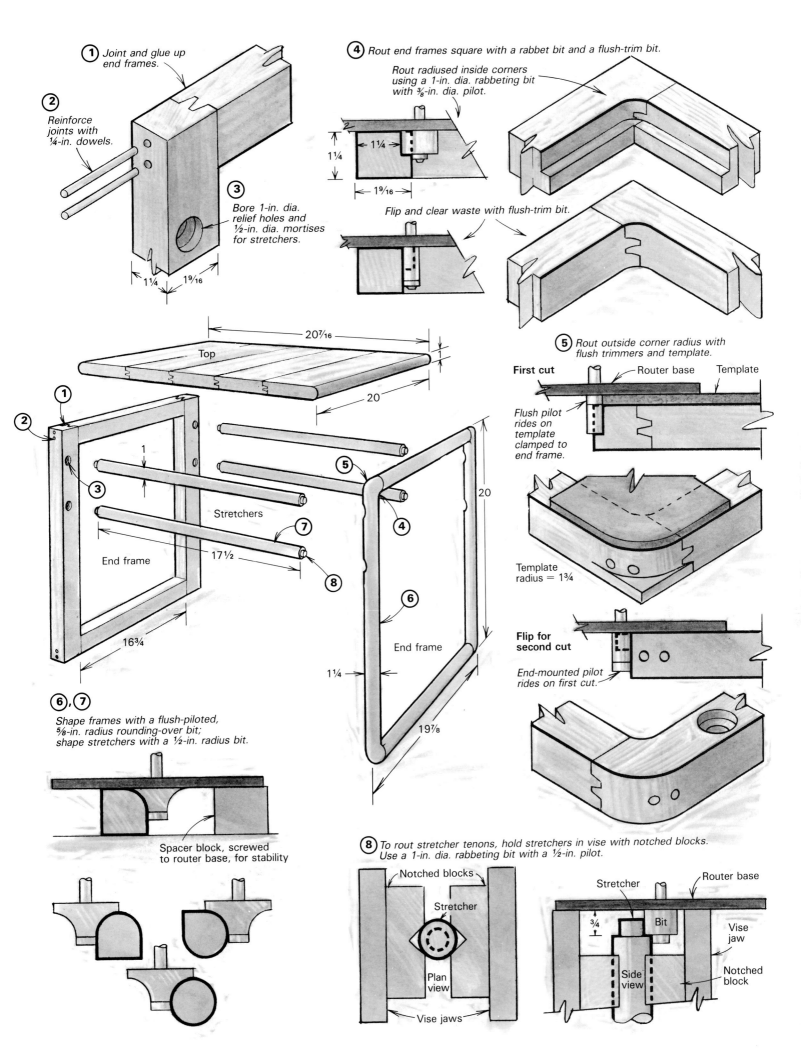

1 Joint and glue up end frames.

2 Reinforce joints with ¼-in. dowels.

3 Bore 1-in. dia. relief holes and ½-in. dia. mortises for stretchers.

1¼ 1⁹⁄₁₆

4 Rout end frames square with a rabbet bit and a flush-trim bit.

Rout radiused inside corners using a 1-in. dia. rabbeting bit with ⅜-in. dia. pilot.

1¼   1¼   1⁹⁄₁₆

Flip and clear waste with flush-trim bit.

20⁷⁄₁₆

Top

1

20

5 Rout outside corner radius with flush trimmers and template.

First cut

Router base   Template

Flush pilot rides on template clamped to end frame.

Template radius = 1¾

Flip for second cut

End-mounted pilot rides on first cut.

1
2
3

1

Stretchers

End frame

17½

5
7
4
6
8

20

End frame

1¼   19⁷⁄₈

16¾

6, 7

Shape frames with a flush-piloted, ⅝-in. radius rounding-over bit; shape stretchers with a ½-in. radius bit.

Spacer block, screwed to router base, for stability

8 To rout stretcher tenons, hold stretchers in vise with notched blocks. Use a 1-in. dia. rabbeting bit with a ½-in. pilot.

Notched blocks   Stretcher   Router base

Stretcher   Bit

¾

Plan view   Side view

Vise jaws   Vise jaw   Notched block

From *Fine Woodworking* magazine (November 1984) 49:58-59

Building a Stand-up Desk

It all hinges on your router

by Charles Prowell

My grandfather was a cabinetmaker, and my father a carpenter, so most of my designs spring from the handcrafted techniques of the cabinetmaker pitted against the practicality of the carpenter. When a San Francisco, Calif., securities analyst ordered a stand-up secretaire desk, my forebearers began arguing over veneers versus glue-ups and inlays versus profit margins, even before the customer could explain how difficult it is to sit at a desk for 10 hours a day. His only stated requirements were that the desk be 30 in. deep, have a lift-up top and accommodate his 5-ft., 7-in. frame. The rest was up to me.

Because I had been mulling over designs for a stand-up desk for years, I quickly worked up a prototype and preliminary drawings, all

Photo: Madeline Schnapp

This stand-up secretaire desk features inlaid accents and wooden hinges, as well as ample storage, pigeonholes and a drawer. The joinery and detail work are easily accomplished with a router.

the while trying to balance my forefathers' concerns for craftsmanship and profit with some of my own prejudices, such as a fondness for wooden hinges. Deciding on a desk frame of California walnut inlaid with quilted maple accent strips was easy for me because I liked the impact of the quilted maple grain and the contrast between the light wood and the dark walnut. The top would be Peruvian walnut because of its rich color and warp-resistant straight grain.

The final design is basically an oversize lap desk fitted into rabbets routed in the legs of the base, which is mortised and tenoned together; the sculpted caps on top of the legs hide the rabbets and endgrain. Tapering the legs creates a more delicate appearance. The desk is doweled together after being fit with pigeonholes and a drawer. The last and most challenging task was to fit the wooden hinges to the top, which would form the slanted writing surface.

Routing the joints—My construction techniques are straightforward and rely heavily on a hand-held router guided by a stock router-mounted fence, a straightedge with stop blocks or bearing-guided bits, such as rabbet and roundover bits. These guides provide maximum control, versatility and quick yet effective cuts. I used three routers for the various jobs this desk entailed: a Makita #3612BR 3-HP plunge router for mortising the legs, plunge cuts and the heavy work; a Milwaukee #5660 1½-HP router for straight rabbets and grooves for inlay and shaped edges; and a small Porter-Cable #309 laminate trimmer for detail work. If you don't own a variety of routers, you can cut the joints with a single table-mounted router or modify my methods to suit your equipment.

I generally rout in a left-to-right direction when facing the work, against the clockwise rotation of the bit so the router is pulled into the work. When cutting across the grain to form tenons, however, I start routing in the same direction as the bit rotation. With this operation, known as climb-cutting, I make light cuts, a maximum of ⅛ in., and remove a small section along each edge to prevent tearout, before finishing the cut in the normal left-to-right direction. Climb-cutting can be dangerous, because the router tends to self-feed and may get out of control, so you may want to start out with a ⅟₁₆-in.-deep cut.

Building the base frame—To ensure a matching grain pattern on the front legs, I rough out both pieces by ripping a walnut 2x4 down the middle. Because the legs extend to the top of the tapered desk, the front legs are naturally shorter than the back legs. After dimensioning the leg stock, lay out the mortises, measuring up from the bottom to accurately locate the joints at the correct height. The legs are not trimmed to final length until the carcase is test-fitted to the base.

I rout all mortises with a plunge router, using a ½-in.-dia. bit set

From *Fine Woodworking* magazine (July 1989) 77:74-77

Fig. 1: Stand-up secretaire desk

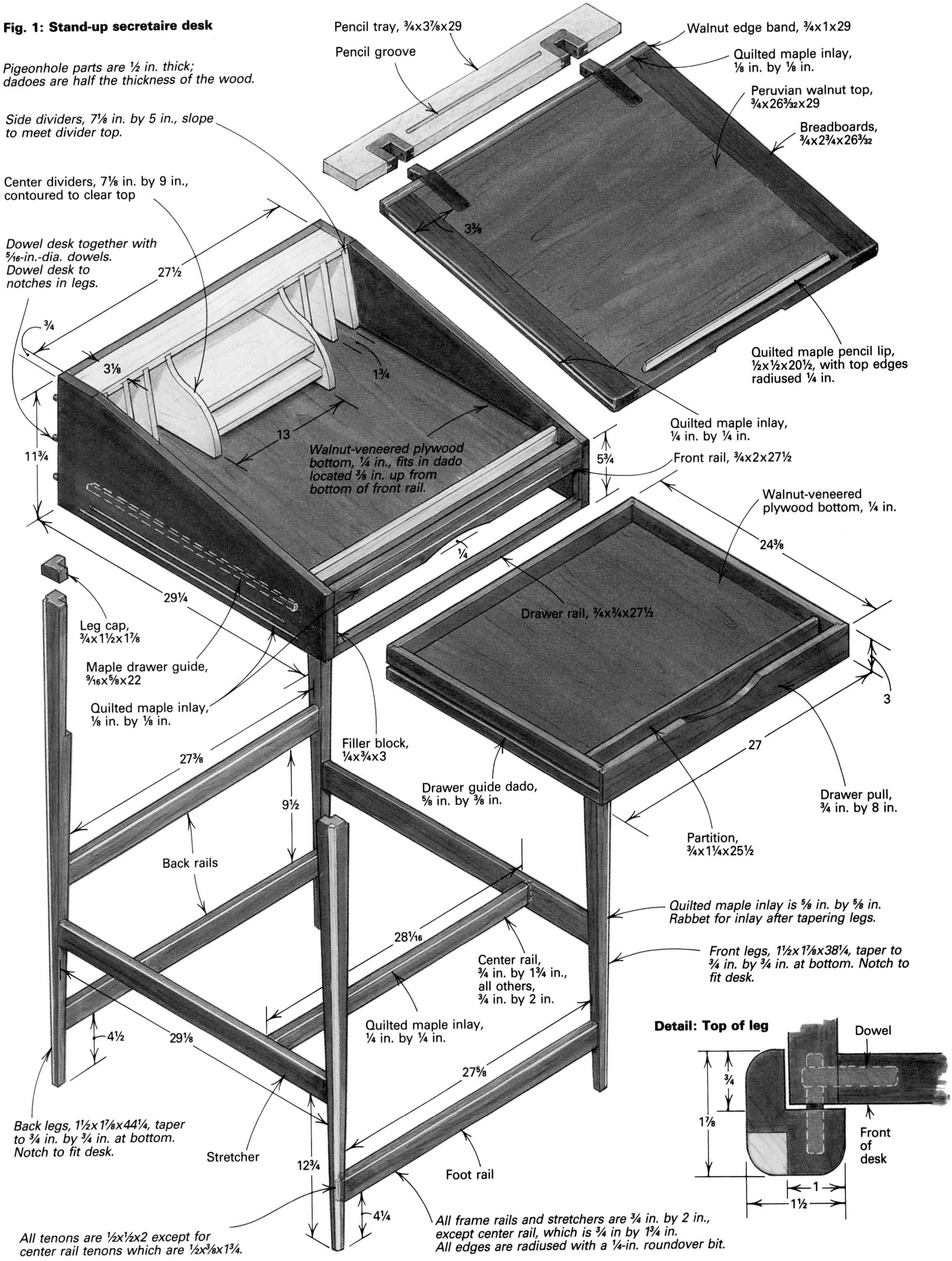

Pigeonhole parts are ½ in. thick; dadoes are half the thickness of the wood.
Side dividers, 7⅛ in. by 5 in., slope to meet divider top.
Center dividers, 7⅛ in. by 9 in., contoured to clear top
Dowel desk together with 5/16-in.-dia. dowels. Dowel desk to notches in legs.
27½
¾
3⅛
1¾
13
11¾
Walnut-veneered plywood bottom, ¼ in., fits in dado located ⅜ in. up from bottom of front rail.
5¾
29¼
¼
Leg cap, ¾x1½x1⅞
Maple drawer guide, 9/16x⅝x22
Quilted maple inlay, ⅛ in. by ⅛ in.
Pencil tray, ¾x3⅞x29
Pencil groove
Walnut edge band, ¾x1x29
Quilted maple inlay, ⅛ in. by ⅛ in.
Peruvian walnut top, ¾x26 3/32x29
Breadboards, ¾x2¾x26 3/32
3⅜
Quilted maple pencil lip, ½x½x20½, with top edges radiused ¼ in.
Quilted maple inlay, ¼ in. by ¼ in.
Front rail, ¾x2x27½
Walnut-veneered plywood bottom, ¼ in.
24⅜
Drawer rail, ¾x¾x27½
3
27
Filler block, ¼x¾x3
Drawer guide dado, ⅝ in. by ⅜ in.
Drawer pull, ¾ in. by 8 in.
Partition, ¾x1¼x25½
27⅜
9½
Back rails
Quilted maple inlay is ⅝ in. by ⅝ in. Rabbet for inlay after tapering legs.
28 1/16
Center rail, ¾ in. by 1¾ in., all others, ¾ in. by 2 in.
Front legs, 1½x1⅞x38¼, taper to ¾ in. by ¾ in. at bottom. Notch to fit desk.
4½
29⅛
Quilted maple inlay, ¼ in. by ¼ in.
27⅝
Back legs, 1½x1⅞x44¼, taper to ¾ in. by ¾ in. at bottom. Notch to fit desk.
Stretcher
12¾
Foot rail
4¼
All tenons are ½x½x2 except for center rail tenons which are ½x⅜x1¾.
All frame rails and stretchers are ¾ in. by 2 in., except center rail, which is ¾ in by 1¾ in. All edges are radiused with a ¼-in. roundover bit.
Detail: Top of leg
Dowel
¾
1⅞
Front of desk
1
1½

Drawings: Kathleen Creston

to a final cutting depth of ½ in. and a router-mounted fence fitted with stop blocks to control the length of the mortise. Because the router fence needs a straight surface to run against, I don't taper the legs until after cutting the joints. The fence and stop blocks are also used to rout the ¾-in. by 1-in. stopped rabbet needed to fit the legs to the carcase. Next, the legs are tapered on three sides, as shown in figure 1 on the previous page. You could taper the legs with a jig on a tablesaw, but I prefer to rough-cut them on the bandsaw and then true them up with a handplane.

Once the tapers are satisfactory, I rout a ⅝-in. rabbet along the outside corner of each leg for the maple inlay with a ball-bearing guided rabbet bit. The inlay is glued proud of the leg and belt-sanded flush after the adhesive cures. The belt sander is a concession to the miserable working qualities of quilted maple, which is very difficult to plane without tearout. I radius the inlaid corner with a ⅝-in. roundover bit and the other three corners of the leg with a ⅜-in. roundover bit.

Before continuing with the legs, rout the tenons on the frame rails and stretchers, as shown in figure 1. To cut ½-in. tenons for the mortises, I set a ball-bearing guided, ½-in. rabbet bit to cut ⅛ in. deep. Run the bearing against the end of a rail to cut one tenon cheek. The rail is then flipped over and the operation repeated for the other cheek. To compensate for the leg taper, I angle the shoulders of the tenons ¹⁄₁₆ in. with a chisel. The ⅜-in. tenons for the center rail are routed in the same manner. Then, rout the rails with a bearing-guided ¼-in. rabbet bit and install the inlays as shown in the drawing.

After routing the mortises for the center rail, assemble the piece and glue the stretchers and legs together to form the left and right sides. Then, I glue in the rails and clamp up the assembled base on a flat surface, and leave it to dry while I work on the carcase.

Carcase construction—The sides, back and top are glued up from several strips of walnut. The sides will be identical if you clamp them together and bandsaw them simultaneously, then clean up the edges with a handplane. The side pieces can be fit into the leg rabbets and used as templates to mark the height and angle for trimming the legs with a fine handsaw. If you want to further emphasize the caps on the legs, you can sand or carve a slight chamfer around the top of the legs to create a reveal.

The back, front rail and drawer rail are now cut out as shown in figure 1. Note: The upper edge of the front rail is ripped at a slight angle to align with the tapered sides. After routing a dado in the front rail for the walnut-veneered plywood bottom of the pigeon-hole compartment, I dry-fit the front rail to the sides. Then scribe the dado location from the front rail onto the side pieces, carrying the layout lines onto the back piece, and rout the dado. After sawing the lower edge of the front rail to the curve shown to counterbalance the drawer's finger pull, I dowel the carcase together. Don't forget to position the bottom into its dadoes before gluing up. After the carcase dries, glue filler blocks to the sides to eliminate the gap formed between the carcase and the drawer when the rabbeted legs are glued to the carcase. Next, rout out the quilted-maple pencil tray as shown, using a ½-in.-dia. cove bit and a router-mounted fence, then glue and clamp it to the carcase.

Figure 1, on the previous page, shows how I dowel the carcase into the rabbets cut in the legs. Even though the base has been glued together, the legs can still flex enough to allow the carcase and protruding dowels to drop into place. Apply glue to the dowels and rabbets, and clamp the assembly together.

Carcase detailing—You can make any style drawer you want. Because I prefer router joinery, I cut lapped rabbets for the corners.

The joints also cover the dadoes holding the drawer bottom. A small curve, ¾ in. high by 8 in. wide, bandsawn on the top edge of the drawer front serves as a finger pull. After gluing a partition for a pencil tray inside the drawer, rout the drawer sides to fit the maple guides screwed inside the carcase.

The ½-in.-thick maple pigeonhole dividers are installed in dadoes routed in the divider top. The side dividers taper from 3⅛ in. to 5 in., top to bottom, while the center dividers have an S-curve profile to accommodate the paper shelves and to fit under the closed top. The stopped dadoes for the paper shelves are routed with a straightedge guide and a stop block, while the through dadoes in the divider top are guided simply by a straightedge. After gluing the divider top to the underside of the pencil tray, glue the paper shelves to the center dividers. I then apply a thin film of glue to the top and bottom of the center dividers and slide this assembly into position between the divider top and the plywood bottom. The side dividers between the divider top and the plywood bottom are installed in a similar fashion, using temporary spacer blocks between the bottom of the dividers to maintain alignment.

My top is based on a breadboard construction, which works fine in California, where humidity levels are fairly constant; you might want to avoid this construction if the humidity fluctuates significantly in your area, because the resultant wood movement will ultimately break the glue joints. Inlays, like those on the top of my desk, are optional. If you want to use inlays, you can cut grooves as shown in figure 1, with a straight bit and router-mounted fence or with a slotting bit and an oversize guide bearing. You should, however, rip the upper edge of the top to the same angle as the side taper, to prevent the hinge from binding when the top is closed.

Routing wooden hinges—You'll learn a lot when you make your first wooden hinge. I know I did, so I'll suggest some improvements I've come up with. Three major steps are involved in routing wooden hinges: making and fitting the pencil-tray hinge leaves; making and fitting the top hinge leaves; and mating the leaves together. Starting with the pencil tray, rout out a 1⅞-in.-sq. mortise ¾-in. deep with a straight bit. Using a ball-bearing guided, ½-in. rabbet bit, rout a recess around the top of the previous cut, then rout a keyway using a ³⁄₁₆-in. slotting bit (see the hinge detail in figure 2 on the facing page). When fitted with a purpleheart spline, the keyway secures the hinge leaf into the pencil tray. If I could do it over again, I'd do all this work before gluing the tray on, bandsawing away most of the waste before performing any routing operations.

To make the pencil-tray leaf, I transfer the measurements from the pencil-tray mortise to a 2⅞-in.-sq. block of Peruvian walnut. Clamping this block in my bench vise, I rout the ⅜-in.-deep rabbet around the bottom with the ball-bearing guided ½-in. rabbet bit, then rout the keyway slot with a ³⁄₁₆-in. slotting bit. After fine-tuning the fit on a bench-type Dremel sander, I scroll-saw a 1-in.-sq. cutout for the hinge knuckle and sand over the edges.

To form the top-leaf mortise, I set up a straightedge guide so I can rout a ½-in. slot 4½ in. long through the top. Routing rabbets on both the top and bottom face of these slots produces the tongue shown on the facing page.

The top leaf is also easy to make, because I can lay the walnut block on top of the cutout and trace it, allowing an extra inch for the knuckle. I cut the groove with the ¼-in. slotting bit in my Porter-Cable router after clamping the leaf in the bench vise. After the knuckle is cut to a 1-in. width, the edges are softened on the sander.

Drilling the hinge-pin holes presents the greatest danger of ruining the work. While aligning the two leaves, I cut and adjust

Fig. 2: Wooden hinges

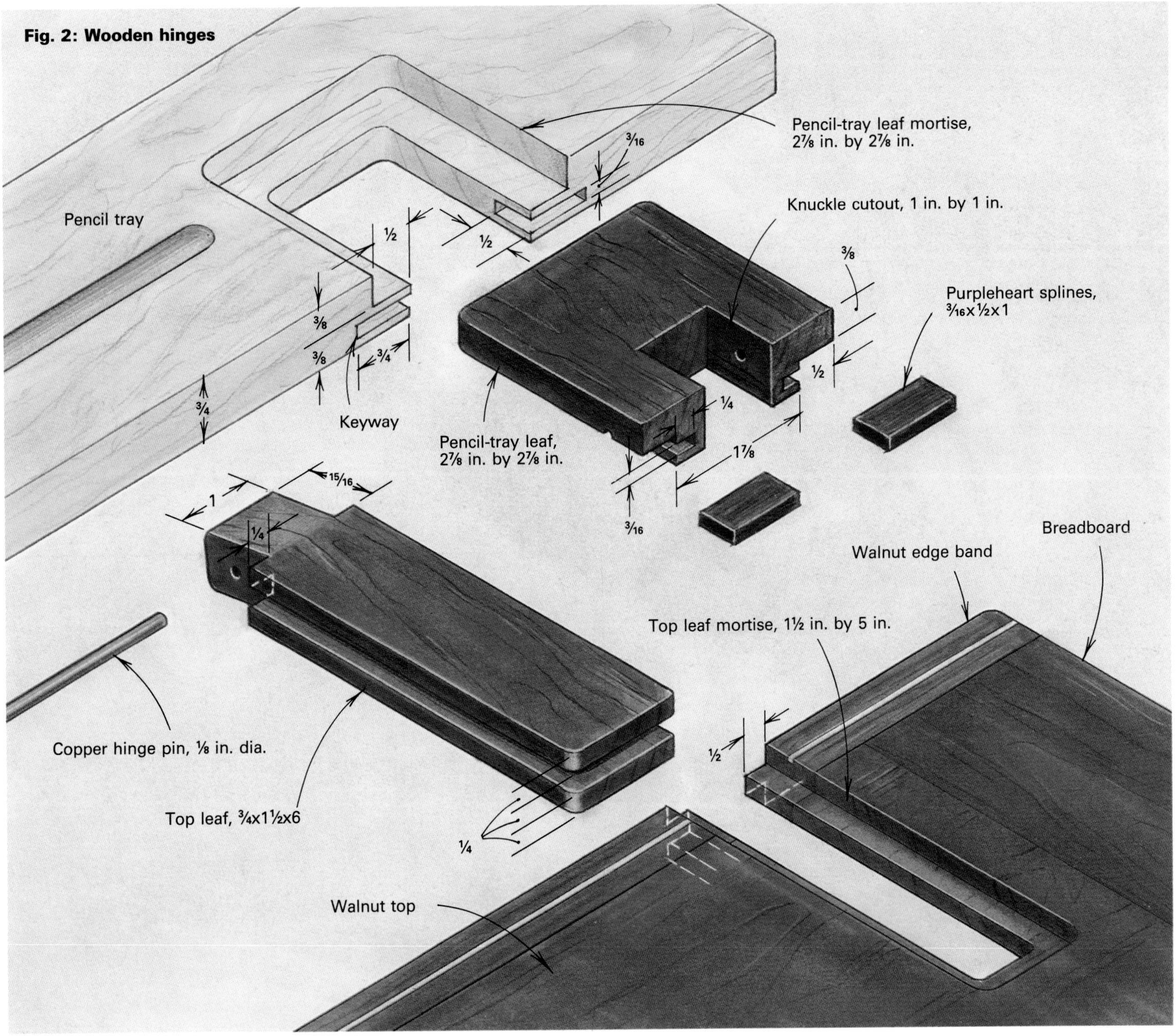
Pencil-tray leaf mortise, 2⅞ in. by 2⅞ in.
3/16
Knuckle cutout, 1 in. by 1 in.
Pencil tray
½
½
⅜
Purpleheart splines, 3/16x½x1
⅜
⅜
¾
½
¾
Keyway
¼
Pencil-tray leaf, 2⅞ in. by 2⅞ in.
1⅞
15/16
1
¼
3/16
Breadboard
Walnut edge band
Top leaf mortise, 1½ in. by 5 in.
Copper hinge pin, ⅛ in. dia.
½
Top leaf, ¾x1½x6
¼
Walnut top

the knuckles for a snug fit all around and clamp the fitted hinge between two boards to maintain alignment. After locating the hinge on the drill press, bore a ⅛-in.-dia. hole through the pivot point of the two leaves. A drill press is essential for a straight bore; otherwise, the procedure becomes hopelessly random.

Proper hinge action entails assemblying and disassemblying, each time sanding the knuckles until the movement is satisfactory. My hinge uses a copper hinge pin to reduce any chances for chemical reaction between the pin and the resins in the wood. Next, the purpleheart splines are glued into position and then the leaf is glued to the fixed pencil rail. With a thin glueline applied to the tongues and grooves (a miniaturist's syringe helps here), the top is slipped and fitted in place on its leaf.

Pieces of walnut, shaped by a ¾-in. roundover bit and sanding, cap the legs. Pencil trays are formed with strips of quilted maple, as shown in figure 1 on p. 103. I thought I was finished with the decorative inlays, but after evaluating the piece, I decided to rout ⅛-in. grooves in the sides and front and install quilted maple strips. I rounded the ends of the strips with a file to match the router bit's profile. The strips were installed proud of the surface and later block-planed and belt-sanded flush.

The finish—I do all of my sanding before putting on any finish; once I start finishing, I don't sand. I sand all surfaces working progressively from 80-grit paper to 220-grit, then I give the surfaces a lighter sanding with 400-grit and a final, quick rubdown with 600 grit. At this stage, the wood is as smooth as glass and ready for my favorite finish: a mixture of ⅓ thinner, ⅓ linseed oil and ⅓ polyurethane. This mixture is heated by placing the can containing the finish in a pot of boiling water after it has been removed from the stove. This mixture is brushed on liberally, allowed to dry for 30 minutes or so, then wiped dry. I build up to six coats, allowing 24 hours between coats, then top the piece off with a coat of paste wax. The wax is a lot like putting on a coat in 50° weather: You don't really need it, but it makes you feel better.

Once the desk was completed, all that remained was a final critique, a process endured in the wake of my forefathers' passing with the completion of every job. I imagined an analysis by my grandfather, searching for flaws, and my father, questioning the profitability with his usual "Time is money, boy." □

Charles Prowell owns and operates Charles Prowell Woodworks, building custom furniture in Sebastopol, Calif.

Routing a Rule Joint

Precise hinge placement for a smoothly swinging drop leaf

by Mac Campbell

A rule joint is the traditional method for shaping the mating edges of a tabletop and a drop leaf. The cove on the leaf rests on the roundover of the tabletop to help support the raised leaf; when the leaf is down, the rule joint forms a decorative molding.

A drop leaf dramatically increases or decreases a table's size quickly and easily, while at the same time eliminates the hassle of storing loose table leaves. Drop leaves are adaptable to either modern or traditional tables, but the key to making this design tool work well is the traditional rule joint.

The principle of a rule joint is very simple: The tabletop has a shouldered roundover cut along its edge, and the hinged leaf has a corresponding cove cut along its edge. When the leaf is raised, the cove rests directly on the roundover so the weight of the leaf, plus serving dishes, elbows or any other objects that might get placed near the joint, is carried by the joint itself and not just the hinge screws. When the leaf is down, the rule joint forms a decorative ovolo molding along the edge of the table. A cross section of this molded edge resembles the brass joint on a traditional carpenter's rule, hence the name rule joint.

To operate properly, a rule joint requires a specially designed hinge (see figure 1 on the facing page). One side of the hinge is longer than the other to span the radius of the cove on the table leaf. Screw holes are countersunk on the reverse side from the knuckle, the opposite of a normal hinge. In use, the hinge knuckle is mortised into the underside of the tabletop so the center of the hinge pin can be placed at (or near) the center of the arc of both the roundover and the cove.

Theory versus reality—Before getting into how to cut and fit a rule joint, it is worth looking at the areas where the theory of the joint, and the reality of making it work, part company. Certainly, you can make a rule joint exactly as shown in figure 2A on the facing page, with the roundover's arc traveling through exactly 90°, so the arc's center is on the underside of the tabletop. On a ¾-in.-thick top with a ⅛-in. quirk, for example, this would require a ⅝-in. radius cutter for the roundover. However, with this arrangement, the tabletop and extension leaf will rub throughout their full range of motion. At the very least, this abrasion will wear and scratch the finish on these parts, especially if any small crumbs or debris get caught in between the pieces, and the damage will seriously detract from the decorative molding formed by this joint. Also, if the leaf should distort due to seasonal humidity changes, the fit can become so tight it will be unworkable. In addition, because the hinges are mounted on the bottom surface of the leaf,

From *Fine Woodworking* magazine (January 1990) 80:48-52

Fig. 1: Table hinge

Q, height of quirk
R, radius of roundover
A, height of hinge pin center above face of hinge leaf

To determine the depth of the hinge mortise, add the height of the quirk, the radius of the roundover and A, the height of the hinge pin center above the hinge leaf, and subtract the total from the thickness of the tabletop.

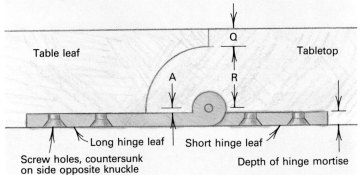

Table leaf · Q · Tabletop
A · R
Long hinge leaf | Short hinge leaf
Screw holes, countersunk on side opposite knuckle
Depth of hinge mortise

the leaf does not hang straight down, but swings in slightly toward the table base. If the joint is constructed as in figure 2A, this extra tilt will open up a gap between the edge of the leaf and the table and spoil the continuity of the edge.

The solution to these problems is to slightly alter the layout of the joint and the placement of the hinge pin as shown in figure 2B at right. Again, assume you have a ¾-in.-thick top and an ⅛-in. quirk; if a ½-in.-radius roundover is used instead of one with a ⅝-in. radius, the center point of the roundover will be moved up ⅛-in. from the bottom of the tabletop. Reducing the radius and raising the center point of the hinge in this way significantly affect the joint by raising the edge of the leaf when the leaf is down, so that it overlaps the roundover. This overlap eliminates the open gap caused by the leaf's tilt in the down position. In addition, raising the center point of the hinge pin lets you recess the hinges into the bottom surface of the top and leaf. Although recessing the hinges is not necessary—many older tables have their hinges surface-mounted with only the knuckles recessed—it does give the table's underside a more finished look.

Another minor alteration in the placement of the hinge pin solves the problem of the parts rubbing on each other as the leaf is raised or lowered. If the hinge pin's center is moved 1/32 in. toward the leaf, the leaf will still close tightly to the quirk at the surface of the tabletop when it is up, but will gradually draw away from the roundover as it is lowered (see figure 2B). This also allows a little leeway for seasonal distortion, but still retains the joint's load-carrying capacity.

Cutting a rule joint—Before putting tool to wood, you must obtain the hinges. When selecting hinges, the critical factor is that the distance from the knuckle to the nearest screw hole on the long hinge leaf must be greater than the radius of the joint so the hinge leaf can span the cove that was cut on the table's drop leaf (see distance R in figure 1). Hinges on old tables were usually made of iron, since they can't be seen on the finished table, but you can get brass drop-leaf hinges from Paxton Hardware Ltd., 7818 Bradshaw Rd., Upper falls, Md. 21156 or Lee Valley Tools, Box 6295, Station J., Ottawa, Ont., Canada K2A 1T4, and several other supply houses.

A rule joint can be cut entirely by hand, but it is much easier to use power equipment. I use a hand-held router for cutting the cove and the roundover and for recessing the hinges. To cut the roundover on the tabletop, I use a bearing-guided roundover bit, and to cut the cove on the leaf, either a bearing-guided cove bit or

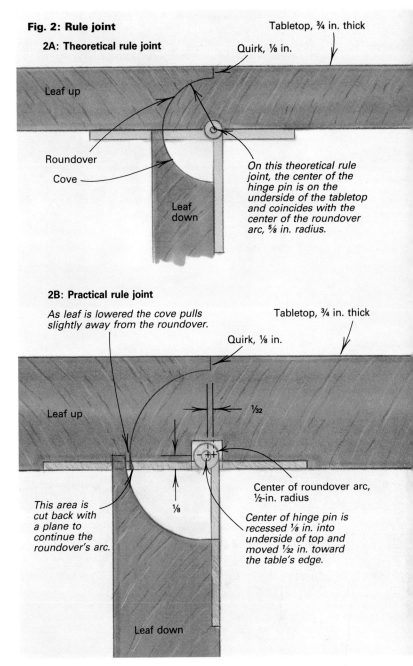

Fig. 2: Rule joint

2A: Theoretical rule joint

Tabletop, ¾ in. thick
Quirk, ⅛ in.
Leaf up
Roundover
Cove
Leaf down

On this theoretical rule joint, the center of the hinge pin is on the underside of the tabletop and coincides with the center of the roundover arc, ⅝ in. radius.

2B: Practical rule joint

As leaf is lowered the cove pulls slightly away from the roundover.

Tabletop, ¾ in. thick
Quirk, ⅛ in.
Leaf up
1/32
This area is cut back with a plane to continue the roundover's arc.
⅛
Leaf down
Center of roundover arc, ½-in. radius
Center of hinge pin is recessed ⅛ in. into underside of top and moved 1/32 in. toward the table's edge.

Shown above are two setups for routing the cove on the extension leaf. Whenever possible, the author uses a bearing-guided cove bit, as shown on the right. However, because he was unable to find a cove bit with a radius larger than ½ in., he uses a ¾-in.-radius core-box bit with a guide fence clamped onto the router base, as shown on the left, for thick tabletops.

A few passes with a block plane are required to round over the flat portion of the table's edge left uncut by the roundover bit.

a core-box bit, as shown in the photo on the previous page. Because I couldn't find a bearing-piloted coving bit with a radius larger than ½ in., I was forced to turn to the core-box bit when I needed a ¾-in. cove for a 1¼-in.-thick tabletop. To cut a cove with the core-box bit, mount a fence on the router with an arc cut out of the fence, so that half of the bit's cutting edge is exposed, and run the fence along the leaf's edge. I have mated pairs of cutters in ½-in. and ¾-in. radii. By varying the size of the quirk and the depth of the hinge mortise, these two radii work for most tabletop thicknesses. For a ¾-in.-thick top, I use a ½-in.-radius set of cutters, and leave a ⅛-in. quirk; for a 1¼-in. top, I use the ¾-in.-radius set, and leave a quirk of about ¼ in.

Begin by jointing the mating edges carefully, as you would for a glue joint; these edges are used to guide the router cuts, so your final fit will be only as good as the original edge-to-edge joint. Bear in mind that some wood is removed so the leaf can overlap the top. For this reason, it's best to work the joint and recess the hinges before final-sizing the top and leaves. This is essential to end up with a continuous curve on the edge of a round or oval table.

Once you have your hinges and decide on the radius of the arc and the size of the quirk, you're ready to begin. When using a router to cut the joint, it's not necessary to actually lay out the joint on the wood; instead, you can just rout the roundover on the table and fit the cove on the leaf to it. Make several passes to cut the roundover, lowering the bit a little each pass until you've reached the desired depth based on the height of the quirk. The final pass should be very light (around 1/32 in.) to give the smoothest possible surface. While you're at it, cut the same profile on a piece of scrap to use as a sanding block for cleaning up the cove on the leaf. It's not necessary to leave the quirk on the sanding block.

Next, change bits and cut the cove on the leaf, again making several passes. If you're using a core-box bit, make sure the fence clamped to the router base leaves exactly half the bit exposed so you get a true 90° cove. As you approach the final depth, hold the leaf up to the edge of the table and check the fit. The top surfaces of the table and leaf should be flush when the cove is resting on the roundover. Again, cut a duplicate cove profile on a piece of scrap for a sanding block. After both profiles are cut and fitted, smooth away any machining marks with 150-grit paper wrapped around the sanding block. Remove as little wood as possible to avoid loosening the fit.

The two pieces should now snugly fit together when the leaf is up. However, as the leaf is lowered, it will not rotate smoothly through its arc because of the uncut area near the bottom edge of the table where the pilot bearing of the roundover bit ran on its last pass (see figure 2B on the previous page). This uncut area must be rounded over to at least continue the arc of the router cut. I prefer undercutting it slightly more than that, so when the leaf is down, any small debris that falls into the crack will fall all the way through. I usually shape this area with a block plane, as shown in the photo at left, and finish up with a scraper and sandpaper.

Laying out and fitting the hinges—Now you're ready for the heart of the process: fitting the hinges. To lay out the hinge locations, place the tabletop and leaves upside down on the bench, and clamp them together along the rule joints. For joints up to about 4 ft. long, I usually use two hinges, each placed one quarter of the joint length in from the end. For longer joints, I often use three hinges: one centered and the others a little less than a quarter of the total distance from each end. After marking the location of each hinge, place one of the hinges upside down (so the knuckle won't interfere) at each mark in turn, and draw pencil lines along the sides of the hinge on both the tabletop and the leaves. Don't mark the ends of the hinge leaves at this time; you must first determine the exact placement of the hinge knuckle. To do so, unclamp the top and leaves.

As pointed out earlier, the center of the hinge knuckle should be 1/32 in. from the center of the roundover arc measuring toward the edge of the tabletop. Set a marking gauge to this measurement (15/32 in. for a ½-in.-radius roundover) and scribe a line on the underside of the tabletop at one of the hinge locations. Carefully place a hinge on this scribe line with the hinge's short leaf pointing toward the center of the table and the center of the hinge pin exactly over the scribed line. Scribe along the end of the short hinge leaf with a sharp scratch awl. Now, with the marking gauge's fence against the table's edge, reset the gauge to this scribed line, and mark the end of the hinge leaf at each hinge location. To finish the layout, reclamp the tabletop and leaves together, place a hinge, upside down, exactly on the lines you just marked out and scribe the location of the long end of the hinge on the table leaf. Again, separate the pieces, set your marking gauge to this line and mark at each hinge location. You now have a complete layout for the hinges and you're ready to rout the recesses for them.

The depth that the hinges are to be recessed is critical to the correct placement of the hinge pin, so you must first measure the exact distance from the face of the hinge to the center of the hinge pin (distance A in figure 1). Add this measurement A to the radius of the roundover and the height of the quirk, and then subtract that total from the thickness of the tabletop to give you the depth of the hinge mortise.

The hinge mortises can be cut with a number of different methods, but I prefer a router because of the precise depth control. Using a ¼-in. bit, set the router to the depth you calculated earlier. Because the placement of the hinge is so critical, mount a fence on the router base to stop the cut just as you get to the scribe line at the end of the hinge mortise (see the photo on the facing page). You could set up a jig to register the router side to side, but I prefer to rout the mortises freehand, stopping just short of the layout line on each side of the mortises and cleaning them out with a chisel later.

Rout and clean out all the hinge mortises, and then clamp the tabletop and leaves together again and check each mortise for fit with an upside-down hinge. Trim with a chisel where necessary. Now, you have only to rout a deeper mortise to recess the hinge knuckle.

Once again, separate the top and leaves. Select a router bit at least as wide as the hinge knuckle. The bit may be as much as 1/16 in. wider without hurting anything, because a tight fit side to side isn't important, although adequate depth is. Set the depth of cut equal to the depth of the hinge mortise plus the height of the hinge knuckle above the face of the hinge. Then, clamp a fence on the router so the distance from the fence to the center of the bit is equal to 1/32 in. less than the radius of the joint's arc. Carefully rout a recess for the hinge knuckle in each mortise in the table-top, and square off the ends of these mortises with a chisel. A plunge router is useful for this operation, but not essential since the bit diameter and depth of cut are small and the fence on the router base provides the needed stability when starting the plunge cut with a regular router.

Clamp the leaves and the top together, and test fit a hinge into each mortise. I've found enough variation in overall size and screw hole placement from one hinge to the next to warrant numbering the hinges and the mortises to make sure the same hinge goes into the same mortise each time. With all the hinges in their mortises, set a screw in one of the holes closest to the knuckle of each hinge. Don't drill all the pilot holes yet, in case minor adjustments must be made later. At this stage, I use steel screws that are the same diameter and 1/8 in. shorter than the ones used in the final assembly. This helps to ensure that the holes aren't stripped out when removing and replacing the screws. Using the preliminary steel screws is especially important when finishing up with brass screws because the steel screws can be driven and removed with less danger of breakage.

With one screw in each leaf of each hinge, carefully turn the whole assembly over and, with the top resting on the bench, raise and lower each leaf. It is possible that everything will work perfectly, but it's more likely that there will be a few stiff spots. The easiest way to locate the points where the joint is binding is to slip a piece of carbon paper in the joint when the leaf is down, and then raise and lower it a couple of times. Do this along the length of the joint, and then remove only a little wood at the carbon-marked spots with sandpaper or a cabinet scraper. Repeat this procedure as often as necessary until the joint works smoothly. Now, you can mark the ends of the top and leaves and, if necessary, disassemble them and trim them to length or, in the case of a curved or round top, bandsaw the final shape of the table. Then, reassemble the parts and set the rest of the screws, again using slightly short steel screws.

With the hinges fully installed, set the whole assembly right-side up on the bench, and use a long level or straightedge to make sure the top and leaves are perfectly flat. If the table base and leaf supports (see the sidebar below) are already built, you can place the top assembly on this. Because there will probably be slight variations where the leaves meet the top, use a cabinet scraper or a handplane (or, when nobody is looking, a belt sander) to smooth

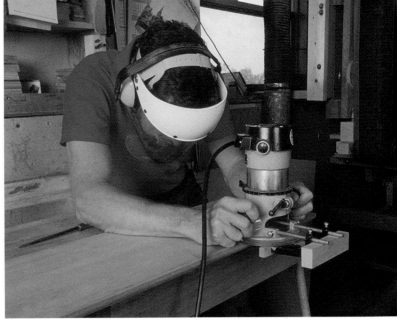

To ensure proper hinge placement, Campbell uses a fence when routing the hinge mortises.

the joint between the two; then, rout a decorative profile on the table's edge if it gets one. Finally, sand the whole top in preparation for applying the finish.

Your rule joint is now complete. Remove the hinges and finish the top and leaves separately. When the finishing process is complete, reinstall the hinges with the proper screws and make a final check of the action of the leaves. Depending on your original fit and the thickness of your finish, there may be a trace of rubbing. If so, it can usually be relieved by going over the joint with steel wool. A light coat of wax should eliminate any squeaks.

There is one more thing to consider when designing a drop-leaf table. The wood for the leaves must be as stable as possible, since the leaves just hang, completely unrestrained against movement. If they are to be made from one or two wide boards, try to pick a very stable wood, and avoid reaction wood or wood cut from an area of the tree near knots or other defects. No matter how attractive the figure, these pieces are more likely to distort over time. Clear, straight-grain mahogany or walnut are the ideal choices. If you are laminating from narrower stock, try to alternate the direction of the annular rings so any cupping will produce a washboard effect, but leave the overall line of the leaf flat. □

Mac Campbell operates Custom Woodworking in Harvey Station, N.B., Canada, specializing in furniture design and construction.

Supporting a drop leaf

Once you've mastered the intricacies of the rule joint, you still need a way to support the leaf in the raised position. Though the solutions are limited only by your ingenuity, there are three basic systems that have been developed through the years: gate leg, pull out and swing arm.

The gate-leg support is probably the best known of the three. In this system, a table leg is attached to an arm that is hinged in some way to the table frame. To operate it, hold the leaf in the raised position with one hand, while you swing the leg out under it with the other. The movable

leg may be one of the four main legs, as in the table shown in the photo on p. 106, or an extra leg tucked in behind one of the main legs. In either case, it is usually attached to the table skirt with a wooden hinge.

The hinge, which is little more than a rotating finger joint, is relatively simple to make. The layout for the hinge is shown in figure 3 on the following page. Draw a circle on the edge of each piece so that it is tangent to both faces and the end of the piece. Next, draw diagonals from the corners of the piece so they intersect at the circle's center and continue to the edges of

the piece. With a square, carry three lines down both sides of each piece: The line where the diagonals meet the edges indicates the back of the chamfer, the line that is carried down from the point where the diagonals intersect the circle will be the centerline of the chamfer and the line that designates where the circle is tangent to the edges of the board is where no wood should be removed when rounding over the knuckle.

Next, I lay out the knuckles for the hinge, so each knuckle is about as high as the board is thick. Make the saw cuts be-

Fig. 3: Wooden hinge layout

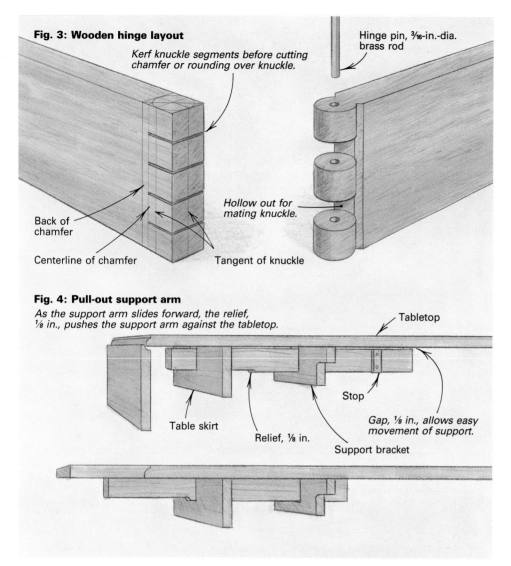

Kerf knuckle segments before cutting chamfer or rounding over knuckle.

Hinge pin, ³⁄₁₆-in.-dia. brass rod

Hollow out for mating knuckle.

Back of chamfer

Centerline of chamfer

Tangent of knuckle

Fig. 4: Pull-out support arm

As the support arm slides forward, the relief, ⅛ in., pushes the support arm against the tabletop.

Tabletop

Stop

Table skirt

Relief, ⅛ in.

Support bracket

Gap, ⅛ in., allows easy movement of support.

A hinged swing arm supports a drop leaf that extends a cabinet top. A small wedge glued to the extension leaf lets the arm swing freely through most of its arc and, when used with an adjustable stop, provides a way to fine-tune the level of the leaf.

tween the knuckles, but don't chisel them out yet. First, cut the chamfers and round over the ends of the boards to form the knuckles' shape. I use a chisel and a rabbet plane to cut the cross-grain chamfer; and to prevent tearout, I score a line with the marking gauge along the pencil line at the back of the chamfer. This chamfer can also be cut with a backsaw and chisel or with the tablesaw tilted to 45°. The ends of the boards may be rounded now as well, using either a small plane or a roundover bit in a router.

After both mating pieces have been chamfered and rounded, chisel out the alternate knuckles just as you would for a dovetail. Once the waste is removed, hollow out the base of each cut to provide clearance for the mating knuckle to fit into.

When all the shaping is completed, assemble the hinge with the two pieces at right angles to each other. Carefully line up the knuckles and, using a drill press, make a hole for the hinge pin. I use a ³⁄₁₆-in. uncoated brass brazing rod for a pin, and peen a head on what will be the upper end. Drilling from both the top and bottom of the hinge toward the middle minimizes

any misalignment. Insert the pin in the hole and try the action of the hinge. There are usually a couple of tight spots to clean up; shave a little here and there until the action is smooth. Make sure the knuckles on the moving arm don't project past the inner face of the fixed arm as the hinge opens; this will cause the hinge to bind once installed on the table.

If a gate-leg support doesn't fit your design, the most common alternative is a pull-out support. This support rides in a slot cut in the skirt, and by using the skirt as a fulcrum, transfers the weight of the leaf to upward pressure on the bottom of the tabletop. For ease of action, relieve the bottoms of the pull-out arms except where they actually bear on the skirt (see figure 4 above). For heavy leaves, use two or three pull outs and connect them with crosspieces to form a pull-out frame.

The final alternative for supporting a drop leaf is the swing arm, as shown in the photo above. This is ideal when extending the top of a cabinet with a drop leaf because the arm is simply hinged to the cabinet side and swung out when needed. I used brass hinges on the swing arm in the

photo, but a wooden hinge can be substituted by setting individual knuckles to the cabinet side at the top and bottom of the swing arm and using separate short hinge pins. In this case, the long grain of the swing arm should run perpendicular to the side of the cabinet to keep the grain from splitting at the base of the hinge knuckle. The problem with this approach is that if the wood of the swing arm contracts during the dry times of the year, the hinge will loosen and the leaf will sag.

The swing arm can also be used on tables, but because of the large torque it exerts on the skirt to which it is attached, this support system should be used only for small, relatively lightweight leaves. A spreader installed between the table skirts where the arms are hinged will help resist the tendency for the skirts to deflect. For this type of swing arm, cut a wooden hinge as described for the gate leg.

All of these support systems have one potential problem in common: since the rule joint prevents the leaf from being raised above the level of the tabletop, the support system drags along the bottom of the leaf as it's pulled into position. My solution in all cases is to screw a small wedge to the bottom of the leaf where it will rest on the support. By screwing the wedge to the leaf through a slot, or adding an adjustable stop, as shown in the photo above, you can regulate where the support rests on the wedge and thereby compensate for any sag or wear that will develop over time. In addition, this wedge system lets you cut the gate leg or swing arm just a hair low, making it much easier to move into position.

—M.C.

Tambour-Top Jewelry Box
Pull the drawer and the top rolls open

by Jamie Russell

Trick tambour boxes are functional objects with a surprise: Opening the dovetailed drawer reveals a compartment under the tambour top. The system works with two-drawer models and various shapes of tambours.

ustomers at craft shows are always mystified but delighted by the way my boxes work: The tambour top automatically opens as the drawer is pulled out. When I first used this "trick tambour" to push out the writing surface on a desk I made, I thought I had an original idea. But, an acquaintance shattered my illusions when she showed me an old Japanese crayon box with a tambour attached to its drawer. It may be an old idea, but tambour-top boxes are fun to make.

In addition, small projects like these boxes offer a craftsman lots of design possibilities. You can afford to experiment with different ideas without risking much material or time, you don't need a lot of room or equipment and you can turn cutoffs from other projects into money-makers. It's also much easier to sell three pieces involving 40 hours of labor and $50 worth of material than it is to sell one piece requiring the same labor and $200 in materials. Personally, I find my optimum attention span for a given project is one week; after a week, my interest loses its fine edge and I get sloppy. It's simple to tailor a batch of jewelry boxes like the ones shown above to make a perfect week's work.

Even though I work in batches, this article will deal only with how to build one single-drawer jewelry box. You can come up with your own production techniques or design variations for drawer-and-tambour boxes, but the basic principle is simple: Any tambour needs a track to carry it out of sight when it's opened. I take advantage of this fact and screw the slat at the rear of the tambour to the drawer bottom and run the track groove under the drawer, as shown in figure 3 on p. 113. Because the tambour top is fairly light and the drawer is barely 8½ in. wide, the drawer easily pulls the tambour open. The tambour also acts as a drawer stop then it reaches the end of the track. The base and molded

shelf-supports tenoned inside the box align the gable sides and keep the box square and rigid—important features for a smooth-running tambour.

Rough-milling stock—Because thick wood has a tendency to move after it is sliced into thin pieces, the first step is to resaw all the box components about a week before you want to build the boxes. This gives the wood time to stabilize before you work it. So far, my best sellers are boxes in oak and walnut. For stability and attractiveness, I prefer stock with a grain pattern somewhere between quartersawn and rift-sawn. Depending on the exact thickness of your stock and your bandsaw blade size, you should end up with three pieces about ⅝ in. thick, which will finish out after planing to either 7⁄16 in. or ½ in. thick, depending on how badly the wood cups. Because it's safer and easier to handle 12-in.- to 13-in.-long sections rather than individual pieces, I lay out both gables, or case sides, on a single board, as shown in figure 2 on p. 112, then bandsaw them out after cutting the tambour track and mortises for the shelf and bottom.

I also cut the 3⁄16x⅜x8½-in. tambour slats a week or so before I need them, to let them stabilize. The slats are glued to a canvas backing and their ends run in a groove routed in the inside of each gable. To help the vertical-opening tambour run smoothly, I also rabbet the slats slightly to create tongues on the ends. The front end of the tambour is a thicker piece dadoed to fit over the edge of both the slat and cloth, as shown in figure 3. I read an excellent article by Alphonse Mattia (*FWW Techniques 2*, p. 88), which taught me most of what I know about making tambours; I recommend you study Mattia's method if you need more information on tambour construction.

Photo: Michele Russell Slavinsky

Designing router jigs—Jigs are essential for quick, accurate and safe work, and I don't think you should avoid them even if you decide to make just one box. To make router jigs for routing the box gables, I generally construct one template for the horizontal grooves (and vertical grooves used on some of the larger boxes), one template for the tambour track and one for the escape/entry slot that allows the tambour to slide in and out of the assembled case. As you can see in figure 2 below, the grooving template has a rim on three sides to index the board to the workpiece. It's easier to glue up the grooving template from separate plywood strips than it is to machine it from a single piece of plywood. I use screws to attach the templates to the workpieces during routing, and the screw holes in the grooving template are indexed to the two other templates so all three can be mounted in turn in exactly the same location on the stock. Thus, the grooves cut with one template will align perfectly with those cut with the other template. The screw holes are located so they'll be hidden by the drawer once the box is assembled.

I cut the horizontal grooves first, then the curved tambour track and finally the escape/entry slot. When routing the track, cut counterclockwise and push the router firmly toward the center to keep

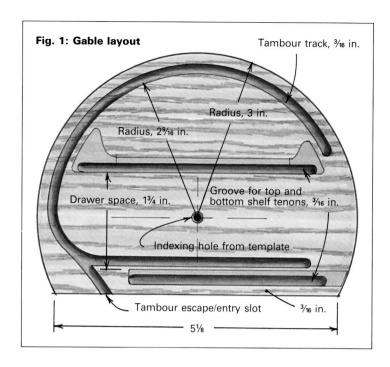

Fig. 1: Gable layout

Tambour track, ³/₁₆ in.

Radius, 3 in.

Radius, 2⁹/₁₆ in.

Groove for top and bottom shelf tenons, ³/₁₆ in.

Drawer space, 1¾ in.

Indexing hole from template

Tambour escape/entry slot

³/₁₆ in.

5⅛

Fig. 2: Jigs for cutting grooves in gables

Step 1:
Grooves for shelf and bottom of box are routed in two gables cut from single board.

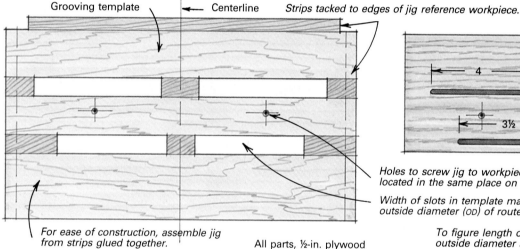

Grooving template — Centerline — *Strips tacked to edges of jig reference workpiece.*

Stock for pair of gables

4   1¹⁵/₁₆

Groove for shelf

3½   1⁹/₁₆

Groove for bottom

For ease of construction, assemble jig from strips glued together.

All parts, ½-in. plywood

Holes to screw jig to workpiece are located in the same place on all three jigs.

Width of slots in template matches outside diameter (OD) of router bushing.

To figure length of slots, subtract bit diameter from bushing outside diameter and add it to the desired length of groove.

Grooves are routed ⁵/₁₆ in. deep.

Step 2:
Routing tambour track

Tambour track template

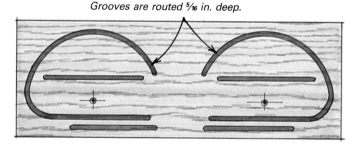

Router bushing follows outside of template.

Block stops groove under drawer.

Step 3:
Routing escape/entry slot

Escape/entry slot template

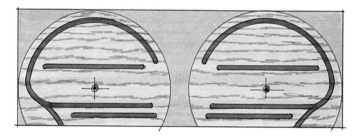

Width of template guides router bushing past edge of workpiece.

This part of template is shaped to match tambour track.

Slot allows tambour to be installed or removed after box is assembled.

After routing, workpiece is ready to be cut in half and radius of gables bandsawn out. Screws holes from jig also serve as center point for compass in laying out gables after the grooves are cut.

Drawings: Joel Katzowitz

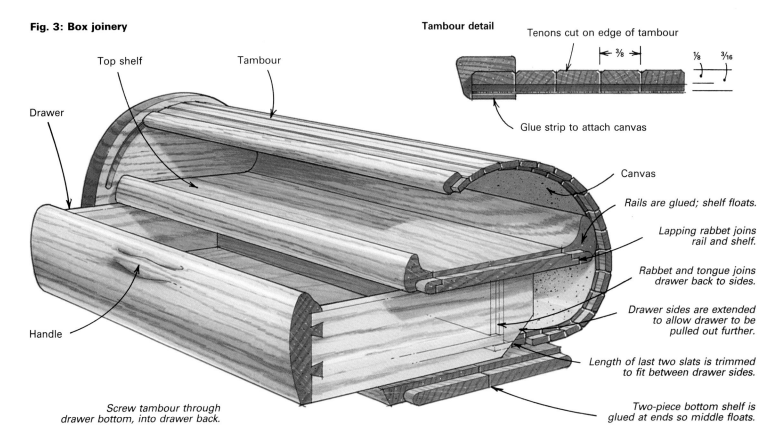

Fig. 3: Box joinery

Drawer

Top shelf

Tambour

Handle

Screw tambour through
drawer bottom, into drawer back.

Tambour detail

Tenons cut on edge of tambour

⅜ ⅛ ³⁄₁₆

Glue strip to attach canvas

Canvas

Rails are glued; shelf floats.

Lapping rabbet joins
rail and shelf.

Rabbet and tongue joins
drawer back to sides.

Drawer sides are extended
to allow drawer to be
pulled out further.

Length of last two slats is trimmed
to fit between drawer sides.

Two-piece bottom shelf is
glued at ends so middle floats.

it from taking off for parts unknown. After roughing out each slot, I rotate my router 180° and make a final pass to compensate for any guide-bushing eccentricity.

Constructing the box interior—The next step is to cut all the shelves and rails to width and then to length, using a single table-saw setup in each operation to ensure all the parts are identical. As shown in figure 3 above, cut tenons on the ends of the rails and on the two halves of the bottom shelf to fit the grooves routed in the gables. For accuracy in cutting the tenons, I set the saw fence so all the tenons will be the same length, then move the blade up and down to adjust for the various thicknesses of the rails and shelves. I cut the tenons with a few passes over a good carbide blade to avoid tearout, then glue up with West System epoxy (available from Gougeon Brothers, 100 Patterson Ave., Bay City, Mich. 48706; 517-684-7286). Epoxy has excellent gap-filling qualities, in case the tenons aren't a perfect fit. The ridges left on the tenons by the multiple sawcuts help lock the joint; should you need to adjust the tenon for a tight fit, it's easy to pare the ridges with a chisel. I make pairs of rails from a single piece to keep my fingers farther from the cut and to give myself solid contact with my router fence and table when I cut the inside coves. For the convex edges of the rails, I rough out the curve by cutting a series of bevels on my tablesaw. Then, after I've ripped the rails apart, I round the bevels over on a 6-in. by 48-in. belt sander. Next, I cut the lapping rabbets on the shelves and rails and try them in their grooves for fit and tambour clearance. Scrape and sand the shelves and rails prior to assembly. I leave the front edge of the bottom shelf square and shape it to the gable's curve after assembly.

I clean up both sides of the gables with a cabinet scraper but only final-sand the inside. I final-sand the outside to 400 grit after assembly. Because these gables are part of a circle, I put the point of my compass in the screw hole left from mounting the template and draw the outside of the box. I rough-out the gables on the bandsaw, fair up the curves on my stationary sander and roundover and clean up the edges with a spokeshave and sandpa-

per. After dry-assembling the box to make sure everything fits, I glue up the box and leave it while I finish-sand the tambour.

Shaping drawer fronts—I build my drawers square, then shape the front curve after fitting them into the box's opening. This enables me to match the drawer front's curve to the gable's curve. You can build the drawer anyway you like, but I prefer drawer sides of contrasting wood and hand-cut dovetails. The graphics of the dovetails are classy, and I don't think there is enough wood or glue surface to cut a strong rabbet in a small drawer like this. And, after several days of machining and sanding, it's a pleasure to shut off the power tools, sharpen my chisels and be a hand-tool woodworker for awhile.

I also enjoy shaping the drawer front mostly with hand tools. I prefer to carve a pull directly into the drawer front, but you may choose to use a separate pull glued or screwed on the front, or even eliminate it entirely, as I did on the oak box shown in the photo on p. 111. With no pull, the tambour itself is slid back, pushing the drawer open in the process. Starting with a 4/4 piece of the same stock as the gables, I cut the drawer front into a rough curve with several beveled cuts on the tablesaw, running the back of the drawer against the saw fence. Then, I fair the curve and match it to the gables using rasps, planes, spokeshaves and sandpaper, leaving enough stock to shape the lip-like drawer pull with carving tools.

Fit the drawer into the box, slide the tambour into its track and attach it with a single screw to the bottom of the drawer back. Now you're ready for finishing. I use Watco oil mixed three to one with gloss alkyd urethane or varnish and a bit of Japan drier (available from paint and hardware stores)—about ¼ teaspoon to a pint. After the finish dries, try the tambour by pulling on the drawer. It should open smoothly; if it doesn't, you may have to detach the tambour and either adjust the fit of the drawer or lubricate the tambour ends and drawer bottoms with a bit of wax. □

Jamie Russell is a self-employed furnituremaker. He would like anyone who makes trick tambour-top boxes to write him at Box 43, Ruddell, Saskatchewan, Canada S0M 2S0.

Wooden Combs
Pattern routing builds the blank

by Ric Carpenter

When my customers tell me how they like my wooden combs, I usually hear the word "love" in the first sentence. Using a wooden comb is a revelation to someone whose hair has always been tortured by plastic combs and brushes. Plastic causes static electricity and split ends—plastic is the reason for all the hair-repair shampoos! Wood, on the other hand, is organic and similar to hair in its molecular structure. Just leisurely combing your hair for a few moments a day not only treats your hair right, it releases a great deal of stress from both mind and body.

I've chosen to be a combwright as the way of making my livelihood. I left white-collar work 10 years ago, when I was 33, and first tried making bandsawn burl boxes. The reality of the craft circuit, however, is that no matter how beautiful the work, nobody buys except at Christmas time. After three years of horrendous effort, I realized that, if I wanted to continue expressing my creativity and, at the same time, add to the reservoir of positiveness in the world, what I needed was a unique item that could be sold year-round by mail.

In the days before plastic and rubber, wooden combs were once common—millions are still made each year in China. The Chinese combs are made from one piece of wood with the grain running with the teeth. This means there's weak cross-grain along the spine of the comb. Sooner or later, the comb will break. I've eliminated that cross-grain problem by making my combs from two pieces of wood glued together, as shown in the photo above.

I work with 16 different woods, from oak to ebony, allowing many combinations. I'll explain the production methods I use, but it's possible to make a couple of combs with little more than a bandsaw (or a scroll saw) and a belt sander (see box, p. 116).

My standard combs are just under 3 in. wide and range in length from 4¼ in. to 9¾ in. I prepare the ½-in.-thick by 10-in.-long by 3-in.-wide handle blanks in advance. I can get one large comb or two small combs from one of these blanks. The tooth blanks are also cut from ½-in. stock.

I pattern rout both the tooth blank and the corresponding opening in the handle blank, as shown in the drawing and photos on the facing page. Before routing, I bandsaw the work slightly oversize so the router doesn't have to remove much wood. My router is mounted on the column of my drill press with a homemade mounting bracket made from steel plate and a piece of 3½-in.-dia. steel pipe. (I call this a poor man's pin router.)

The tooth blank is bonded into its cut-out in the handle with fast-setting epoxy, tinted black with a little graphite. The resulting dark black glueline fills any gaps and looks like purposeful decoration. I prefer West System epoxy resin #105 and hardener #205, sold by Gougeon Brothers, 100 Patterson Ave., Bay City, Mich. 48706. I prepare the surfaces for gluing by scuffing with 50-grit sandpaper and wiping each surface with alcohol. I apply a first coat of epoxy to both surfaces and allow it to soak into the wood. After 20 minutes, I apply another coat and clamp the two pieces together with rubber bands.

The next step is to cut the teeth. The teeth and the slots in between are ¼ in. wide. I've made a gang saw that cuts all the slots in one pass, either 11, 16, or 23, depending on the size of the comb. As you can see in the photo at right, the blades are graduated in diameter, a job that any saw-sharpening shop should be able to handle. The cross-cut fence that holds the comb blank and feeds it into the blades is designed to stop exactly above the center of the saw arbor. At this point, I switch off the saw and remove the comb. Feeding the comb farther will

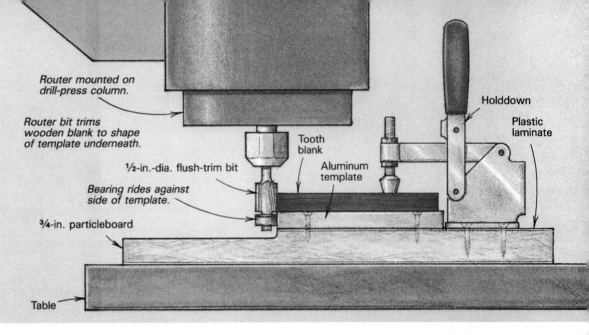

Fig 1: Routing the tooth blank and handle cutout

Each size comb requires two templates.

Male template cuts tooth blank.

Bit — Aluminum

Female template cuts tooth cutout in handle.

Bit

Router mounted on drill-press column.

Router bit trims wooden blank to shape of template underneath.

½-in.-dia. flush-trim bit

Bearing rides against side of template.

¾-in. particleboard

Holddown

Plastic laminate

Tooth blank

Aluminum template

Table

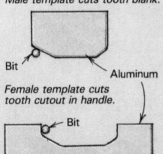

A bracket welded from steel plate and a section of 3½-in.-dia. steel pipe mounts a router on the drill-press column (above)—the jig cuts the tooth inlay blank for a large comb. Each comb requires two templates (right). The male jig (top) cuts the tooth blank and the female jig (bottom) cuts the corresponding cutout in the handle. The router pilot bit rides against the edge of the template to trim the stock on top.

A gangsaw (above) cuts all the teeth in one pass. The cross-cut fence that holds the comb is designed to stop over the center of the arbor. At this point, the saw is switched off and the comb removed. Carpenter's sanding machine (right) consists of six ¼-HP motors mounted on a lazy Susan. Each padded sanding disc sports a different grit paper.

Photos this page: William B. Ivy

William B. Ivy

result in shattered teeth. After cutting the teeth, I saw out the handle profile on the bandsaw.

For contouring and finish sanding, I made a sanding machine from six ¼-HP sealed 1,725-RPM motors mounted on a lazy Susan. A 9-in.-dia. aluminum sanding disc from Sears is mounted on each arbor. I glued 1-in.-thick foam rubber to each disc with contact cement, then covered the foam with two drawstring cloth bonnets. I glue sandpaper to the outer bonnet with contact cement. Each disc gets a different grit (50, 120, 220, 320, 400 and 600).

Starting on the 50-grit disc, I grind the initial contours. The comb is shaped so that it tapers in section from about ⅜ in. at the spine to a point at the business end of the teeth. The 120-grit paper removes any lumps and bumps and finishes the taper. I sand between the teeth with a 1-in. narrow-belt sander. It's important to remove any rough spots that may grab the hair.

Next, the comb is put in a vise and, using a carbide cutter (Dremel #1009) in a Foredom flexible-shaft handpiece, I relieve the gaps between teeth at the spine. I bevel each tooth edge and round the points by hand with 120-grit paper.

The combs are finished with Howard Feed-N-Wax (made by Howard Products, Inc., 411 W. Maple, Monrovia, Calif. 91016), an aromatic mix of beeswax, carnauba and orange-oil. □

After cutting the teeth, the top of each groove is relieved with a carbide cutter in a Foredom flexible-shaft handpiece.

Ric Carpenter can be reached at Sierra Legacy, P.O. Box 563, Lotus, Calif. 95651.

Making combs the hard way
by David Sloan

You don't need special equipment if you only want to make a couple of wooden combs. I made one with a bandsaw, tablesaw, belt sander and thin rat-tail file. It took me about 4 hours from start to finish, but that included lots of head scratching and some scrounging around for materials.

First, I bandsawed the tooth blank to the shape I wanted. Then, I traced the tooth blank shape on the handle blank and bandsawed the opening in the handle, staying inside the pencil line. I had to sand and file a little, but I got the two pieces to fit pretty well. I smeared 5-minute epoxy on both pieces and clamped them with thick rubber bands.

I cut the teeth on the tablesaw, but the bandsaw would be safer. The setup I used to space the teeth works on either machine. First, cut into some scrap and measure the width of the kerf. You will need some spacers twice as wide as the kerf so the teeth and the spaces between them will be equal. I rummaged through some drawers and found some nuts that were ¼ in. thick—twice the thickness of my ⅛-in. kerf. The drawing shows how I used the nuts to space the teeth.

Finally, I sanded the comb to shape on an upside-down belt sander, sanded between the teeth by hand (whew!) and relieved the gaps between the teeth with a rat-tail file. □

David Sloan is a former associate editor of Fine Woodworking.

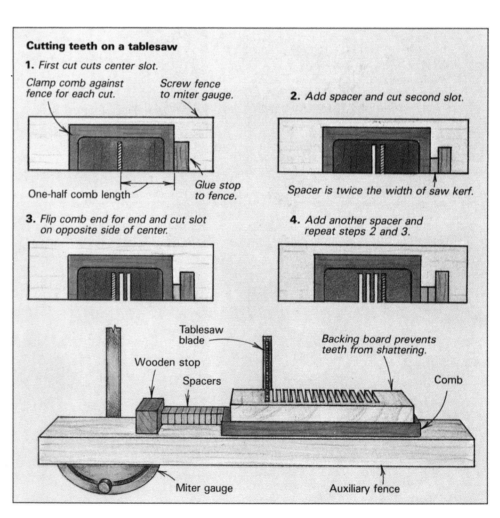

Cutting teeth on a tablesaw

1. *First cut cuts center slot.*

Clamp comb against fence for each cut.

Screw fence to miter gauge.

One-half comb length

Glue stop to fence.

2. *Add spacer and cut second slot.*

Spacer is twice the width of saw kerf.

3. *Flip comb end for end and cut slot on opposite side of center.*

4. *Add another spacer and repeat steps 2 and 3.*

Tablesaw blade

Wooden stop

Spacers

Backing board prevents teeth from shattering.

Comb

Miter gauge

Auxiliary fence

Production Hand Mirror
Machine jigging needn't compromise design

by Michael Fortune

When I began woodworking ten years ago, the opportunities for designing and building furniture weren't all that plentiful. So in between my sporadic furniture commissions, I'd design and produce smaller objects, such as the hand mirror described in this article. The scale of these smaller pieces spared me from investing much on materials, no matter how exotic the wood. More important, producing them helped me develop my design, construction and organizational skills.

My first mirror evolved from some sketches of Gingko-tree leaves. I did most of the work by hand with gouges, rifflers and sandpaper. Shaping the nooks and cranies was murder. My worn fingers prompted me to go back to the drawing board, but I wanted to avoid the common production trap of limiting myself to easily reproduced shapes, thereby letting machines compromise my designs. After making a few sketches and mock-ups, I realized that, by separating the head from the handle and using jigs and power tools to produce the two pieces individually, I could preserve both my design and the mirrors' handcrafted look.

The hand mirror is a good example of the evolutionary process that leads to most of my production procedures: I design an object, make it, then simplify the process with jigs and machines. Perhaps the ability will come after a few more years of experience but, right now, I can't completely plan out the sequence of machine operations and jigs before I actually build a piece. At best, I have a positive attitude toward the purpose and design of jig construction.

My first batch of jig-produced mirrors was a group of six. The head of each mirror consisted of two pieces of hardwood, bookmatched along a centerline paper joint which became the major reference line for measuring pieces and aligning them to jigs throughout the process. My subsequent batches were groups of ten—a number better-suited to my studio size, profit margin and attention span. I always stick with even numbers, so the parts stack evenly and it's obvious if anything is missing.

On another style of hand mirror, I continued to work from the centerline, but divided the head into eight wedges. This allowed me to develop more graphically interesting grain configurations by arranging and rearranging each board individually. I glued up the wedges in groups of four to make right and left mirror halves, then assembled the halves with a paper joint. Sometimes, I selected stock with a consistent grain pattern so that the gluelines and individual segments wouldn't be very noticeable; other times, I accented the gluelines with veneer strips.

Making the mirror involves such a variety of pieces—squares, rectangles, wedges and circles—that jigs are essential in order to obtain consistent results from batch to batch. As you can see in the photographs on the following pages, my jigs fall into several broad

From *Fine Woodworking* magazine (July 1987) 65:37-41

Wedges are cut on the bandsaw with the simple jig shown at top— a 6-in. by 9-in. plywood rectangle, notched so that a wedge is cut when the carrier is pushed along the fence and past the blade. The jig for gluing up the wedges (above) is designed so that bar clamps spanning the front edge of the jig and the backs of the wedges pull the segments into angled battens, tightening the glue joints.

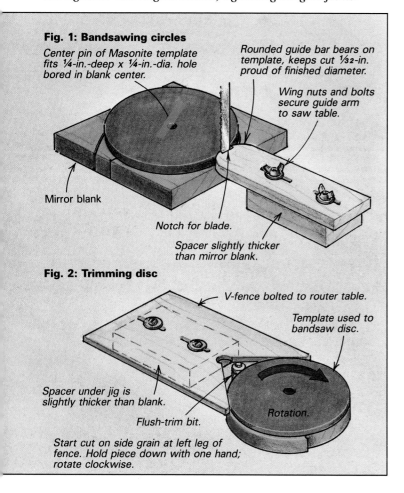

Fig. 1: Bandsawing circles

Center pin of Masonite template fits ¼-in.-deep x ¼-in.-dia. hole bored in blank center.

Rounded guide bar bears on template, keeps cut ¹⁄₃₂-in. proud of finished diameter.

Wing nuts and bolts secure guide arm to saw table.

Mirror blank

Notch for blade.

Spacer slightly thicker than mirror blank.

Fig. 2: Trimming disc

V-fence bolted to router table.

Template used to bandsaw disc.

Spacer under jig is slightly thicker than blank.

Flush-trim bit.

Start cut on side grain at left leg of fence. Hold piece down with one hand; rotate clockwise.

Rotation.

categories: cutting jigs, to rough out discs and wedges; router jigs, to shape edges and cut joints; and clamping fixtures, to hold irregularly shaped pieces during glue-up. Whenever possible, I try to key the jigs and operations together. The bandsaw, router table and shaper have holes drilled and tapped (¼–20 thread size) in the surface, on the same centers and at the same distance from the center of the cutters, so that jigs and setups can be transferred from machine to machine. For ease of measurement, all the holes are located on 2-in. centers, measured from the center of the cutters.

For segmented heads, I begin with 6-in. by 6⅝-in. by ¾-in.-thick blanks, cutting each into wedges with a taper jig on the tablesaw or bandsaw. The jig I use (see top left photo) is a notched 6-in. by 9-in. plywood carrier that bears against the fence and produces a wedge as it's pushed past the blade. The sawn edges should be adequate glue surfaces. If not, flatten them by lightly rubbing the wedge on sandpaper double-face-taped to plate glass or another hard, flat surface, such as a jointer table. I assemble the wedges with West System epoxy glue (Gougeon Brothers, Inc., 100 Patterson Ave., Bay City, Mich. 48706) and clamp them on the jig shown in the photo at left—two angled battens screwed to a plywood base. The wedges are placed between the battens so that bar clamps can pull them into the angled pieces, closing up the glue joints.

The segmented or book-matched blanks can be cut round freehand or with any number of jigs. To ensure that the jigs fit all the parts, it's important that every blank be cut 5⁹⁄₁₆ in. in diameter. I use a circular tempered-Masonite pattern and a flush-trim router bit. A center peg in the template fits a center hole bored into the blank, so the template can be accurately located before being press-fit in place. I bandsaw the discs ¹⁄₃₂ in. proud of the line, as shown in figure 1, then true the circles on a router table with a flush-trim bit. I strongly suggest the use of a V-fence like the one shown in figure 2. This device serves as both a cutting guide and an important safety device—when I was a design student, I nicked myself with a round-over bit before realizing the circular bit can spin the workpiece and draw your hand into the cutter.

I begin the cut by bearing on the left leg of the V-fence and moving the side grain into the cutter, holding the piece down with one hand and rotating it clockwise into the cutter with the other. Speed is dictated by the sound and quality of the router cut. Go too fast and tearout will occur; move too slowly and burning may result.

The next operation uses the same setup with a different bit to cut a groove in the edge of the blank so it can be mounted on a lathe faceplate with the locking blocks shown in figure 3. I set a ½-in. dovetail bit so it protrudes ⅜ in. from the router table, then align the V-fence so that the bit leaves a slight ¹⁄₆₄-in.-high flat between the table and notch. Now, I turn the mirror cavity with a lathe gouge and scraper until it's exactly 4⅞ in. in diameter by ⁷⁄₃₂ in.

Slips of veneer are epoxied between the wedge-shaped mirror segments as a design accent. The basic shape of Fortune's hand mirror was inspired by sketches of Gingko-tree leaves.

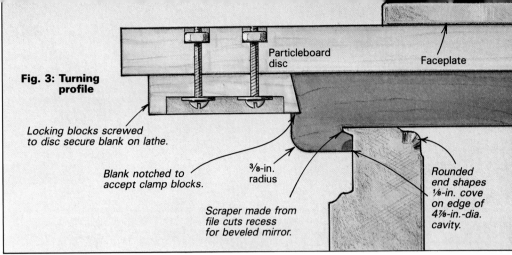

Fig. 3: Turning profile

Locking blocks screwed to disc secure blank on lathe.

Particleboard disc

Faceplate

Blank notched to accept clamp blocks.

³⁄₈-in. radius

Scraper made from file cuts recess for beveled mirror.

Rounded end shapes ¹⁄₈-in. cove on edge of 4⁷⁄₈-in.-dia. cavity.

Fortune cuts the mirror groove on a lathe with a scraper ground from a file, above. The cutting wedge is slightly thicker than the mirror bevel to allow for seasonal wood movement. To shape the back, he mounts a template off-center on the blank, below, then guides the disc into a cove bit with a V-fence on a router table.

Fig. 4: Offsetting back of blank

V-fence flat on router table.

Loosen screws and slide V-fence to vary amount of offset.

Rotation.

Double-face-tape offset template to head, align centerline of pattern with paper joint.

Make three passes with ⁵⁄₈-in. core-box bit to cut ³⁄₈-in. depth.

V-fence

Offset cove

Masonite template

Router table

deep around the perimeter. I dish the cavity to ⁹⁄₃₂ in. deep at the mirror's center.

The shape of the outside radius and the undercut that holds the mirror are cut next. In a two-step process illustrated in figure 3, I cut the mirror-holding undercut, then flip the tool and cut the adjoining cove. (I ground the two-sided tool—also visible in the top photo, above—from a file.) The exact dimensions of the undercut are determined by the shape of the beveled mirror (Floral Glass and Mirror Inc., 895 Motor Parkway, Hauppauge, N.Y. 11788 or Sterling Equipment Co., 6700 Distribution Dr., Beltsville, Md. 20705), plus an allowance for the wood's seasonal contraction and expansion. While the piece is still on the lathe, I also sand the cove and outside roundover to 320 grit.

You now have two options for completing the head. The first is to use woodworking methods and tools everyone knows (i.e. files, gouges, rasps, sandpaper blocks), but which can't easily or quickly generate—let alone duplicate—sculptural shapes. Another option is to utilize a carving duplicator, as I do. This method bypasses some of the steps, time and risk of shaping, but it's likely to be too expensive for anyone not headed into full-scale production.

The simplest, most straightforward approach to shaping the head involves a router table, a ⁵⁄₈-in.-dia. core-box bit and an offset pattern double-face-taped to the back of the blank. The amount of offset is largely an aesthetic decision, but I've found that the adjustable V-fence/router table setup shown in figure 4 works well. Make

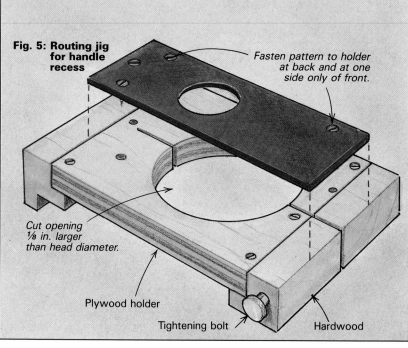

Fig. 5: Routing jig for handle recess

Fasten pattern to holder at back and at one side only of front.

Cut opening 1/8 in. larger than head diameter.

Plywood holder

Tightening bolt

Hardwood

After routing the offset cove, Fortune bandsaws the angle on the back using a cradle, left, which supports the workpiece as it passes the blade and keeps the operator's fingers out of the way. Strips of sandpaper lining the cradle prevent the piece from rotating. Most of the final shaping is done with a die grinder, right, moving the cutter diagonally to the grain. Wood will disappear quickly if you carve into the rotation of the cutter, but you'll gain more control by rolling with the cutter. Grinding marks are later removed with files.

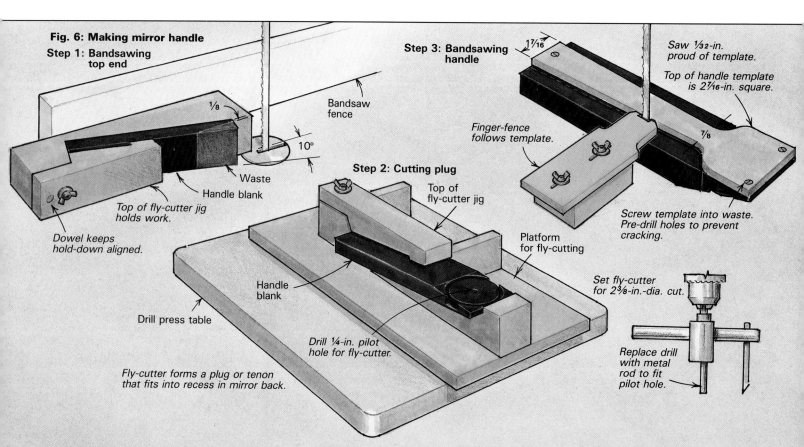

Fig. 6: Making mirror handle

Step 1: Bandsawing top end

Bandsaw fence

1/8

10°

Waste

Handle blank

Top of fly-cutter jig holds work.

Dowel keeps hold-down aligned.

Step 2: Cutting plug

Top of fly-cutter jig

Handle blank

Platform for fly-cutting

Drill press table

Drill 1/4-in. pilot hole for fly-cutter.

Fly-cutter forms a plug or tenon that fits into recess in mirror back.

Step 3: Bandsawing handle

1 7/16

Saw 1/32-in. proud of template.

Top of handle template is 2 7/16-in. square.

Finger-fence follows template.

7/8

Screw template into waste. Pre-drill holes to prevent cracking.

Set fly-cutter for 2 3/8-in.-dia. cut.

Replace drill with metal rod to fit pilot hole.

three passes to rout the outside cove to a depth of ⅜ in., but take care—at the end of this operation, you're routing the underside of the blank, which is cantilevering over the router bit.

My original sketches suggested that the overall form would be most successful if the handle were slightly out-of-plane with the head. I decided to saw a 6° angle on the back of the mirror head, which would allow a 3-in.-wide recess for fitting the handle. Since I make batches of mirrors, I use a box cradle with hold-downs (see photo, far left) to ensure accuracy and keep my fingers well out of harm's way during the cut. For a single hand mirror, I'd just hot-melt-glue the head to a carrier and tilt the bandsaw table to cut the angled surface. Either way, the next step is to cut the ⅛-in.-deep recess for the handle with a router and jig (see figure 5) that clamps the blank between a Masonite template and a holder.

Now, I shape the head's back. A regular marking gauge is fine for scribing a line round the offset cove to define where handshaping should begin to rise up to meet the handle recess. The blank is difficult to hold, so I hot-melt-glue a round 1½-in.-thick softwood disc into the mirror cavity. The disc can be clamped in a bench vise during shaping operations and rotated as necessary.

The shaping can be done by whatever method you prefer, but careless mallet-and-gouge work may pop the paper joint. I've found an electric die grinder with coarse ¾-in. bits (available from Severance Tool Industries, Inc., 3790 Orange St., P.O. Box 1866, Saginaw, Mich. 48605; part no. JLT) effectively removes most of the waste, especially when I make crisscross strokes diagonal to the grain direction, as shown in the near photo, left. Level out the scallop marks left by the grinder with a #49 random-tooth patternmakers' rasp (available from Jamestown Distributors, 28 Narragansett Ave., P.O. Box 348, Providence, R.I. 02835), and finish the surface with a gooseneck scraper and 150-, 180- and 220-grit sandpaper wrapped around a small piece of Formica.

I always expect a wood-splitting disaster when I separate the two halves of the head along the paper joint, but I haven't had a single failure in the 60 or so joints I've done. My method is to gently rock a 1½-in.-wide chisel along the paper joint inside the mirror cavity until the halves separate. The edges must be scraped and sanded before the mirror is test-fitted. Insert enough shimming behind the mirror to push its bevel gently against the lips that hold the glass in place. My shims are the front page of the day's newspaper, along with a business card. Should the hand mirror crash to the floor someday, at least the owner will get a surprise: the address of where to buy a new one. The hydroscopic nature of wood requires that the mirror be slightly loose in the head, but to prevent rattling, I put four drops of clear, flexible silicone under the lip.

One last crucial detail is to paraffin either side of the joint and along the centerline of the newspaper shim touching the wood. The wax prevents the epoxy from freezing the mirror in place, or from lifting the silver off the glass. Epoxying the two semi-circles together appears to be a tricky clamping job, but several heavy rubber bands crisscrossing the disc will handle it. Be very careful with the alignment or you risk having to re-level and resand everything. The final sanding finishes the mirror with 320-grit silicone-carbide paper.

Making the handle is an exercise in visualizing and extracting a form from a block of wood. I prefer oval handles, but you could make any shape you want. I've used East Indian rosewood, Ceylon and Macassar ebony, curly koa and curly maple, but ebony generates the best response. Shape and proportion are the key considerations. My handle is 2⁷⁄₁₆ in. wide, ¾ in. thick and 10 in. long. The whole handle-making process can be done freehand, but I use the jigs shown in the drawings below to gain speed and accuracy.

Before assembling the pieces, I fair all the curves and refine the shapes with a scraper and sandpaper. For easy cleanup, paraffin the perimeter of the head recess and the handle before the final epoxy glue-up. Take care to align the axis of the handle with the center glueline in the head. A 6-in. square of particleboard on the mirror side of the head and a softwood block on the paddle end will protect the mirror as the handle is clamped up. Finally, seal the hand mirror with the clear finish of your choice. □

Michael Fortune is a furniture designer/builder in Toronto, Canada. His mirror-making techniques are demonstrated in Router Jigs and Techniques, *a Taunton Press videotape. Drawings shown here were adapted from a booklet accompanying that tape.*

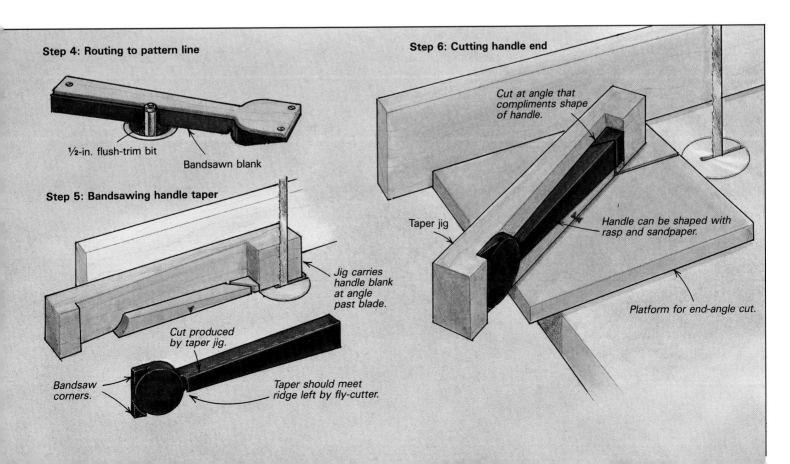

Step 4: Routing to pattern line

½-in. flush-trim bit

Bandsawn blank

Step 5: Bandsawing handle taper

Jig carries handle blank at angle past blade.

Cut produced by taper jig.

Bandsaw corners.

Taper should meet ridge left by fly-cutter.

Step 6: Cutting handle end

Cut at angle that compliments shape of handle.

Taper jig

Handle can be shaped with rasp and sandpaper.

Platform for end-angle cut.

Wooden Pulls for Drawers and Doors

Getting a handle on homemade alternatives

by Paul Levine

Drawer and door pulls are a personal item, much like an earring or a tie tack. They are important design details that, when well crafted, add visual texture to what might otherwise be a featureless expanse of plastic laminate in the kitchen. Along with the cabinet faces, they help to establish a kitchen's feel.

There are plenty of good pulls on the market. In recent years, European hardware manufacturers have exported to the United States a rich variety of well-designed pulls and knobs made of wood, metal and plastic. These pulls are well suited to European-style cabinets, and many are available by mail order.

But if you're bored by the thought of store-bought pulls or just want something different, you can make your own. Making pulls involves a lot of extra work and certainly isn't for everyone, but I've seen many a prospective client run an appreciative hand over my custom-made pulls. They sell casework every time.

Wood, metal or plastic pulls, whether ready-made or custom-made, are most easily added to a door or drawer by screwing them directly to the face surface. Personal taste will determine where on the door or drawer they ought to go. As a general rule, however, surface-mounted pulls look best centered on a drawer face, while door pulls should be mounted near the top edge of a base cabinet door and the bottom edge of an upper cabinet door. Another option is to use a stile glued to the edge of a plywood face, which provides plenty of raw material from which to shape a pull. Finally, you can rout or carve a pull right into a solid-wood face.

Cylindrical pulls—The simplest pulls I've used are cylindrical button pulls, like those shown in the top, left photo on the facing page. These wooden pulls can be turned on a lathe, but I find it easier to cut them on the drill press, using a plug cutter. Plug cutters are available up to 1½ in. in diameter and up to 3 in. long. I make my pulls 1 in. in diameter and about ⅞ in. long. My drawers are plywood with solid-wood edging. I use the same type of wood for the pulls and begin with stock a little thicker than the pulls will be long. With the board clamped to the drill press, I run off an entire job's worth of pulls at once, making a few extras in case of mistakes, poor grain or unattractive color. For reasons you'll understand in a moment, I stop the plug boring just shy of the full thickness of the board, so the plugs remain temporarily captive in the holes.

Cylindrical wooden pulls are fastened to the cabinets with machine screws passed through holes in the door or drawer face and into brass or steel threaded inserts let into the back of each pull. Threaded inserts come in various sizes and shapes (available from most woodworking mail-order supply houses), and the size hole required for an insert will depend on several factors. Inserts

that are meant to be hand-threaded into the hole will require a slightly larger-diameter pilot hole than those that are meant to be power-driven. For example, brass inserts require a larger hole than steel ones of the same size, because brass is softer. Also, in the very hardest woods, like ebony, the hole should be just a hair smaller than the diameter of the external threads. If the hole is too small, either the insert won't go in or it will split the pull. I bore the holes for the inserts while the pulls are still attached to the board so I won't have to clamp them individually to the drill press.

I don't generally use brass inserts, because they're too soft, particularly in hardwoods, where the extra toughness of steel inserts makes them easier to drive. True, steel may react chemically with oak, but the insert is concealed by the pull, so any staining won't be visible. Even steel inserts can be difficult to drive in straight, though. I've found a neat trick for accomplishing this, which saves me lots of effort, especially if I have dozens of pulls to make. I cut off the head of a hex-head machine bolt sized to fit the insert's inside threads (usually ¼ in. dia.) and chuck it in the drill press with the bolt threads on the bottom. I thread an insert onto the bolt and turn the chuck by hand as I lower the insert into its hole. When all the inserts have been screwed in, I resaw the board on the bandsaw to cut the pulls free. This operation is quite safe, as long as you keep your cut well away from the inserts. If you should accidentally saw into the inserts, though, you will ruin the blade and the pulls.

These round pulls look good on just about any cabinet design, but they're not always appropriate. Some people find their smooth sides hard to grasp, and they are especially difficult on heavy drawers or doors. You wouldn't want them on a file drawer, for example. You can improve the grip on this pull by cutting a notch into one or both sides of the cylinder. I do this by boring a hole across the pull while it's still attached to the board or by sanding a notch into the pull after it's cut free.

Yet another simple pull can be made by using the plug cutter to cut half-wafers in stock about ⅜ in. thick. Clamp two pieces of stock together at their edges, center the plug cutter on the seam and bore away. The resulting half-wafers can be attached with glue and drywall screws driven in from the inside of the door or drawer. Wafer pulls are suitable only for delicate applications, not for large or heavy drawers.

Stile pulls—Of all the various pulls I make, I like glued-on stile pulls best. Their chief advantage is that they require no pattern at all. Over the years, I've experimented with various stile widths, finally settling on 2 in. as the best choice, as shown in the bottom photo on the facing page. The stile can be glued to a vertical or horizontal edge, depending on whether the pull will be for a

From *Fine Woodworking* magazine (November 1988) 73:80-83

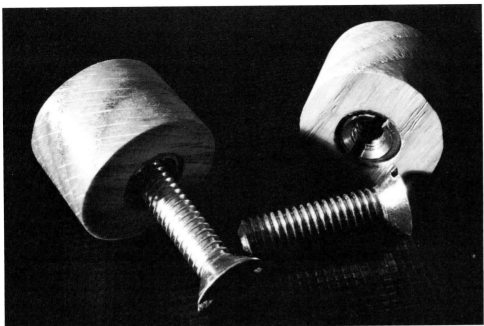

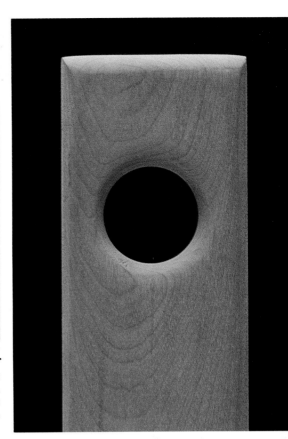

Button pulls, above, are simple to make and install. These are shaped using a plug cutter on a drill press and will be held in position with screws through the back of the drawer faceplate. Also easy to make is the stile pull, right, which requires only a drilled hole with smoothed edges. Stiles, 2 in. wide and glued to the drawer face in place of edging, provide plenty of material for routing pulls. The photo below shows routed maple stiles glued to the top of the door and bottom of the drawer face to form matching pulls.

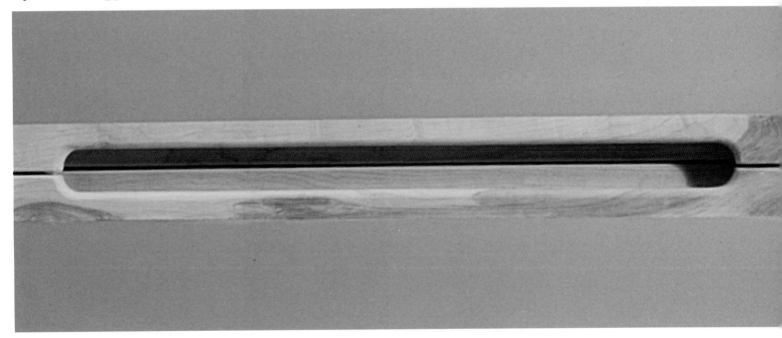

door or a drawer. In either case, the size of the plywood panel will have to be adjusted to allow for the stile's width.

The stile can be added to an already edged face, or it can be glued on in place of one of the ¼-in. edging strips. The method you choose depends on the look you want. If the stile is glued to edging that has been chamfered or rounded, a shadow line results, highlighting the stile. A stile installed in lieu of edging will appear cleaner and will form a more integrated part of the door or drawer face. Obviously, if you want wooden stile pulls, you'll have to make and install them as you're edging the faces. If you've chosen commercial pulls, you can install the faces when the edging is complete and add the pulls later.

The simplest stile pull is the round pull shown in the top, right photo above. The cutout is a hole, 1⅛ in. in diameter or larger, bored on the drill press using a Forstner bit. Once you've decided on the location of the pull, simply bore the hole and then shape the edges of the hole to provide a comfortable and secure finger-hold.

After the hole has been bored, clamp the workpiece in a vise so the front of the stile faces up. Then, round the edge using a ¼-in. bearing-guided roundover bit, as shown in the top photo on the next page. Flip the piece over, and use a ⅜-in. bearing-guided cove bit to hollow out the back of the pull for the finger-hold (see the middle photo on the next page). Although I used to be rather precise about the exact depth of this cut, I don't bother to measure it anymore. Instead, I start by making a small cut, then drop the bit a little on each successive pass. After three or four passes with the cove bit, the pull is done, except for sanding.

The pull is the first place you touch a cabinet, so it should be

After the overall shape of the stile has been cut out, the pull's front edge is rounded over, above, using a router.

The back is shaped with a cove bit, above, guided by a pilot bearing (cut-away view shown for clarity). The finished pull, below, has a thin piece of wood glued to the back of the stile to close off the back of the pull.

silky and inviting. Don't spare the labor here, because you'll regret it every time you open a drawer. I find that the best approach to sanding pulls is to use a combination of hand and machine sanding. I start with an orbital sander, then sand by hand. I begin with 100 grit, then go to 120, 180, and finally 220 grit. Sand all the parts evenly and be sure to get the finger-hold as smooth as possible.

You can vary the design further by making a split-round pull, which I often use on adjacent door stiles. To make one, rip a board into two 2-in.-wide stiles, then clamp them together and bore the hole. This method preserves the wood's grain and the cutout's circular shape. Now round over the front edge of the hole and cove the back, as you do for round stile pulls. A split-round stile pull needs a backup plate (see the bottom photo on this page) to close off the opening so the pull won't look like a bottomless, dark hole in the front of the cabinet.

Yet another variation of the basic round pull is the elongated version. To make one, bore two holes to form the ends of the cutout pull and remove the waste between them with a jigsaw. To get the waste cut perfectly straight, I follow with a router and trimmer bit, guided by a straight piece of plywood clamped to the back of the stock along the outside edges of the holes.

Inset pulls—An inset pull is a shaped hole or slot cut through the door or drawer face. To provide a finger-hold, a cove is routed into the backside of the opening, as described for the stile pulls. Generally, I only make an inset pull in solid wood, because through-routed slots in plywood aren't very attractive. However, it is also possible to cut the pull in a piece of hardwood let into a plywood drawer face or door.

The inset pulls shown in the photo on the facing page are one of my favorite inset designs. It was inspired by furniture I once saw in a book about Charles and Henry Greene, two turn-of-the-century architects best known for their skillful blending of Arts-and-Crafts style with Japanese motifs. I wanted to incorporate the Greene brothers' sense of rich, individual character in my own cabinets. This pull can be routed directly into a solid-wood drawer front or into a stile, which is then glued to a door or drawer face. If you choose the stile approach, the pull's shape can be routed into a pair of stiles that have been temporarily clamped together. When they are separated and glued to faces, the stiles will form pulls in adjacent doors or drawers.

The process for making inset pulls is called pattern routing, and it ensures consistent results, because the same pattern is used to guide the router for each pull. Making an accurate pattern is really the only tricky part of making the pull; using the pattern as a guide makes the machining go pretty quickly. To begin, I draw a full-size outline of the cutout portion of the pull on a piece of ¾-in. plywood. As the drawing on the facing page shows, the pull's shape is defined by a series of ¼-in.-radius circles joined by straight lines. When laying it out, though, I don't bother drawing in the radii. Instead, I simply mark the centers of the eight circles and bore them out with a ½-in.-dia. Forstner bit. This method produces a cleaner, smoother curve than I could ever achieve by hand.

When the holes have been bored, I jigsaw the lines that connect their outside edges. With a mill file and 80-grit sandpaper, I shape the outside radii and smooth the pattern so the pilot bearing on the router bit will have an even surface to run against.

Once the pattern is completed, I make a test pull on a piece of scrap. Using the pattern as a guide, I bore the holes at each outside corner first. Then, I jigsaw almost up to the edge of the pattern. I then turn the pattern over and use a 1-in.-long bearing-guided trimmer bit to shape the cutout to the pattern. Finally, I

The inset pulls above were made by using the pattern-routing technique described in the text. This design can be used in solid-wood drawer fronts, or if routed into a stile then ripped in half, on adjacent door or drawer fronts.

Pattern routing an inset pull

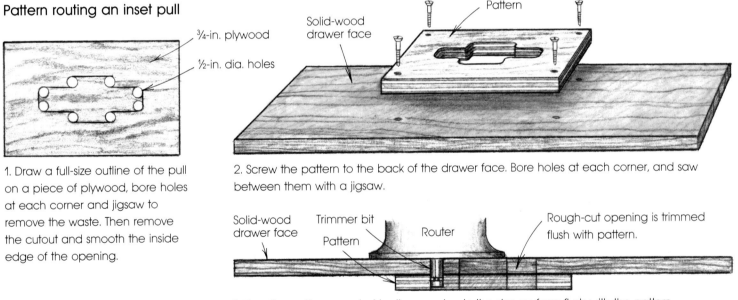

¾-in. plywood

½-in. dia. holes

1. Draw a full-size outline of the pull on a piece of plywood, bore holes at each corner and jigsaw to remove the waste. Then remove the cutout and smooth the inside edge of the opening.

Pattern

Solid-wood drawer face

2. Screw the pattern to the back of the drawer face. Bore holes at each corner, and saw between them with a jigsaw.

Solid-wood drawer face

Trimmer bit

Pattern

Router

Rough-cut opening is trimmed flush with pattern.

3. Turn the pattern over to trim the opening in the drawer face flush with the pattern.

round the inside edges of the pull, cut the cove on the backside and sand the pull smooth, as described for the stile pulls.

When I'm satisfied that the shape is exactly right, I perform each machining operation on all the pulls. Working this way ensures that all the pulls will be identical, and it saves endless resetting of the router's cutting depth. Also, if you are working on a stile, it makes sense to shape the pull before the stile is glued to the drawer or door face. This way, if you make a mistake cutting it, you haven't ruined the whole face. If you are shaping a drawer pull, the pattern can be screwed to the back of the face, because the screw holes will be hidden when the face is mounted.

Once the pull is cut into a drawer face, the face can be screwed directly to the front of a drawer, provided the front is made of the same material as the face. If it isn't, the contrasting wood will show through the cutout. To remedy this, you can let into the drawer front a piece of wood of the same species used for the face, or you can glue a ³⁄₁₆-in.-thick hardwood plate to the back of the cavity. □

Paul Levine is a cabinetmaker and furniture designer in New Milford, Conn. This article has been adapted with permission from the Taunton Press book "Making Kitchen Cabinets," ©1988, The Taunton Press, 63 S. Main St., Box 5506, Newtown, Conn. 06470. Photos are by the author.

Index